T0350524

PROCUREMENT
AT A CROSSROADS
Career-Impacting
Insights into a Rapidly
Changing Industry

JON HANSEN · KELLY BARNER
FOREWORD BY DAVID CLEVENGER

Copyright © 2016 by Jon Hansen and Kelly Barner

ISBN-13: 978-1-60427-117-1

Printed and bound in the U.S.A. Printed on acid-free paper.

10 9 8 7 6 5 4 3 2 1

Library of Congress Cataloging-in-Publication Data
Hansen, Jon, 1959- author. | Barner, Kelly, 1978- author.
  Procurement at a crossroads : an industry in transition or turmoil? /
by Jon Hansen and Kelly Barner.
  Plantation, FL : J. Ross Publishing, [2015] | Includes index.
  Identifiers: LCCN 2015041296 | ISBN 9781604271171 (pbk. : alk.
paper)
  Subjects: ILCSH: Purchasing.
  Classification: LCC HF5437 .H274 2015 | DDC 658.7/2—dc23 LC
record available at http://lccn.loc.gov/2015041296

This publication contains information obtained from authentic and highly regarded sources. Reprinted material is used with permission, and sources are indicated. Reasonable effort has been made to publish reliable data and information, but the author and the publisher cannot assume responsibility for the validity of all materials or for the consequences of their use.

All rights reserved. Neither this publication nor any part thereof may be reproduced, stored in a retrieval system, or transmitted in any form or by any means, electronic, mechanical, photocopying, recording or otherwise, without the prior written permission of the publisher.

The copyright owner's consent does not extend to copying for general distribution for promotion, for creating new works, or for resale. Specific permission must be obtained from J. Ross Publishing for such purposes.

Direct all inquiries to J. Ross Publishing, Inc., 300 S. Pine Island Rd., Suite 305, Plantation, FL 33324.

Phone: (954) 727-9333
Fax: (561) 892-0700
Web: www.jrosspub.com

Dedication

It is mandatory for anyone with 4 children under the age of 10, who is in the final stretch of writing a book during summer vacation, to thank their significant other. If you have children, the reasons are obvious ... so thank you Jennifer! You are indeed the love of my life—and yes, they will be a comfort to us in our old age.

The above being a given, there is a group of people whom I would like to both thank as well as dedicate this book to—my readers and listeners.

Over the years, as one dedicated follower put it, I have tackled head-on the topics that few would dare to cover. In fact, by consistently challenging the mainstream pundits and purported power influencers, I have been accused of being on the fringe of common sense or worse, being at risk of "becoming the Fenimore Cooper of procurement blogs." By the way, I actually considered the Cooper comparison to be a compliment—especially when sound research warrants challenging the purported sacred cows of the industry.

Even my intrepid coauthor, Kelly Barner, was "warned" about me. Someone close to her even questioned whether it was good for her reputation to be associated with me in terms of the writing of this book. Queue Michael Jackson's *Bad* video. Between you, me, and the gatepost, Kelly can more than hold her own in the bad department—and I offer this as the highest compliment that I can to someone with whom I have enjoyed working with these past few months.

In the end though, it is you, the readers and listeners, whose voice has ultimately spoken in the form making both the *Procurement Insights* blog and *PI Window* radio show two of the most popular sources of information in the industry.

It is because of your support that I have the opportunity to do the two things that I love to do—write and host a talk radio show. For this, I not only thank you but dedicate this book, because in the end, it is your voice that ultimately matters to me the most.

Jon Hansen

To my Mom, whom I absolutely adore, and who always feels better when my "Jon Hansen work" is done.

I also want to express my gratitude for our amazing network of colleagues—without any one of whom this book would not have been possible. If their generous spirit and genuine curiosity continues and spreads to others, we will have no trouble building a very bright future for procurement. There are many people who have offered up their energy and encouragement during this project, but I would particularly like to thank Tim McCarthy, David Clevenger, Drew Gierman, Cindy Allen-Murphy, Kate Vitasek, Phil Coughlin, Rob Handfield, Gerard Chick, Susan Avery, Tom Derry, Sadie Smith, Erin Vadala, and Alan Holland.

Kelly Barner

Contents

Foreword

When I entered the supply chain space in 2000 there were grumblings and theories. The consultants who had helped to reshape the space were beginning to enter leadership roles within corporate procurement organizations. Reverse auctions, eProcurement, spend visibility, and numerous other technological advancements were altering our capability to manage suppliers, conduct negotiations, and manipulate data. It was more than an exciting time, it was an interesting time, and the idea was beginning to spread that the procurement function could be something substantively different than it had once been. It felt as though we were all on the cusp of something big.

More than 15 years later, I'm surprised to see how little things have changed. Certainly the discipline has become more sophisticated. Better tools have resulted in better analytics, but this increase in visibility hasn't translated into an enhanced vision. The organizational stature of procurement departments falls about where it always has: as an underutilized and largely underappreciated function within too many businesses. We have pointed fingers in hopes of finding a reason for this—at our internal customers for not seeing value in our solutions and at our leadership for not measuring our contributions accurately—but there is no mystery to how we ended up here.

Our profession has repeatedly failed in its collective attempt to be viewed as strategic contributors for one simple reason: procurement is out of step with the broader strategic goals of the companies for whom we work.

Companies are in business to grow and innovate, not to save money. In fact, saving money often runs perpendicular to growth and innovation. In that environment, the individuals who are responsible for saving money are not just less useful, they're outright counterproductive. As a result, procurement ends up begging different functions to work with them, and those functions end up being resistant. It shouldn't come as a surprise, because too often these groups have conflicting goals, despite playing for the same team.

You cannot be relevant without being a meaningful contributor to the overall goals of the organization, and the goal of every organization is to grow. New markets, better margins, improved products, more share; every eye is focused on what's next. That brings us to the crossroads that Kelly and Jon are asking us to carefully consider.

So here we stand: we can stay the course or we can veer off in a new direction. In choosing the former we continue to plod ahead as we always have, leaving us safely confined to familiar roles as solid, tactical contributors. By selecting the latter we incur both risk and possibility. A change in direction means that we may get lost, but it also allows for the potential to achieve new and better things we could never have seen along the traditional path.

THE ROAD TO RELEVANCE

Any productive new path for procurement must result in greater importance and thus begins with a question: "Are you important today?" Are the activities of you and your teammates making a meaningful impact on the goals of the business?

I'm reminded of a recent Ford Motor Company earnings call, during which CFO Bob Shanks outlined the effectiveness of their supply chain efforts. He spoke not in terms of cost improvements, but rather about better engagement with suppliers to achieve design changes, new features, and other innovations that have provided Ford with the ability to command a higher price for their cars. This is procurement running in stride with executive leadership, facilitating innovation, and enabling growth.

Organizations must innovate to grow and to sustain growth, and those advancements will increasingly come from outside their four walls. Think of the thousands of suppliers already servicing your company. Each of them possesses deep expertise in their area of specialization. Still, we are only using the majority of them to deliver, rather than to help our business excel. We remain locked in adversarial relationships with our suppliers resulting from repeated price negotiations and monitoring delivery. This dynamic is not conducive to increasing productivity or identifying new solutions. In other words, it is not creating either tactical or strategic value.

Procurement is already set up as the mechanism through which providers gain access to companies, and therefore, is best positioned to become the innovation portal for companies. Instead of issuing requests for

proposals in the hopes of squeezing another 5% out of, say, our reloca-
tion services provider, why aren't we working with them to understand
how our company can optimize our approach to workforce mobility to
deploy our talent globally to meet our changing business requirements?
It's faster and more impactful, and would make procurement a more
useful partner to human resources and the broader organization.

Then look beyond one category, at the literally thousands of supplier
partners servicing your company today. Of the 10,000 or so providers
working to supply you with goods and services, how many are being
asked to create solutions or prescribe alternatives? How many of them
are being told about the goals your organization has and are being challenged to support them? Probably 500, or 5% of those suppliers have
people dedicated to your account. They spend a total of about one million hours of resource time annually: one million. Are you capitalizing
on that commitment of time and effort from subject matter experts to
expand the resources and productivity of your enterprise, or are you
waiting for them to drop a box on your dock?

THE EVOLUTION OF A FUNCTION

The migration from a bid or governance mentality to serving as brokers
of resources, intelligence, and knowledge requires a fundamental change
in how we view ourselves. If we expect our internal and external stakeholders to take us seriously as we redefine our roles, we have to hold
ourselves to a different standard than we ever have in the past.

Becoming relevant, and staying relevant, is about more than doing
things differently. It's about hiring and cultivating the kind of talented
professionals that will enable procurement to be seen as contributors:
people with a strategic and commercial mind-set. It's about recognizing
that the way we've saved money in the past (sourcing, identification of
historic weaknesses, increasing spend volumes, demand management)
are not the ways we will be able to demonstrate improvement in the
future.

Gaining alignment with our leaders necessitates better communication with them, so that we understand their goals and how to support
them. Was it, for example, more important for Apple to be first to market with a smartphone, or to have better margins than Samsung, or to be
cheaper than Google? Understanding that speed might supersede cost
means being closer to decision makers.

Making decision makers and supply partners pay attention also means that we must become expert promoters of our value. Procurement professionals have rarely been confused with slick *marketeers*, but in the future we must be. As our discipline evolves, and as we change individually, it's critical that we let people know. Procurement has historically generated support by maintaining anonymity and by allowing others to take credit for their achievements. It's time to lay claim to our impact, to show that we can add scale, ideas, and resources to our organizations and that it's the type of meaningful change that warrants a seat in the boardroom. Promotion is not arrogance; it is procurement challenging our peers to view us differently and to appropriately value our contributions.

So we arrive at the crossroads with a choice to make. We can go on bidding stuff and seeing if we can secure enough stakeholder alignment to implement whatever improvements we think we've identified, or we can take a new tack. We can recognize our opportunity as vast and significant and largely untapped. We can change our professional fate by changing the way business is done and by teaching our organizations that there is more to be gained by leveraging our network than there is by continuing to simply buy and sell. It begins here, today, with this book and with these ideas and with your desire to incorporate them into the next generation of procurement and your commitment to being important tomorrow, five years from now, and ever on.

—David Clevenger, Senior Vice President of Strategy and
Organizational Development, Corporate United, Cleveland, Ohio

July 2015

About the Authors

JON HANSEN

The editor and lead writer for the PI Social Media Network's *Procurement Insights* blog, and the host of the *PI Window on The World* radio show, Jon Hansen is a two-time Ernst & Young Entrepreneur of the Year Finalist. Through funding from the government's Scientific Research & Experimental Development program, Jon built a software company that he eventually sold for $12 million. Based on his business experience and his work with major clients in developing programs that dramatically improved their procurement practices, he is considered to be a leading expert on subjects as diverse as supply chain practice, public sector policy, emerging business trends, and social media.

KELLY BARNER

Kelly Barner is the managing editor of Buyers Meeting Point, an online resource for procurement and purchasing professionals, and has a decade of experience working in procurement and supply chain. Her unique perspective on supply management is based on her time as a practitioner, a consultant at a solution provider, and now as an independent thought leader.

Ms. Barner's introduction to procurement was in the not-for-resale (indirect) procurement organization for a global grocery retailer. While there, she developed a specialization in sourcing location-based and corporate services. After earning her MBA, she took a position on the consulting team at Emptoris, a procurement solution and services provider that was acquired by IBM in 2011. She has led projects involving members of procurement, supplier, and purchasing teams and has practical skills in strategic sourcing program design and management, opportunity assessment, knowledge management, and custom taxonomy design.

Ms. Barner is a popular and regular guest content contributor to publications and blogs such as *Procurement Insights*, the *Selectica's Social Contracting* blog, the *Ivalua* blog, and *Design News*. Since 2011 she has delivered a weekly procurement Internet radio update that covers the coming week's events and a guest soundbite with editorial commentary.

Ms. Barner has her MBA from Babson College, an MS in Library and Information Science from Simmons College, and a BA in English and History from Clark University. In 2012, 2013, 2014, and 2015 she was awarded a Provider "Pro to Know" designation by *Supply & Demand Chain Executive Magazine*, and in 2013 she was also recognized as one of 28 "Top Female Supply Chain Executives."

Introduction

When asked about the future of procurement during an October 2014 interview about his book, *The Procurement Value Proposition*, Dr. Robert Handfield, Professor of Supply Chain Management at the North Carolina State University Poole College of Management, and the director of the Supply Chain Resource Cooperative, observed that while many of the ideas "have been kicking around for quite some time, the conditions under which they might flourish have yet to materialize in more than a handful of organizations."[1]

He then went on to talk about "corporate responsibility, technological advances, geopolitical and macroeconomic change, and demographic shifts." In short, from the standpoint of today's procurement professionals, the world as we knew it no longer exists. In fact, Handfield went so far as to suggest that unlike any other time in the past, our profession is in the midst of a seismic shake-up that will not only divide, but sever the procurement professionals of today and tomorrow from their predecessors.

This means that any book discussing the future of procurement must go beyond the mere recognition of this shift. To be truly useful, a book must also embrace the unique challenges of developing practical approaches to conditions that do not yet exist from a generational business perspective. It must also take into account the ripple effects of any changes, including but not limited to solution providers, analysts, associations, standards-setting bodies, and news/opinion sites. In this book, we aspire to better understand the choices procurement professionals are faced with, both individually and collectively, and how the decisions that are made today will affect the trajectory of their careers and of the profession as a whole.

For example, how will someone who has been in procurement for ten to twenty years take the information from this book and apply it, as opposed to someone who is early in his or her career? How about the emergence of a third potentially influential group—those who have chosen the procurement profession as a second career? This last group is particularly interesting in that they seem to represent the best of both the seasoned buyer and the up-and-coming *Generation Next* professional. These three groups have very different backgrounds, expectations, and perspectives on the future. The experienced professionals and second career procurement professionals have a depth of knowledge about the business world, while Millennials and second career procurement professionals share a fresh perspective on corporate commercial activity that introduces the innovation and enthusiasm that our field so badly needs.

While the prospects for this brave new world of tomorrow may prove daunting, perhaps we can take solace in the fact that similar, albeit less dramatic, changes are taking place elsewhere in the enterprise—namely in finance and information technology (IT). In all defined functional groups, questions remain about whether experience is an advantage or a hindrance. In the face of significant shifts, seasoned professionals have the added burden of *unlearning* (or essentially, ignoring) the knowledge and instincts they have worked hard to acquire. It is possible that they will have to relinquish their perspective on the role they play in the enterprise simply to survive.

In this context, Handfield's notion that "the integration of procurement across the business is not the responsibility of a few, but rather a challenge that must be embraced company-wide" rings true.[2] This dynamic creates some interesting synergies as well as conflicts. The disparity between positive and negative consequences creates a choice as well as an opportunity for those of us who would work in the field. In fact, it creates many choices. Every time we are exposed to a new set of circumstances we get the opportunity to make a choice that changes our current position and future trajectory.

Hope is by no means lost for the procurement profession—not even for those who have been in the industry for some time. In fact, if we are prepared to capitalize on the current opportunity, we may be able to take the evolutionary shifts that are emerging and use them to reshape our role for the better. We have identified the following three tensions as the primary shifts vying for procurement's attention:

1. The difference between what procurement was designed to do and what we are being expected to accomplish;
2. The changing relationship between a company and its suppliers, as more of each operation is fulfilled in the supply chain rather than by the company itself; and

3. The fact that despite all of the changes—be they in the areas of procurement talent, corporate expectations, or implemented technology—very little has changed about how the rest of the organization perceives procurement or how surrounding entities (associations, blogs, analysts) cover the field.

In this book, we will consider nine timely and major questions regarding procurement's role in the enterprise and the crossroads at which we now stand. Our goal is not to provide directions for the next step in a hypothetically *correct* path, but to illuminate the relative benefits of each choice available to the profession. We will also consider what the next phase of procurement's evolution will be like by sharing the observations of others and taking some creative (but enthusiastic) license of our own.

Regarding this last point, the authors have traveled on different professional paths to reach this collaborative crossroads. While we can't promise that we will agree with each other about the role of history in determining procurement's present, the relative priority of our current challenges, or what the days to come will hold, we can assure you that ours will be a lively dialogue. In fact, we have taken advantage of every opportunity to provide a diversity of understanding—called out, so that you know which of us holds each opinion and why, in the hopes that providing multiple perspectives on a series of relevant issues will help you determine your own position.

We also hope that by comparing and contrasting our positions with those of other respected thought leaders, our readers will increase their likelihood of making optimal choices of their own at their own professional crossroads. In the end, we aspire to enable you to make the best decisions about your own future in procurement, regardless of your starting point.

Chapter 1 Preview: Who Is Procurement?

"Some executives used to think of procurement as the place you send staff away in order to never see them again." (*Leading Procurement Strategy*, Carlos Mena, Remko van Hoek, Martin Christopher[3])

Most discussions of procurement overlook the fact that while we generalize the characteristics of the professionals in the field, the procurement community is made up of a diverse pool of individuals that share varying degrees of similarity with the collective, and in some cases stereotypical, procurement persona. As we explore the actual makeup of the profession as it stands today, these differences come into focus.

We are also able to see new and distinct perspectives forming. Many of the factors contributing to procurement's changing identity exist on an individual level, such as generational shifts and nontraditional career paths. As these and other dynamics reshape the procurement profession, there are implications for our professional associations, skills development priorities, collaborative technologies, expectations about loyalty to the profession (or the company), the path to chief procurement officer (CPO), and how we organize ourselves as a function. What remains to be seen is how much of a resemblance the procurement team of the future will share with the role that exists today.

Chapter 2 Preview: Has Procurement (Finally) Come of Age?

"Among procurement leaders, the CPO is twice as likely to report to the CEO and to be a member of the top management team as is the case at the average performers." (*Procurement 20/20*, Pete Spiller, Nicholas Reineke, Drew Ungerman, Henrique Teixeira[4])

Since many procurement professionals have a traditional mind-set about influence and advancement, we often view the fact that the CPO is not a standard executive level role as evidence that we have not *made it* yet. But this can be as much of an advantage as an obstacle. For procurement organizations without a direct representative at the executive table, current priorities and future opportunities are largely dictated by the function they report in to (finance, operations, etc.). In addition, the responsibilities that have traditionally defined the chief financial officer (CFO) and chief information officer (CIO) positions within an enterprise are going through major transformations of their own. This means that while traditional reporting hierarchies still exist, at least for the time being, the dynamics and boundaries within this framework are fluid. The opportunity this represents for change, or more specifically the ability to grow one's relative influence, is the same for all areas of practice, be it finance, IT, or procurement. As individual professionals within procurement, we need to embrace this reality in order to grow our responsibilities and grab the opportunity to build on the work we have already done.

Chapter 3 Preview: Is Procurement Strategic?

"The fundamental problem is that deeply ingrained structures and systems designed to extract maximum value from a competitive advantage become a

liability when the environment requires instead the capacity to surf through waves of short-lived opportunities." (*The End of Competitive Advantage,* Rita Gunther McGrath[5])

Although the procurement function evolved out of tactical purchasing through the adoption of new technology and increased strategy, procurement is no longer simply about acquiring products and services. We are driven to extract maximum value from every dollar spent by the enterprise, from every supply relationship, and through every executed contract. At one time, savings were realized through efficiency gains due to supply base consolidation—leveraging projected volume to achieve maximum economies of scale. While we met our short-term objectives using this approach, we created difficulties for our future selves by inadvertently embedding unseen pockets of risk and dependency within the supply chain. The intelligence vacuum created as a result of operating within a tactical bubble now requires us to play catch-up in terms of understanding the needs of those with whom we must work. But how? How do we move beyond a narrowly defined scope of performance measurements, centered around objectives such as best price, to a broader horizon perspective that embraces supplier liquidity and mutual gain?

Chapter 4 Preview: Is There Truth Behind the Numbers?

"Almost all data analysis is about crunching numbers from the past and extrapolating these numbers into the future. For obvious reasons, the past does not include data on things that haven't happened or ideas that have not yet been imagined. As a result, data analysis of the future tends to underestimate or even ignore past events or conditions that can't be measured while overestimating those that can." (*The Moment of Clarity,* Christian Madsbjerg and Mikkel B. Rasmussen[6])

To the extent that procurement is a data-driven discipline, we are closely linked to the capabilities of our technology. And while quality data is an essential foundation for all of procurement's efforts, the time required to make it actionable comes with a high opportunity cost. In many cases, we are slaves to data cleansing and report creation. Our solutions, despite how they are characterized, often serve as no more than accessible, segmented storage. Making sure that enabling technologies are doing as much heavy lifting and enrichment as possible frees up procurement professionals to do the strategic work required to create value and competitive advantage for the organizations and colleagues we support. At the same time, increasing the level of task and workflow automation allows us to leave a data trail that can later be mined for trends and improvement opportunities.

Chapter 5 Preview: Are Win-Win Collaborations Really Possible?

"As with any relationship, it cannot just be turned on, it needs to be courted, pursued, built, and reinforced with consistency and persistence. Both sides need to want it and need to invest in making it happen." (*Supplier Relationship Management*, Jonathan O'Brien[7])

In our opening paragraphs we made reference to Robert Handfield's statement that the "integration of procurement across the business is not the responsibility of a few but rather a challenge that must be embraced company-wide."[8] Handfield's point is crystal clear: building real and productive relationships is as much an act of will as it is intent, but intent can be so abstract that it is unlikely to be a motivating factor for the enterprise at large. What this means from a procurement perspective, however noble the intent or pressing the need to redefine the collaborative process, is that we must ensure that both shared and individual objectives are achieved. This is particularly true of the buyer-supplier relationship. Evolving from transactions to relationships to partnerships requires a new level of transparency that will seem both foreign and even contradictory for many in procurement who are accustomed to the *knowledge is power*, one-sided approach to resource maximization.

Chapter 6 Preview: Do We Really Need Another Chapter about Finance?

"Procurement does not just work in a vacuum where we only negotiate with suppliers. A CPO needs to work well with the rest of the executive team so that they will accept that procurement deserves to have a decision-making role." (*The* CPO, Christina Schuh, Michael F. Strohmer, Stephen Easton, Armin Scharlach, and Peter Scharbert[9])

Procurement's somewhat troubled relationship with finance has received so much coverage to this point, that we felt it only fair to ask ourselves and our readers whether enough has changed between the two functions to require a rewrite of the topics that have already been covered ad nauseam. Our historically myopic focus on this one internal relationship, important though it might be, has blinded us to all of the other changes and shifts taking place. It may also have blinded us to some of the challenges that start with us and prevent better relations with *all* internal functions. Recognizing the need to collaborate and implementing a viable plan of action to ensure that channels of communication are not only opened but remain open is more challenging today than it has been at any other point in time. While procurement has gone through a *profession altering* transformation, so have those who occupy the executive suites in both finance and IT. Within the context of this change, identifying the points of connection that will facilitate greater collaboration is tantamount to trying to hit a moving target.

Chapter 7 Preview: Can Procurement Technology Benefit from the Uber Effect?

"Uber is a $3.5 billion lesson in building for how the world *should* work instead of optimizing for how the world *does* work." (Aaron Levie Tweet, August 23, 2013[10])

Since our early days as procurement (rather than purchasing), we have been identified and defined in large part by the technology we use. Rather than being a positive bridge to the rest of the organization, in some cases it has created a new set of difficulties around adoption and compliance. Given its importance to our potential, you would think that procurement would carefully evaluate our providers as companies as well as solutions, and that we would hold solution analysts to a high standard as well. Unfortunately, we have fallen into the same trap that many of our stakeholders did, evaluating the products and services being purchased in too narrow of a scope. Given the rise of the cloud for delivery and security, and the level of commoditization that has taken place in procurement technology, we should have moved beyond a features and functions approach to technology decision making by now. We have not, nor have our analysts. Until we all start looking more closely at the people behind the solutions—and the evaluations, for that matter—we will not be able to see them clearly.

Chapter 8 Preview: Are the Differences Between the Public and Private Sectors Real or Perceived?

Each side of the divide has strengths and weaknesses, but in every case the public sector is providing something the private sector cannot: A backup that's there if and when you need it; a benchmark for private providers; and a backstop to make sure costs don't spin out of control. (When Government Competes Against the Private Sector, Everybody Wins by Eric Schnurer[11])

If there is any idea that needs to *go the way of the dinosaurs*, it is the pervasive belief that public sector procurement is the *goofy cousin* of the private sector. While the public sector is not without its challenges and past failures, neither is the private sector. The difference is that the public sector, especially procurement, receives a disproportionate amount of news coverage for their failures. If the two groups are to work together effectively, there needs to be mutual respect and understanding. When this is made possible, and when the public sector takes control of the effort, there is almost no limit to the value that can be created: just ask Elon Musk.

Chapter 9 Preview: The Media and Procurement: Are We Really Covered?

"All you have to do is write one true sentence. Write the truest sentence that you know. So finally I would write one true sentence, and then go on from there. It was easy then because there was always one true sentence that I knew or had seen or had heard someone say." (A Moveable Feast,[12] Ernest Hemingway)

The role of the media sector is to cover developments in their area of expertise for the sake of their readers or audience. In order to be truly effective, they must do so without any distorting self-interest. Although procurement has long had a robust media sector, the lines between analysts and bloggers have blurred, creating a situation where organizations are reliant upon the same companies and organizations for revenue that they are supposed to be covering objectively. Although under normal circumstances this might require no more than taking a *grain of salt* approach to reading coverage, when major or controversial developments occur, it presents those in the media with a difficult dilemma: do you print a negative or questionable story if it jeopardizes your revenue? For the practitioners that are reliant upon the media for truthful and complete coverage, there is a dilemma as well. How can they stay informed when only a subset of information is being conveyed? Can anything that is reported upon be trusted?

Chapter 10 Preview: Where Does Procurement Go from Here?

"It's quickly dawning on us instead that our education was at best a thin foundation that needs to be continually refreshed in order for us to stay

competitive." (*The Power of Pull*, John Hagel III, John Seely Brown, and Lang Davison[13])

American author and social philosopher Eric Hoffer once said, "In times of change, learners inherit the earth . . . while the learned find themselves beautifully equipped to deal with a world that no longer exists."[14] In this one simple yet powerful statement, Hoffer sums up the procurement professional's greatest challenge, as well as his or her greatest opportunity. The only question left to be answered is this: what does making the transition from being learned to learning entail, and are we up to the task?

In this final chapter of our book, we will examine what it means to change the way we see our profession, including our understanding of its role within the modern competitive enterprise. From moving beyond the adversarial aspects of past supplier engagement practices, to becoming relational and collaborative in our interactions with external as well as internal partners, readers will hopefully find this chapter an essential survival and transformational guide for their careers.

Change is on the near horizon. We can no longer deny or avoid it any more than we can precisely predict what it will look like. We can, however, adapt and become relevant beyond what we ever thought possible.

REFERENCES

1. Jon Hansen, "The Procurement Value Proposition: A Discussion with Robert Handfield PhD," *PI Window on the World*, November 5, 2014, http://www.blogtalkradio.com/jon-hansen/2014/10/30/the-procurement-value-proposition-a-discussion-with-robert-handfield-phd.
2. Gerard Chick and Robert Handfield, *The Procurement Value Proposition: The Rise of Supply Management*, (Philadelphia: Kogan Page, 2015), xii.
3. Carlos Mena, Remko van Hoek, Martin Christopher, *Leading Procurement Strategy: Driving Value Through the Supply Chain*, (Philadelphia: Kogan Page, 2014), 36.
4. Pete Spiller, Nicholas Reineke, Drew Ungerman, Henrique Teixeira, *Procurement 20/20: Supply Entrepreneurship in a Changing World*, (New Jersey: Wiley, 2013), 22.
5. Rita Gunther McGrath, *The End of Competitive Advantage: How to Keep Your Strategy Moving as Fast as Your Business*, (Boston: Harvard Business Review Press, 2013), 5.

6. Christian Madsbjerg and Mikkel B. Rasmussen, *The Moment of Clarity: Using the Human Sciences to Solve Your Toughest Business Problems*, (Boston: Harvard Business Review Press, 2014), 43.
7. Jonathan O'Brien, *Supplier Relationship Management: Unlocking the Hidden Value in Your Supply Base*, (Philadelphia: Kogan Page, 2014). 319.
8. Gerard Chick and Robert Handfield, *The Procurement Value Proposition: The Rise of Supply Management*, (Philadelphia: Kogan Page, 2015), xii.
9. Christina Schuh, Michael F. Strohmer, Stephen Easton, Armin Scharlach, and Peter Scharbert, *The CPO: Transforming Procurement in the Real World*, (New York: Apress, 2012), 23.
10. Aaron Levie, Twitter post, August 23, 2013, 1:16 a.m., https:// twitter.com/levie.
11. Eric Schnurer, "When Government Competes Against the Private Sector, Everybody Wins," *The Atlantic*, March 11, 2015, http:// www.theatlantic.com/politics/archive/2015/03/when-government -competes-against-the-private-sector-everybody-wins/387460/.
12. Ernest M. Hemingway, *The Poetry Foundation*, Accessed July 6, 2015, http://www.poetryfoundation.org/bio/ernest-m-hemingway.
13. John Hagel III, John Seely Brown, and Lang Davison, *The Power of Pull: How Small Moves, Smartly Made, Can Set Big Things in Motion*, (New York: Basic Books, 2012), 13.
14. Eric Hoffer, *Between the Devil and the Dragon: The Best Essays and Aphorisms of Eric Hoffer* (New York: Harper & Row, 1982), 146.

This book has free material available for download from the
Web Added Value™ resource center at *www.jrosspub.com*

At J. Ross Publishing we are committed to providing today's professional with practical, hands-on tools that enhance the learning experience and give readers an opportunity to apply what they have learned. That is why we offer free ancillary materials available for download on this book and all participating Web Added Value™ publications. These online resources may include interactive versions of material that appears in the book or supplemental templates, worksheets, models, plans, case studies, proposals, spreadsheets and assessment tools, among other things. Whenever you see the WAV™ symbol in any of our publications, it means bonus materials accompany the book and are available from the Web Added Value Download Resource Center at www.jrosspub.com.

Downloads for *Procurement at a Crossroads: Career-Impacting Insights into a Rapidly Changing Industry* consist of:

- Links to on-demand audio interviews with thought leaders in the fields of procurement and supply chain that were key to the formation of the thesis of the book
- The Purchasing Professional's 10 Commandments
- Purchasing and Supply Management Salaries by Point of Entry, 2015
- A process diagram for supply market intelligence that is designed to guide procurement professionals through the process of gathering intelligence in order to make informed sourcing decisions and develop negotiation strategies
- Survey results of CFO's View of Procurement
- Links to the blogs and podcasts of both authors so readers can stay up to date on how procurement and the rest of the enterprise continue to progress and evolve in response to internal and external forces

1

Who Is Procurement?

"Some executives used to think of procurement as the place you send staff away in order to never see them again." Leading Procurement Strategy, Carlos Mena, Remko van Hoek, Martin Christopher[1]

In 1913, Elwood "E.B." Hendricks was a representative for the Thomas Publishing Company in New York City.[2] He was a salesperson, busy providing reference materials to purchasing agents at many of the largest companies of the day. The Thomas Register of American Manufacturers was the supplier network or business network of its time, and it allowed purchasing agents to locate products across the United States. Although information on suppliers and their capabilities had been consolidated, most purchasing agents were still focused on their own local community and were skeptical of the need to network in an extended fashion—even with other agents.

In a time long before e-commerce and before use of the telephone was commonplace, business was conducted in person and in writing. As he made his rounds of sales calls, Hendricks recognized how professionally isolated purchasing agents were, even in densely populated New York City. Known by his contemporaries as *an idea man*, he "saw a need for a professional organization that would bring them [purchasing agents] together to network as well as provide educational opportunities to improve their performance."[3] The organization he envisioned, which would become the New York Chapter of the Institute for Supply Management (ISM) was formally launched in January of 1914. It still exists today, and although it conducts business in a different way and with a vastly different membership profile, it has achieved the national status intended by Hendricks.

Despite the fact that ISM is well-known in the field of procurement, few practitioners know that we owe our oldest professional institution to the vision of a salesperson. This piece of our collective history is indicative of the stereotypical procurement *personality* and the challenges that it creates for us today. In a field stereotyped as being risk averse, full of professionals who feel most comfortable following or enforcing preapproved guidelines, opportunities to blaze new trails or foresee strategic changes may pass us by.

As was the case in the early 20th century, procurement today is in need of vision and direction. The characteristics of the average practitioner are changing in terms of demographics, qualifications, background, and aspirations. At the same time, companies are looking to accomplish more than managing economies of scale and standardizing specifications to reduce costs. Just over a century after Hendricks helped found ISM-New York, the procurement profession is primed to seize an opportunity for better corporate positioning and unlimited potential. Whether or not the changing profile of modern procurement practitioners and the expanding expectations of the enterprise will come into alignment, and where our next visionaries will come from, remains to be seen.

PATHS INTO, THROUGH, AND OUT OF PROCUREMENT

Now that we have established a historical basis for the collective procurement persona, we must ask:

- What does the history of the profession and its evolution to this point mean to today's purchasing professionals on a practical level?
- Or, to put it another way, just as Hendricks' vision resulted in the establishment of a professional community: what will be the next big shift, when will it happen, who will serve as the visionaries, and what impact will it have on us?

The answers to those questions will, for each individual, have a lot to do with how they found their way into the procurement profession in the first place.

To gain this important perspective, each practitioner must first identify into which one of the following three career categories he or she falls—traditional purchaser (or buyer), *Generation Next* procurement professional, or second career procurement professional. If, over a period of time, we were to ask a variety of procurement audiences all the same question—How many of you *chose* purchasing as a career?—the audience response would vary greatly.

It used to be that if one or two hands were raised, it was considered a big number. In the past, it seemed that the majority of traditional purchasing people *fell* into the job. Back then it was considered a job rather than a profession, and it was more likely to be determined by circumstance than by choice. Starting a career in purchasing was reminiscent of the classic childhood scenario where the captain of the team had to pick the guy with thick eyeglasses and two left feet because he had no other choice. Accepting a career in purchasing was similar to the captain's choice in that no one else seemed to want the job, so you took it and its two left feet rather than forfeit the game.

Equally important is the sentiment captured by the quote that opens this chapter. Sometimes having a career in purchasing had more to do with a manager or executive not wanting to see you any more than it did any choice you might make for yourself. The authors of *Leading Procurement Strategy* made this statement before going on to discuss the increasing breadth and depth of required procurement capabilities. Not only do our organizations want us to be more strategic with regard to the responsibilities we have had in the past, but also to expand our influence and relevance into areas such as corporate social responsibility, risk management, and supply base innovation.

Whether traditional buyers ended up in purchasing because it was the path of least resistance or because they were banished there from some other function, it did not bode well for their success. It also does little to suggest that the role will survive beyond them. By allowing purchasing teams to be staffed with people who had so little inner direction (or so much ability to offend), corporations inadvertently doomed the role. These professionals had no ability to make the choices necessary to succeed in an increasingly complex and quickly changing landscape. In the process of corporate natural selection, they went extinct after failing to offer enduring value.

Generation Next: Fresh Procurement Faces

Fortunately, and like the tagline from the old Virginia Slims ad proclaimed: "You've come a long way, baby!"—things in purchasing are much different today, largely because people in purchasing (or procurement as it is more commonly known now) are much different. Ambitious professionals choose procurement, either as their first step out of college or as a second career. While even these two deliberate paths bring different strengths and qualities to the profession, they share the recognition that procurement is a promising career choice and hold ambitious ideas about what can be accomplished from a position within it.

This point was driven home when a young woman from what we will call *Generation Next* (no Pepsi required), approached us with great enthusiasm about pursuing a career in procurement and supply chain management. In stark contrast to the bygone days of dog-eared supplier catalogs and a *you don't get what you deserve, you get what you negotiate* adversarial mind-set, her interest was based on the opportunity to get a diverse, global business experience. Far from being trapped in a functional role focused on getting the best price, she saw procurement as a compelling way to make a strategic organizational impact.

With a 4.0 grade average from a prestigious university and business experience that included handling sustainable farming and the procurement of pickles from India, she is the poster person for all that the procurement profession can, and will become in the next few years.

Considering these kinds of credentials, it is no wonder that in their book, *The Procurement Value Proposition: The Rise of Supply Management*, Gerard Chick and Robert Handfield talk about the definite and definitive chasm between the purchasing people of the past, and today's strategic procurement professionals, "As businesses turn their attention from compliance to growth and innovation, businesses must focus, too, on developing their strategy to enhance the commercial acumen and professional capability of their procurement people, beyond the skill sets traditionally required in their roles."[4]

Let's face it, procurement today is a brand-new game, with new rules requiring new skill sets that older generations did not need to possess. The fact of the matter is that the role and value of procurement as defined by those outside of the profession has changed dramatically. It has evolved from being a functional *job* to a high value *career*. Or, to put it another way, in the past you would not waste the talents of a person with a 4.0 grade average from a prestigious university on a buying position. Nor did you, early in your career, need to have experience in dealing with a globalized supply base or in working within the framework of socially responsible mandates.

There are, of course, studies that to varying and debatable degrees, attempt to quantify the above evolution of the profession. For example, in her January 15, 2014 article on procurement changes over the last decade,[5] My Purchasing Center's Susan Avery summarized the findings from a 2013 industry survey, excerpted in the text box and illustrated in Figure 1.1.

Changes in Procurement Practitioners from 2003 to 2013

On average, the age of the procurement professional is staying roughly the same. In 1993, the average age was 44 years. In 2003, it was 46 years. But 70% of procurement professionals in 2013 were 45 years or older.

In 2013, 84% of procurement professionals had college degrees; the majority of these were business degrees. In 2003, just 67% held degrees. In 1993, the figure was 61.2%. Again, most of the degrees were in business. Ten years ago, 21% had graduate degrees—most of which were Master of Business Administration (MBA) degrees. Today, 44% have graduate degrees—again, the majority are also MBAs.

Given these figures, it's probably not surprising that many more procurement professionals today report to the chief financial officer (CFO) than in 2003. Specifically, 40% now call the CFO their boss; 10 years ago, just 6% worked for companies with this reporting structure. More reported to the chief executive officer (CEO) back then—35% compared to 30% now.

It is left up to each one of us what we will take away from the My Purchasing Center survey. This is a pivotal point in time for procurement that will redefine both the profession and the professionals' future for many, many years to come. Needless to say, the expectations are great. *Procurement 20/20*, written by a team of high-level McKinsey executives, offers the following challenge in its last chapter: "By 2020, procurement's role will have become even more important for sustaining constant supply, best cost, reduced volatility, faster and improved innovation, and clean corporate-brand image."[6] If the majority of this promised transformation is to take place between now and the year 2020, we had better get going.

Impact of Second Career Procurement Professionals

Of course we would be remiss if we limited this discussion to purchasing traditionalists and the emerging Generation Next procurement

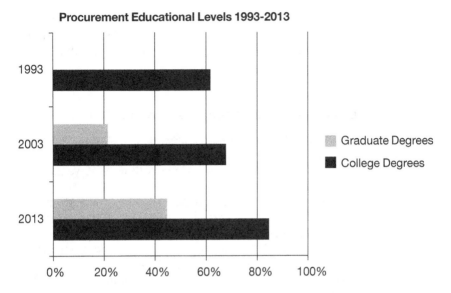

Source: My Purchasing Center (Note: Information on graduate degrees was not available in the 1993 data)

Figure 1.1   Procurement educational levels 1993-2013

professionals. There is a third, less vocal but increasingly influential group that is starting to make their mark.

Here is the story of Giuliana, who, while participating in a Public Sector Supplier Forum group on LinkedIn, was asked: "Why did you choose purchasing as a second career?" She provided an interesting perspective that until recently may not have received the weight of consideration it was due.[7]

"To answer your question of—*Why procurement?*—we had just come out of 2007-2008 with the major turmoil in the financial & property markets. I wanted to be more active civically, but certainly didn't want to be in political office. It seemed like every level of government seemed unable to cut their spending. Then a simple position in the Purchasing Department was posted at our local municipality—I had the administrative qualifications and applied.

I feel that if government is to be responsible, then we, as citizens, have to step up and be more active. I had the work experience, and as I am strong in organizational skills, this seemed like an area that I could make a difference—be a part of the solution. It's behind the scenes (which I prefer), but can have a positive impact, if the work is done well. Since I first started, I have had to [sic] opportunity to get certified, which certainly helped broaden my understanding of the industry—both public and private sector.

That choice to work in procurement was the way I participated in local government. And yes, in these last five years, I have seen a slow transition from the mind-set of just purchasing/ buying materials for the city, to buying/planning within the broader scope of the city's strategic goals. Purchasing is slowly becoming a topic that is considered at the planning stages— questions such as: 'Should we even buy?' and 'Is the purchase necessary for the long-term goals?' Once these questions become routine within the whole organization, along with the choices made, I would say we will have succeeded in reincorporating the procurement department back into the organization as a recognized integral part of the planning process."

Somewhere between the buyers of yesteryear (the majority of whom fell into the job) and the up-and-comers who deliberately look to procurement as their first career choice, the second career generation is almost a hybrid—representing the best of both. They have the depth of experience in the business world and the focused energy associated with choosing to pursue a new and exciting challenge.

It would be reasonable to suggest that since most people from the traditional practitioner group fell into the procurement profession, they are in the same category as those who have chosen procurement as a second career. After all, these individuals were doing something else before assuming the purchasing mantle. Although it is technically a second career for both groups, the fact that traditional buyers were led to it by circumstance rather than free will prevents them from having the same impact as those who consciously chose to make the switch to procurement rather than stepping away from something else. Unlike Giuliana who, for example, had a clear vision as to what entering the profession would mean in terms of organizational impact—purchasing people tend to be functionally driven. A job needed to be done and someone had to do it so—why not them?

In the same LinkedIn discussion stream, a group member named Phillip seemed to echo the second career professional sentiments expressed by Giuliana when he said:

"I myself did not start out in purchasing and I can appreciate proven professionals coming into the profession with new eyes and ideas. That is where best practices come from. I agree, things are changing, and it is not the recent graduates that are doing this. It is people like you and myself and many other talented professionals."

Of course, the impact of generational divides and second career integration relative to the modern workforce applies to all career paths, not just procurement, and it includes changes related to years of experience versus fresh energy and the natural turnover cycle. In addition to these changes, procurement organizations need to be particularly aware of adjustments related to changes in chosen career paths. Professionals that make the conscious choice to transition from another path to procurement are enriched with experience, knowledge, and the enthusiasm to learn so that they can make a difference. They may actually be reshaping the profile of the procurement profession more than Generation Next.

Whether they are a silent majority or influential minority, one thing is clear—second career procurement professionals are positioned to effect the greatest change in the shortest time frame, in a field that is already going through the early stages of a major transformation.

WILL PURCHASING GO THE WAY OF THE DINOSAURS?

We are certain that there is bound to be some spirited debate regarding the aforementioned categories, both as we have defined them and as we have described them. We will also leave it open to discussion whether or not it is fair to assign (or confine, depending on your point of view) someone to a predefined label. One thing is certain, however—procurement needs leaders. From where those leaders emerge will have a significant impact on the future of the profession in the coming years and decades.

If, for example, age is not a factor, as suggested by the My Purchasing Center survey findings, then why can't traditional purchasing professionals make the transition from buyer to strategic industry influencer? And why is so much emphasis being placed on the ability of Generation Next and second career professionals to lead the next evolutionary stage on their own, rather than with or after an official handoff from traditional buyers? Usually, there is a passing of the torch between old and new that recognizes the value represented by an understanding of the history held in the minds of those who have gone before. If it is true that traditional buyers have no role in either the future or the transition to the future, what impact will this break in the generational chain have on the industry? After all, doesn't there have to be some commonality between what was and what is and what will be, to ensure a sound progression?

In a recent Blog Talk Radio interview on *The Five Most Important Questions for Procurement in 2015*,[8] Kate Vitasek, author of the *Vested Outsourcing* series of books and a lead researcher at the University of Tennessee, suggested that the procurement function will never fully realize and attain its proper ranking within the organizational hierarchy until "all of the dinosaurs have died off." Vitasek's sharp comments speak to an underlying problem that has plagued the profession for many years, and that is the oversimplification of what we have traditionally done. While stakeholders outside of the profession may have held us back with their attitudes and generalizations, procurement insiders have done little with their own actions to disprove these perceptions.

In a December 2014 blog post, Vitasek offered up an example of how antiquated supply management practices can come back to bite an organization—even at the highest levels. Tesco, a multinational grocery retailer headquartered in the UK, has long been criticized by its suppliers for heavy-handed policies and practices. Far from just having high expectations of its suppliers, the discovery of accounting irregularities led to changes in executive management and a criminal investigation. "In an iNVEZZ news report, [Britain's Business Secretary Vince] Cable said Tesco has a reputation for behaving robustly—another way of saying *squeezing*—towards its suppliers, many of which are small or medium-sized businesses that rely on their contracts with the retailer."[9] What might have been considered perfectly acceptable (if aggressive) business practices in the past, today results in interrupted careers, criminal liability, lost shareholder value, and a damaged brand reputation.

Today's business world is fast, complex, and global, but the market, consumers, and shareholders will not tolerate a bottom line that is bolstered by unfair treatment of suppliers. Instead, more creative approaches are required. Few of the traditionally minded players are equipped to handle the frenetic pace of shifting variables and high stakes. In short, we are well beyond the best-price, volume-leveraging, cost-avoidance focus of the bygone era. Think of it in the context of professional hockey—or any sport for that matter.

While even Wayne Gretzky or Gordie Howe, two standout professional hockey players in the late decades of the 20th century, could be stars if they were young players today, the majority of their contemporaries would not be able to make the transition to succeed in what is a far more complex and faster game. This theory is most clearly proven in the fact that training, equipment, and even the strategy of the game have evolved to the point of being radically different from that with which they were familiar.

More than just simply teaching an old dog new tricks or giving a traditional buyer a world-class eProcurement solution, what is happening now in the procurement world is a reflection of a natural evolutionary process. In sharing the findings of a 2013 Oxford study, International Association for Contract and Commercial Management (IACCM) president Tim Cummins pointed out that 47% of all purchasing professionals today will become redundant over the next few years.[10] This means that we will see nearly half of purchasing people fade into a sunset of irrelevance, left behind by a changing world they can no longer comprehend and which no longer requires their skills or knowledge—whether by skill set or choice (or a little of both).

Do prognostications such as the ones made by Vitasek and Cummins mean that those who have been in purchasing for longer than a few years should stop reading this book and simply accept the inevitable? *No!* In fact, they need to read this book more than any other segment of the procurement community.

Despite the assertions of the senior executives who, in a fateful 2006 Chief Procurement Officer (CPO) Agenda Roundtable,[11] concluded that the people who are most capable of running a purchasing department are the ones who don't have a purchasing background, we do not believe that ongoing relevancy is beyond the grasp of any professional, at least not from an opportunity or aptitude standpoint. In that roundtable, Tom Rae, Senior Vice President of corporate purchasing at the German-based automotive supplier Continental, said, "One of the benefits of more CPOs coming from outside the procurement world is that they tend to be wonderfully connected in their organizations; they bring a network and credibility, and that helps to move procurement into the mainstream."[12] His opinion on this subject is certainly not unique, and it hinges on a few critical assumptions about procurement professionals: we have limited networks, which deprive us of a key source of external credibility. He also clearly believes that procurement is not mainstream and, therefore, needs to be moved closer to the center by outsider CPOs. By accepting that our leaders are likely to have backgrounds in functions other than what procurement brings with it, we create an opportunity to broaden our perspective and increase the diversity of approaches we have at our disposal.

The desire to learn (or unlearn) and adapt to a changing reality is, of course, another matter. But this is the case regardless of the industry in which one pursues their career aspirations. Provided that there is a strong desire to adapt and therefore reinvent the profession and one's occupation within it, the long-time buyer has as much of a chance as a *Top 30 Under 30*[13] new kid or a second career veteran to make a meaningful impact and realize success.

This is where the corresponding evolution of external forces such as association curricula and emerging technologies come into play. In the spirit of Handfield and Chick's observations that the integration of procurement in this brave new world "is not the responsibility of a few but rather a challenge that must be embraced company-wide,"[14] the procurement professional does not stand alone.

In other words, true alignment is not limited to an internalized process of mind-set transformation that must take place on an individual basis. It is also based upon being in sync with both the company for whom you work, and the association or associations with whom you are a member.

If you are with a company that views procurement as a functional extension of finance, as opposed to a strategic focal point to drive bottom-line profitability, you are not likely to gain any significant traction from a career relevancy standpoint. Conversely, if you find that you are on the periphery of a disquieting cyclonic change, relative to your present company's views of how procurement must evolve to assume a more proactive role in the business as a whole, the ball, as they say, is in your court. In either instance, alignment may prove difficult, if not impossible, and either one or both parties must seriously contemplate a change.

With the former, it is time for you to seek a more progressive-thinking organization that will not only foster, but actively facilitate your development into a new generation influencer. If you find yourself in the latter position, then lay low for as long as you can, until you can retire or are laid off. In the meantime, get your resume out there or think about a second career in another field, and start saving a few extra dollars because job security is a thing of the past. The same can be said for your current association memberships.

In the end, change is inevitable. As the old saying goes—you can either lead, follow, or get out of the way. In the context of what we have outlined above, you can opt in, slide over, or move out. The choice is yours. And if the choice isn't yours, or if you don't have the vision to make a choice, the choice will be made for you. Since that option isn't particularly appealing to most professionals, our recommendation is to embrace the change that is certain to come.

IMPLICATIONS OF THE BREAK BETWEEN OLD AND NEW PROCUREMENT

We spent the first part of this chapter talking about the changes in individual procurement career paths as a result of the transition from old procurement to new procurement—assuming we can still call it procurement moving forward. This shift will not just affect procurement professionals and the companies for whom they work. There is a whole industry that has been built up over time to support the networking, analyst, news, and thought leadership needs of the profession. How will they—*will they?*—make the change from old to new?

Real change never comes without some heartache, and just as not all practitioners will survive the coming transition, some familiar institutions will be left behind as well. Unable or unwilling to change their business models or value propositions, they will fight to stay alive until the numbers do not exist to make their operation sustainable. By no means do we rejoice in the fading relevance of these organizations. There is a real sadness associated with saying good-bye, even when the time has clearly come.

Although the specifics in each of the following categories of peripheral organizations differ, there is a troubling trend. Focusing on procurement is worthwhile enough to make a niche organization an attractive acquisition for a large, mass-market provider, but not commercially viable enough to keep it around for long after that. When we look at the associations, analyst firms, news outlets, and thought leaders that serve the procurement industry, we see a disconcerting pattern of brilliant resources and individuals being swallowed up by impressive firms, never to be heard from again.

Professional Associations

The fact that we open this chapter with the founding story behind the ISM over a century ago, demonstrates just how influential such organizations have been and still are to the procurement profession. At this crossroads, however, we need to look at the founding purpose of such professional associations, whether that purpose continues to resonate with the professional community, and how their channels of interaction will be able to adjust to the changing social norms of the 21st century.

Most detrimental to the longevity of professional associations—at least in the traditional form—is the current trend toward virtual networking. Whether through LinkedIn or more practice specific (but entirely online) resources such as Procurious, it is unlikely that young procurement professionals anticipate spending an evening each month meeting in person with colleagues from other companies in their local area. And while these virtual channels are equally available to professional associations, the question remains: how virtual can an association become and still be considered an association?

ISM has made particular efforts to evolve. Thomas Derry, their President and CEO since 2013, has a background in finance rather than procurement. Just as an aside, the appointment of someone from outside the purchasing world, and from finance of all places, to head up the world's oldest procurement association shows that perhaps little has changed relative to the opinions expressed by the executives who participated in the CPO Agenda Roundtable discussion back in 2007. Said irony notwithstanding, Derry took over the reigns at ISM from former CEO Paul Novak only six months after ISM acquired ADR North America. Billed at the time as the meeting of two industry *powerhouses*,[15] it is unclear from an outsider's point of view just what sort of a lasting impact this may have had on ISM's mind-set or strategic direction.

In a PI Window on Business Blog talk radio interview on April 15, 2015, Derry talked about some of the challenges and changes facing ISM as they strive to support their core base of members, while also welcoming and attracting new professionals who have a decidedly different set of needs and wants. He noted that there have been "lots of significant underlying changes in consumer behavior and we [ISM] have to track with those or we just won't be relevant." Derry interestingly described ISM as a content or media business in the interview rather than as a professional or networking association, recognizing the changes in how information is marketed and distributed. "We have to become more digital in the distribution of our information.... We have to understand how our members and customers want to consume and need to consume our information confronting the kinds of lives they live today." Despite how spot-on his comments were, it is worth noting in a sadly ironic way, that ISM did not publicize or distribute the link to the interview on Twitter (a channel perfectly suited to the immediate distribution of podcast content) in the 48 hours before or the 24 hours after.

ISM, as well as other associations, such as the Chartered Institute of Procurement and Supply (CIPS) and the IACCM, the latter of which seems to be more focused on embracing and responding to the virtual revolution, along with the smaller niche players such as the Next Level Purchasing Association and American Purchasing Society, face similar challenges. They must embrace new content formats and marketing channels while not alienating their base membership—professionals that are more likely to expect traditional formats, such as print.

Even small changes in their traditions and legacy give evidence to a growing shift within the field. CIPS held a vote in June 2014 to change the word associated with the *P* in their well-known acronym from *Purchasing* to *Procurement*.[16] The vote passed, and the change caused little if any ripple in the profession. This may be because, by either a stroke of luck or misfortune, CIPS did not have to rebrand. They simply moved from one *P* to another. The name change appears to have been more about keeping up with a change in the common parlance of the profession than an adoption of any strategic or directional change. One day they were CIPS, and the next day they were, well, CIPS. In 2015, Sourcing Interests Group made a similar move, changing the meaning of the *I* in their commonly used acronym, SIG to *Industry*.

In the context of the above, it is not surprising that a 2009 on-air broadcast of a panel discussion focused on answering the question—"Is the Traditional Association Model Dead?"—resulted in some concern about how associations, regardless of the field they serve, could maintain their relevance in a world of faster information availability and alternate distribution channels.[17] The panel, including participants from IACCM, Next Level Purchasing Association (NLPA), Corporate United, and Buyers Meeting Point questioned the need for an organization focused on providing publications and certifications through a local chapter model.

In the discussion, NLPA President Charles Dominick made the seemingly simple but directionally critical statement that "Traditional associations have been around a long time and, like any older organization, they do things the way they have always done them." His point, that part of what makes establishments or traditional associations, well... traditional is that they have endured. But the foundation that has allowed them to pass the test of time becomes an impediment to agility if, as we

Figure 1.2

believe we are seeing in procurement, a shift takes place in the professional community they serve (see Figure 1.2).

Contrary to what one might expect, there has been more activity rather than less in the association space, as shown in Figure 1.3. Since 1990 a number of new associations and networking groups have been founded, with no significant merges or departures of the legacy associations of the early 20th century. What we see instead is more fragmentation. Rather that being a reverse of the rollup that occurred as local chapters joined forces to result in one large, national entity. Instead, the market is being fragmented, based on the interests and needs of different segments of the talent base.

This does not mean, however, that changes have not been taking place, and we can expect this to continue and intensify in the coming years. The recognition or awareness of a coming shift is not enough. What will ultimately determine the continuing relevance of professional associations in procurement is not only the recognition that *the times they are a changing* in terms of the methods of engaging their membership, but a willingness to break away from what were once viewed as being the traditional thought leaders, such as analysis firms and their analysts.

In this regard, you are truly known by the company you keep; and as such, a well-intentioned collaboration with someone who is deemed out-of-touch or no longer relevant will undermine an association's

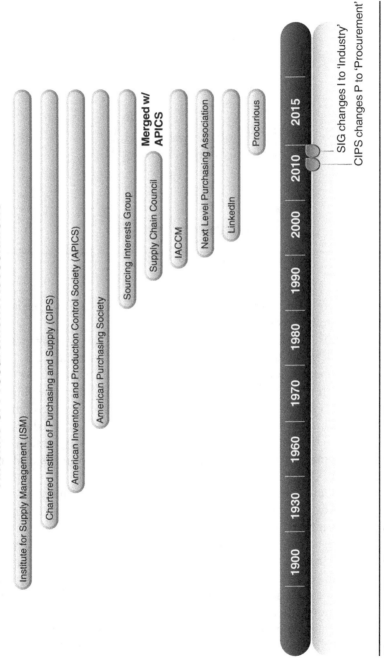

Figure 1.3   Timeline of procurement associations

credibility as an important source of information and insight. In other words, associations must be mindful of not only their ability to connect with their changing membership demographics, they must also identify newer and more relevant sources of intelligence and deliver it in a channel that supports their members' desire to *collaborate at your convenience* as David Clevenger said in the panel discussion. There are long-standing relationships that have become ingrained in any large, established association's hierarchy; to the point that distinguishing between or separating the two—the people and the association's mission—can, in and of itself, be difficult.

Certification, Experience, or Degree?

In the 2009 panel discussion, IACCM president Tim Cummins defined the traditional membership model as delivering a monthly (or so) publication, a localized chapter structure, and a certification program. In the past, whether professionals read the publication or attended local chapter meetings (if available), they saw value in being able to demonstrate their knowledge and skills in a core set of areas generally recognized to be associated with practical success. The certification program also serves an important role as a revenue stream for the association itself, generating income through program administration, administering assessments, and offering ways to earn the requisite professional development credits to maintain certification. If, as Dominick said, traditional associations *do things the way they've always done them,* can they survive the transition—both philosophically and financially—to a world where there was no longer a need for a standardized certification?

We have identified three groups of procurement talent: traditional buyers, Generation Next, and second career professionals. Is there a benefit for each of these groups and the organization they work for to get and maintain such a certification?

Let's stereotype for just a moment and assume that the traditional buyer has a certification and keeps it in good standing on an annual basis. If, as we have suggested, their prevalence in the procurement profession is beginning its long ride into the sunset, their promise to said organizations is limited. They have also, perhaps, been failed by the very professional development organization put in place to validate their skills and help their knowledge keep pace.

Generation Next, fresh out of college, is unlikely to put themselves back into a classroom setting or a virtual educational model. This is particularly true if they are carrying debt from student loans, which may already include the costs of graduate study. According to the My Purchasing Center study referenced previously, in 2013, 44% of procurement professionals had graduate degrees. Since this was a steady increase from 21% in 2003, it is safe to assume that the percentage of procurement professionals with graduate degrees today is even closer to the 50% mark. What Generation Next might be willing to do, however, is pursue a certification through a company sponsored group program— assuming the management team sees value in such an investment. Since even emerging leaders from Generation Next are unlikely to have the influence to promote such an effort themselves, unless a legacy program exists, one is unlikely to be started.

The organization's perspective on procurement certifications also comes into question with our second career professionals. Their desire to be in procurement is not enough to get them the job. The company has to accept them for the position despite the fact that they know the person does not have procurement experience. It would make little sense for them to immediately force the second career professional through a highly standardized education program.

The other question about the ongoing validity of certifications is whether they will be able to capture the sorts of knowledge and skills procurement professionals will need to have going forward. With movement away from the tactical and toward a more strategic, nuanced approach to spend management, assessing a professional's capabilities in a standardized format becomes infinitely more difficult.

As we conclude our discussion of this topic, it does seem appropriate to acknowledge that there are benefits of the traditional association model that are neither part of their recruitment materials or their revenue model, one of which is informal mentoring. Having the opportunity to network with one's own peers in such a way that does not fall within the confines of their potential for promotion or compensation is hugely beneficial. More mature members are opened to the ideas and perspectives of younger members and in return can provide them with sage advice and friendly counseling on any number of topics. One area in which experienced professionals could definitely offer advice is, ironically, in an area with which they likely have the least familiarity, and that is social networks.

The February 19, 2015 Procurement Insights post, "Are these profile images representative of the brand Coupa wants to project?"[18] talked about how our social network profiles, including the pictures we use, have become our calling card. What people see creates a lasting first impression of not only the individual, but the company they represent. Unfortunately, and as demonstrated by the referenced visuals, the up-and-coming generation does not necessarily make this association between what people see and how it likely impacts the viewer's perception—either positively or negatively. Nor do they understand that these social profiles are not personal or professional; they are all public. This is perhaps where, in conjunction with a sound company social media policy in place, the experienced professionals can not only offer useful input, but show the way in terms of leading by example.

Analyst Firms

If major changes are expected in procurement's professional associations, nothing short of a complete evolutionary transformation has unfolded in the analyst realm. As with procurement professionals and their associations, there are the traditional occupiers of this role, most notably Gartner, Forrester, and Aberdeen.

Gartner announced their intent to acquire AMR Research on December 1, 2009.[19] In the acquisition, they got AMR's clients, their intellectual property, and their audience. They also got Mickey North Rizza, characterized at the time by Spend Matters as "the last of the industry analyst greats in the procurement market. A great thinker, strategist, writer. and speaker."[20] And yet she stayed with Gartner for less than three years, leaving in May 2012 to join the solution provider BravoSolution.

What this actually means to the procurement profession is a point where our symmetry in writing this book encounters the first of what will likely be many forks in the road. Does the procurement profession need a cadre of dedicated analysts?

JON'S PERSPECTIVE: *Why Mickey North Rizza Can't Go Home Again...Or Can She?*

In a Procurement Insights post dated June 21, 2013, I wrote the following:

"If after spending years with a vendor, a journalist/analyst may not necessarily possess the required objectivity in terms of effectively covering the market, what are my thoughts if this scenario is reversed? Specifically, what if a former journalist/analyst takes a position with a vendor? Does this draw into question the validity of their assessment of the market in the years prior to their joining their new company?"

That is an interesting thought, especially given the fact that one would not be unreasonable in assuming that there was, at least indirectly, a prior relationship that ultimately paved the way for the present position. Let's look at Mickey North Rizza's situation as an example.

In the June 1, 2012 Supply & Demand Chain article "Former Gartner Analyst Joins BravoSolution," it was reported that North Rizza had joined the company as Vice President of Strategic Services.[21] According to the article, North Rizza "will leverage her practitioner heritage and deep domain knowledge to help BravoSolution's customers accelerate sourcing and procurement performance."

What is most interesting is that with this move, it appears that North Rizza has come full circle. Prior to her joining AMR Research, which was purchased by Gartner in 2009 for $64 million, North Rizza held the position of Vice President of Supply Base Management at Modus Link. That's right, a vendor.

This means that the cross pollination factor that has stirred up so much controversy of late within the realms of the public sector has been at work in the career of North Rizza, as well as other countless journalists/analysts. While it would be erroneous to presume that all such incestuous ties between analyst firms and the vendor market they are purported to be covering objectively is suspect, one cannot help but wonder what impact this has had on the evolution of the market itself.

After all, and as referenced in my March 20, 2009 post "Riding the Crest of a New Wave: How the Original SaaS Companies Have Gained the Upper Hand,"[22] why did the journalists/analysts fail to respond in any meaningful way to a 2000 white paper by the Software & Information Industry Association (SIIA), which predicted the demise of packaged desktop and enterprise applications? It is understandable why Larry Ellison would, for all these years, have poo-pooed the notion of web-based, on-demand applications. But why did the journalists and analysts remain silent?

One can only wonder if objectivity had been shaded or muted by the oligarchical nature of industry relationships that until recently has kept the value of the on-demand, web-based world locked-up in a Pandora's box of mutual, self-serving interest. Or to put it another way, the evolutionary transformation of the industry today would have likely occurred at least 5 to 10 years earlier had the comfortable fox-watching-the-henhouse rapport between vendor and journalist/analyst not existed.

In fact, I believe that had the market been allowed to develop the way it was supposed to, outside of the bipartisan sentiment that governed industry coverage, it would have likely saved end-user clients hundreds of millions of dollars. "How?" you might ask.

Think of all the failed eProcurement initiatives in both the public and private sectors and the exorbitant costs associated with the licensing, maintenance, and consulting fees that were paid largely up front. How could any mainstream journalist/analyst covering the industry during this period claim that they did a good job when so many initiatives failed to achieve the expected results, especially since the decision to move forward with the ill-conceived projects were based largely on their coverage and recommendations?

Once again let's consider the North Rizza appointment to the position of Vice President of Strategic Services at BravoSolution. While I found her to be highly credible during our interview on my radio show,[23] one can only wonder what credibility she would possess outside of the *usual suspects* in terms of influencing anyone's decision to go with that organization's solutions. This is based primarily on the fact that there is an ever-growing cynicism in the industry toward journalists/analysts from her period. You simply have to note the responses to my January 7, 2011 post "Madison Avenue ooops...make that Gartner, names Oracle as a leader in supply chain planning,"[24] to see that the old guard's views are taken with barely more than a grain of salt by today's procurement professionals.

Call it guilt by association but, I doubt that the burgeoning number of young and savvy, up-and-coming procurement professionals will harbor the same inclinations of fealty toward the affiliations that marked and marred the industry's delayed development over the past 10 to 20 years.

This ultimately ties back in to the point raised earlier relative to the sources of market intelligence upon which associations rely to both inform and empower their membership. Perhaps more than anything else, the above commentary regarding Ms. North Rizza speaks to the fact that with Generation Next and second career procurement professionals, the industry is no longer a closed community.

As a result, all sources of expert insight are now subject to increased scrutiny based upon a variety of factors, not the least of which is the ready access to information individuals now have as a result of technology. In short, challenging the status quo is far easier in a hyper-connected Internet world than it was back in the heyday of the traditional analyst era. Or, as Tim Cummins observed during a recent panel discussion at the Virginia 2014 Forum,[25] if you wake up in the morning and you are not feeling well, you are more inclined to do a search of your symptoms on Google than you are to call a doctor.

In the end, and more than an M&A driven compression, it is the self-determination immediacy associated with the market's ever-increasing access to reliable sources of information that will have the greatest impact on the analyst world.

KELLY'S PERSPECTIVE: *It's Not the Analyst Turnover That Worries Me, It's the Lack of Replenishment*

My perspective on the changing field of analyst firms, analysts, and procurement news outlets, is different from Jon's in that I have held three very different positions within the procurement sphere. I was a practitioner, managing back office and location-based services for a global retailer. I worked on the consulting services team at a solution provider. Now I serve my professional community in a capacity that is a blend of analyst, journalist, and tour guide. Depending upon which transition point in my career I met someone; they might make the case that I was going over to the *dark side*.

This reaction to a very common transition within an industry serves as a poignant reflection of the mind-set held by many within procurement, whether they are practitioners, solution providers, or thought leaders. This is a natural flow, and other industries accept it without negativity. Did my time as a practitioner preclude me from being an effective consultant? Absolutely not. It strengthened my understanding of the challenges my clients were facing, and it made finding the right solution an intensely personal effort. Did my time at Emptoris prior to their acquisition by IBM in December of 2011 make it impossible for me to serve in a journalistic role? If anything, it gave me a perspective on the kinds of challenges that solution providers of varying sizes were facing as they competed with enterprise solutions.

I struggle with the idea that North Rizza, by working at a provider, then at an analyst firm, and then at a provider again, has any connection with the many enterprise resource planning (ERP) implementation failures and their puzzling but continued positive market coverage. And North Rizza is just one example in a field of many. The fact that the expiration date on any analyst's firsthand knowledge of a market is set the moment they remove themselves to the commentary sector naturally limits the damage they can intentionally inflict upon that market. My concern about this is equally measured between the undue influence analysts may have on investments or decisions made and the fact that their knowledge depreciates on the same schedule that their *objective* influence increases. I hold this concern for myself, as I get further from my time as either a practitioner or a solution consultant every day. Any publicly facing person who does not purposefully consider his/her own perspective is under-serving their followers.

Part of my concern about the historical disappearance of procurement-focused analysts and publications is about their revenue potential. In my five years of covering the procurement space from the commentary sector, I have seen major players disappear or become diminished. To some extent, that is to be expected, as there is a cyclical nature to any evolving business. Some companies get too big, prompting some groups or individuals to become offshoots, blazing their own trails as smaller, nimbler, self-directed entities. Just like the fragmentation we saw in the procurement association space, a similar dynamic is taking place in the analyst space. In Figure 1.4, I have put together a timeline of major shifts in the procurement analysis and commentary sector. While there are plenty of relatively small players in the space, the major players (such as the Gartners, Aberdeens, etc.) seem to be losing interest in maintaining experts in supply chain.

I wholeheartedly believe in capitalism. If there was a market with sufficient resources and demand to support more procurement publications and analysts, one would exist to serve it. If there were real money to be made by a Gartner or an Aberdeen by keeping a procurement practice alive, they would do it. Just as Mickey North Rizza left AMR Research/Gartner in 2012, Lora Cecere left AMR in 2009, ultimately going on to found Supply Chain Insights in 2012. Andrew Bartolini left Aberdeen's Global Supply Management (GSM) Channel in 2010 to found Ardent Partners. Constantine Limberakis and Christopher Dwyer, two notable players in the GSM Channel, weren't far behind. In 2012, Limberakis left Aberdeen for IASTA (later acquired by Selectica), and Dwyer joined Bartolini at Ardent Partners in 2013. Neither Gartner nor Aberdeen has been able to reestablish their once highly regarded presence.

I have it on good authority that they are very good at math and projections in those analyst firms. The fact that these players have stepped away from the market tells me that there is not, in fact, demand for it, and that worries me as we continue to clamor for the CPO to be a consistently influential role.

Timeline of Procurement Analysts, Bloggers, and Publications

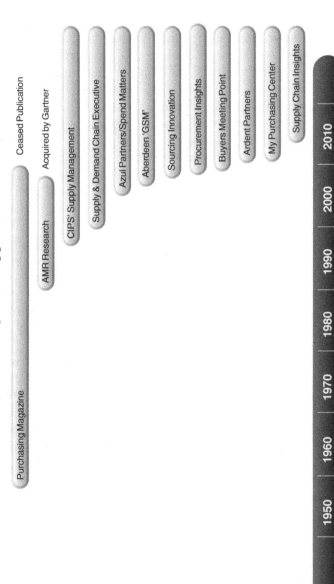

Figure 1.4   Timeline of procurement analysts, bloggers, and publications

IS THIS CROSSROADS PROCUREMENT-SPECIFIC?

Procurement is clearly at a crossroads, and this book is by no means the only one to point out that fact or to attempt to capture the moment and bring clarity to the path forward. But that does not relieve us of the obligation to consider whether or not the crossroads is procurement-specific. Many of the changes we are experiencing, including the rise of the Millennials, increased automation and outsourcing, and the prevalence of virtual models for social networking and association affect the entire employment market and workforce equally. What if procurement is just dealing with the same challenges being seen by any other professional community that has been around for a century?

The January/February 2015 issue of *Industry Week* magazine includes an article by Steve Minter titled, "The New Objective of Continuous Improvement, You."[26] In it, Minter discusses the need to evolve professionally for precisely the reasons traditional buyers are going extinct: they are not open-minded about embracing change and are hesitant rather than self-driven when faced with new knowledge to master. Minter's article was written for a manufacturing audience, and he takes an interesting stand by saying that skills and knowledge gaps are just as much of a challenge in the executive suite as they are on the shop floor. He quotes Edward D. Hess, a professor at the University of Virginia's Darden School of Business and author of *Learn or Die: Using Science to Build a Leading Edge Learning Organization.* "In an increasingly tech-driven world, says Hess, leaders will first and foremost need to be 'adaptive learners'—employing a set of skills that will help them remain relevant even as knowledge rapidly advances and skills become outdated overnight."

Minter is writing from the point of view that it is not too late for manufacturing executives. He encourages them to be open-minded, to drive themselves to master new skills, to be willing to try new things and to make mistakes, and to pursue peer feedback. Procurement commentators, on the other hand, seem to have already seen, or at least visualized, the break between the old and new procurement. No one is writing about how traditional buyers can repackage themselves as strategic procurement professionals. As we have already shared, Vitasek comes right out and says that they need to go before any real progress can be made. Every profession has their *dinosaurs*. Why is procurement less able to accept change than their counterparts in other functions?

The answer to this may be that the changes being seen in procurement are not being driven by an altered attitude in corporate executive leadership, although that, too, is coming to pass. The changes in demographics, skills, technology, and career progression are in response to the external economic environment that companies now must navigate in order to compete and survive. The very first sentence of the Introduction in *Procurement 20/20* makes this point abundantly clear by stating, "It is becoming more and more important for every senior executive to know how to manage the external parts of the company's value chain."[27] The data that they go on to explore in the following chapters supports this point. The percentage of external spend is increasing, as is the amount of revenue expected to be delivered by each employee.

After reading advice like this from McKinsey and any number of other respected sources, executives naturally turn and look at their procurement function, a move many of them may not have made in quite some time. They see a group that is sorely lacking in skills and aptitude. Change—real, sudden, meaningful change—is coming to procurement from the top down. Nothing else could spur such action.

Chick and Handfield acknowledge this executive epiphany in their discussion of the significant external factors impacting procurement and supply management, "Given the ever-increasing logistics costs of globalization, increasing levels of risk and complexity, and the perennial issue of rising labor costs, now seems a good time for a major rethink on procurement and supply management strategy." The results of an executive *rethink*, assuming one happens, is unlikely to be accompanied by a great deal of patience or plans for transitioning traditional buyers forward. It is more likely that they will pursue a combination of new blood, whether fresh from college or distinguished by success elsewhere in the organization and a sort of self-selection for those already in the procurement organization. Anyone that demonstrates an ability to add value will stay. Anyone mired in the ways of the past must go.

CONCLUSION

In the past, it has been common practice to differentiate between purchasing and procurement by marking the line between tactical and strategic. Purchasing is the tactical acquisition of materials and services and has come to mean almost the same as buying. Procurement incorporates the thought and planning—in other words, the strategy—that puts the optimal contracts and supplier relationships in place for purchasers to buy from. The fact that this line is not carved in stone serves as evidence of our profession's discomfort with the range of skill sets and capabilities that must exist within our scope of influence.

Perhaps as a result of the implementation of eProcurement systems that are then used by people outside of the procurement organization to make purchases, the term *procurement* has started to take on a more tactical meaning. If the name of the function is constantly evolving, so must be the professionals in its ranks.

If the collective whole of the procurement profession is equal to the sum of its many (moving) parts, the infusion of new talent and perspectives on an individual level must, by definition, change its progression. As the profile changes, so does the demand for education, networking, and industry coverage. Demand will rule the day when it comes to procurement commentary on an ongoing basis, and a new professional profile, directed in large part by the highest executive levels of the organization, will alter the landscape of both the profession and the peripheral institutions that serve it.

REFERENCES

1. Carlos Mena, Remko van Hoek, Martin Christopher, *Leading Procurement Strategy: Driving Value Through the Supply Chain*, (Philadelphia: Kogan Page, 2014), 36.
2. "Institute for Supply Management," *ISM-New York, Inc. 2013-2013*, (2013).
3. Pat Toensmeier, "ISM-New York Looks to Future in Centennial Year," *ThomasNet News*, October 23, 2013, http://news.thomasnet.com/procurement/2013/10/03/ism-new-york-looks-to-the-future-in-centennial-year.
4. Gerard Chick and Robert Handfield, *The Procurement Value Proposition: The Rise of Supply Management*, (Philadelphia: Kogan Page, 2015), 133.
5. Susan Avery, "Procurement Changes in Past 10 Years," *My Purchasing Center*, January 14, 2014, http://www.mypurchasingcenter.com/purchasing/blogs/procurement-changes-past-20-years/.
6. Peter Spiller, et al., *Procurement 20/20: Supply Entrepreneurship in a Changing World*, (New Jersey: Wiley, 2014), 179.
7. Giuliana Scott, February 2, 2015, comment on Jon Hansen, "Have the previous generation of buyers let down today's professionals?" *Public Sector Supplier Forum*, January 28, 2015, https://www.linkedin

.com/groups/Have-previous-generation-buyers-let-1907269.S.5965
862142233059350?trk=groups_items_see_more-0-b-ttl.

8. "Procurement Unplugged: The Three Most Important Questions for 2015," narrated by Jon Hansen, PI Window on the World, *Blog Talk Radio*, January, 28, 2015, http://www.blogtalkradio.com/jon-hansen/2015/01/28/procurement-unplugged-the-three-most-important-questions-for-2015.

9. Kate Vitasek, "Why Is Integrity Important Only after You're Caught?" *Vested Way*, December 5, 2014, http://www.vestedway.com/why-is-integrity-important-only-after-youre-caught/.

10. Lakshmi Sandhana, "47% of Jobs Under Threat From Computerization According to Oxford Study," *Gizmag*, September 24, 2013, http://www.gizmag.com/half-of-us-jobs-computerized/29142/.

11. Jon Hansen, Procurement's Expanding Role and the Executive of the Future," *Procurement Insights*, August 3, 2007, https://procureinsights.wordpress.com/2007/08/03/procurement%E2%80%99s-expanding-role-and-the-executive-of-the-future/.

12. "Are there any limits to procurement's role?" *Supply Business*, Accessed March 7, 2015, http://www.supplybusiness.com/previous-articles/winter-2006-7/features/executive-debate/.

13. "30 Under 30 Supply Chain Stars," *ThomasNet*, accessed February 22, 2015, http://www.thomasnet.com/30under30/.

14. Chick and Handfield, *The Procurement Value Proposition*, xii.

15. Jean McHale, "ISM Expands Service Offerings by Acquiring ADR North America," *ISM.ws*, January 4, 2012, http://www.ism.ws/about/MediaRoom/newsreleasedetail.cfm?ItemNumber=22120.

16. "AGM vote on CIPS name change and chartered status—results are in," *CIPS.org*, June 24, 2014, https://www.cips.org/en/News/news/AGM-vote-on-CIPS-name-change-and-chartered-status---results-are-in/.

17. "Is the Traditional Association Model Dead?" narrated by Jon Hansen, PI Window on the World, *Blog Talk Radio*, April 9, 2009, http://www.blogtalkradio.com/jon-hansen/2009/04/09/is-the-traditional-association-model-dead.

18. Jon Hansen, "Are these profile images representative of the brand Coupa wants to project?" *Procurement Insights*, February 19, 2015, https://procureinsights.wordpress.com/2015/02/19/are-these-profile-images-representative-of-the-brand-coupa-wants-to-project-by-jon-hansen/.

19. "Gartner Enters into Agreement to Acquire AMR Research, Inc.," *Gartner.com*, December 1, 2009, http://www.gartner.com/technology/about/amr-research-acquisition.jsp.

20. Jason Busch, "The End of an Analyst Era: Mickey North Rizza Leaves Gartner, Joins BravoSolution," *Spend Matters*, May 21, 2012, http://spendmatters.com/2012/05/21/the-end-of-an-analyst-era-mickey-north-rizza-leaves-gartner-joins-bravosolution/.

21. "Former Gartner Analyst Joins BravoSolution," *Supply & Demand Chain Executive*, June 1, 2012, http://www.sdcexec.com/news/10724418/former-gartner-analyst-joins-bravosolution.

22. Jon Hansen, "Riding the Crest of a New Wave: How Original SaaS Companies Have Gained the Upper Hand," *Procurement Insights*, March 20, 2009, https://procureinsights.wordpress.com/2009/03/20/riding-the-crest-of-a-new-wave-how-the-original-saas-companies-have-gained-the-upper-hand-a-procurement-insights-knowledge-leadership-publication/.

23. "Taking Measure of An Acquisition," narrated by Jon Hansen, PI Window on the World, *Blog Talk Radio*, June 10, 2009, http://www.blogtalkradio.com/jon-hansen/2009/06/10/taking-measure-of-an-acquisition.

24. Jon Hansen, "Madison Avenue ooops … make that Gartner, names Oracle as a leader in supply chain planning," *Procurement Insights*, January 7, 2011, https://procureinsights.wordpress.com/2011/01/07/madison-avenue-ooops-make-that-gartner-names-oracle-as-a-leader-in-supply-chain-planning/.

25. Jon Hansen, "Expert Panel Weighs in on How to 'Leverage the Power of Procurement' at Virginia Forum 2014," *Procurement Insights*, November 21, 2014, https://procureinsights.wordpress.com/2014/11/21/expert-panel-weighs-in-on-how-to-leverage-the-power-of-procurement-at-virginia-forum-2014/.

26. Steve Minter, "The New Objective of Continuous Improvement: You," *Industry Week*, January/February 2015, http://www.industryweek-digital.com/industryweekmag/jan-feb_2015?pg=27#pg27.

27. Spiller, et al., *Procurement 20/20*, 9.

This book has free material available for download from the
Web Added Value™ resource center at *www.jrosspub.com*

2

Has Procurement (Finally) Come of Age?

"Among procurement leaders, the CPO is twice as likely to report to the CEO and to be a member of the top management team as is the case at the average performers." Procurement 20/20, Pete Spiller, Nicholas Reineke, Drew Ungerman, Henrique Teixeira[1]

Coming-of-age stories like *The Catcher in the Rye*, *To Kill a Mockingbird*, and *The Adventures of Huckleberry Finn* capture a common but important part of the human experience. Although we may be more familiar with coming-of-age movies and television today, the genre resonates generation after generation because we continue to find ourselves face-to-face with external circumstances that require a reexamination of our internal perspective and priorities.

Also known as *bildungsroman* or *novels of formation*, coming-of-age stories capture the experiences of an individual through a time of change and growth.[2] "Coming-of-age films focus on the psychological and moral growth or transition of a protagonist from youth to adulthood. Personal growth and change is an important characteristic of this genre, which relies on dialogue and emotional responses, rather than action."[3] Since the change experienced in coming-of-age stories is more often marked by contemplation and observation rather than action, it may feel like waiting through a delay—but the associated pause is critical. The result is a hero or heroine who absorbs and combines external impressions and internal reactions before taking any steps based on them. Coming-of-age stories are usually told after the fact, when the storyteller has the benefit of knowing the outcome.

Procurement is in a unique position today because we realize we have reached this transition while it is still underway. While fictional or popularized coming-of-age stories are almost always told about one individual in one set of circumstances, this does not preclude us from applying the concept to procurement in a collective sense. The tensions facing procurement today—old vs. new, tactical vs. strategic, savings generation vs. collaboration, focus on the bottom line vs. top line—have created a context within which we must reconsider our role in the enterprise as well as the skills, approaches, and solutions that will enable us to take action. While any one of us can make personal, individualized changes, the crossroads procurement is standing at today requires something more coordinated because the whole supply paradigm we function within is shifting. While we do not all have to select the same path moving forward, we do have to make a choice. Each one of us has to stop and select a direction.

At this point in our progression, it is critical that we summon the strength to effect change by breaking free from the traditional boundaries of what procurement has previously been thought to entail. The tensions we face are evidence of the intellectual maturation like that seen in coming-of-age stories because they will enable us to take meaningful, self-fulfilling action at some point in the future. The difference between fictional coming-of-age journeys and the one procurement has embarked upon is that fictional journeys come to an end once mature action is taken. The main character's story opens, we come to understand the tensions between them and their environment, and then they observe and consider. Once they act, the story is over.

Because procurement is attempting to stage a collective coming-of-age, there is no plateau we will reach where we can say, "This is it; we have matured." In other words, there is no end in sight to our story, just a visible horizon that we must reach before reassessing and moving on to the next one. The first mature step procurement takes is the beginning of our journey, not the end.

Rather than making a single corrective skill or capability adjustment, procurement needs to adopt a sustained ability to evolve so that our thoughts and actions continue to match the environment in which we work. In *The Procurement Game Plan,* authors Charles Dominick and Soheila Lunney provide what they consider to be *The Purchasing Professional's Commandments,* as shown in Figure 2.1. Their 10th commandment is "Thou shalt commit to continuous improvement of thy skills, never letting a year go by without learning new practices used by other purchasing professionals."[4] While every ambitious professional should continue to invest in his or her skills and capabilities, the situation faced by procurement today is different. We are not working on improving in the context of a known set of skills. We have to accept a new professional mind-set that expects and embraces constant, continual evolution. Then, and only then, will procurement have come of age. Until that time, we remain somewhat mired in the angst and turmoil of a group constantly facing tension that would push us in the right direction but prevents learning enough from our experiences to allow them to change us permanently for the better.

Unfortunately, many procurement professionals want to view the maturation process as a destination rather than a journey. The very suggestion that we are working toward a point at which we can say that we have *arrived* reflects a lack of comprehension that is likely to keep us bound to our past rather than freeing us to embrace the possibilities of the future. We are not in need of a simple Point *A* to Point *B* movement. There is no process revision or governance improvement that can carry us forward.

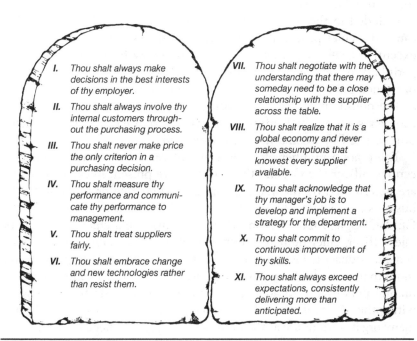

Figure 2.1 The Purchasing Professional's Commandments

It will be our ability to embrace change; to be positive and enthusiastic about change (when possible); and to accept the fact that change will be a constant going forward that will indicate our full maturity.

A MATURE PERSPECTIVE OF POSITION VERSUS INFLUENCE

As a first step towards maturity, procurement must recognize that having a seat at the executive table is not the exclusive end goal. In fact, a myopic obsession with establishing a C-level procurement executive position may actually prove limiting to our growth and potential. The end goal should be to occupy a place of true, sustainable influence within the organizational hierarchy. "Procurement professionals at [the leadership] stage, particularly those at the top, require a very broad set of transformational, visioning, and influencing skills," wrote the authors of *Leading Procurement Strategy.* "They need to be able to convince their internal colleagues of the power of procurement and align their suppliers to create stronger supply chains."[5] Ironically, in order to build influence, power, and achievement we have to eschew the traditional mindset about what constitutes all three.

Included in the old, confined way of thinking is the belief that because the chief procurement officer (CPO) position is not a standard executive level role, procurement has somehow been relegated to the periphery of relevance. We must get beyond assigned titles (and their presumed perks) to find our place in an enterprise where the functions and responsibilities that have traditionally defined the roles of staid executives such as chief information officers (CIOs) and chief financial officers (CFOs) are in a state of flux as well.

There are a number of C-level executives other than the chief executive officer (CEO), and the ones that are present in each enterprise are determined by the value of the associated role or function to the business as a whole. The most common C-level positions today are the CEO, CFO, and CIO. Beyond that, there may be a chief marketing or sales officer, chief human resources officer, and in some organizations, general counsel is included in the C-suite. Each one is responsible for more than just advocating for their particular view. They must use their unique perspective to advance a united corporate strategy and work with other C-level executives as needed. As we will discuss shortly, many organizations are at the point where they may need to consider an additional cross-functional C-level position that manages strategies and standards for collaborating with partners.

While traditional reporting hierarchies still exist, at least for the time being, the dynamics within this framework are fluid. The opportunity this fluidity represents for change, and more specifically the ability to expand and assert one's influence, is equal for all areas of practice. The key, therefore, is not to view the maturation of procurement through the same restrictive lens that so many in our profession have previously done. This is not a question of *our time, our turn* where we expect to ascend the ranks in the same way as other functions have. What is required today is a new, more holistic view of our potential contribution to competitive advantage. The strategic importance of procurement has already been recognized within most organizations as well as the business community as a whole. They accept the expanded role of the supply chain and supply base in creating sustainable advantage and securing revenue.

But even this herculean accomplishment is just the beginning. As procurement professionals, we need to catch up with this expanded view of our potential in order to assume a leadership position equal to our merit. Beyond a change in how we view the bigger world and think about our place in it, we also have to expand the definition of what we do and how our actions impact the modern global enterprise. As authors Handfield and Chick acknowledge of their own vision for procurement in *The Procurement Value Proposition*, the ideas they present are not necessarily new. "It is worth pointing out at this juncture that some of the ideas pointed out in this book have been kicking around for some time, although the conditions under which they might flourish have yet to materialize in more than a handful of organizations. The hope is that— with all that has been accomplished in procurement over the past few decades—the time for these ideas may finally be coming."[6]

If, as Handfield and Chick state, the steps procurement must take toward a more meaningful tomorrow have been clearly laid out before, what is the hold up? Something has to change in order for procurement to finally take these steps, for the enterprise to be ready to receive us in our new role, and for the C-level to welcome someone from procurement into their ranks.

THE MORE THINGS CHANGE, THE MORE THEY STAY THE SAME

It is doubtful that when 19th century French novelist Jean-Baptiste Alphonse Karr coined the phrase "the more things change, the more they stay the same," he was thinking about procurement.[7] His epigram and its application to the procurement profession has been validated and expanded upon by contemporary thought leaders many times. In his foreword to *Leading Procurement Strategy*, Peter Kraljic, creator of the Kraljic matrix and a former Director at McKinsey, wrote, "It is over 30 years ago that I first ran into procurement as a source of strategic value and relevance for the company. ... Since then a lot has happened and I am now convinced more than ever that procurement is critical for enterprise performance enhancement."[8] If over three decades ago Kraljic was able to see the strategic potential of procurement, it is amazing to think that there is anyone left to convince today. It is also worth observing that he does not say a lot has happened *in procurement*. The events he refers to could be larger economic and market events that have resulted in more change in our companies than in procurement itself. Perhaps we have remained relatively still while the world changed around us.

A particularly notable example of this is a March 27, 2014 *Harvard Business Review* article by Proxima Group CEO Matthew Eatough, in which he describes procurement's seeming inability to change. "... procurement doesn't register on the C-suite's radar in a manner proportionate to its growing importance within the organization, and most procurement departments are neither ready nor empowered to take on their new responsibilities."[9] Failing to register on the radar in spite of the growing importance of supply chains and suppliers uncovers a major weakness on the part of procurement leaders and organizations. In fact, if you accept the premise behind Eatough's text, it seems that very few people—including those in our profession—regard procurement as strategically relevant. And if we do, we are not doing an effective job at making the case for it.

Eatough's list of reasons why procurement doesn't register with executive leadership shares a common theme with a *Procurement Insights* post written shortly after the blog was launched in May of 2007. "Procurement's expanding role and the executive of the future"[10] highlighted several critical points from a 2006 *CPO Agenda* roundtable discussion involving senior procurement personnel from organizations such as Nestle, Danone, British Airways, and Merrill Lynch. An example that makes the point about procurement's perceived value particularly well is the assertion by one executive that truly talented individuals "should move out of purchasing after five or six years and do another job, whether it's finance, human resources, manufacturing, or marketing."[11] If time spent in procurement was considered a sure and steady pathway to leadership, no one, least of all *truly talented individuals* would risk rotating out to another part of the company.

Ironically, that executive's belief in the need for internal rotation has to do with the fact that he sees purchasing as an insular function, sheltered and protected from the real operational challenges of an enterprise. "It's easy to be clever when you are only the purchasing guy and you don't have a factory that stops, the pressure of the client to deal with … Purchasing people are not prepared for that, so they need to learn the real operational life."[12] His view of the poor relative value of procurement, and the limited advantages it offers to someone looking to have a large-scale impact on the success of the enterprise, is one that we face, overtly and otherwise, on a regular basis. If we are unable to prevent this from becoming a generally accepted truth, the advancement potential of procurement individuals as well as their organization will be significantly lessened.

It is no stretch to draw parallels between the CPO roundtable and the present-day Eatough *Harvard Business Review* article. This is especially true when you consider the earlier piece's reference to the fact that the majority of the C-suite executives in the roundtable believed the best person to run a purchasing department is someone who doesn't have a purchasing background. As Tom Rae, then senior vice president of corporate purchasing at the German automotive supplier Continental, stated, "One of the benefits of more CPOs coming from outside the procurement world is that they tend to be wonderfully connected in their organizations; they bring a network and credibility, and that helps to move procurement into the mainstream."[13] His justification for non-purchasing professionals having the advantage in leading the function is based on the fact that most procurement professionals are not sufficiently connected and they do not have the same level of credibility that leaders from other functions do. Whether this is true or simply perceived to be true, procurement has a problem that directly impacts our present-day and future influence potential.

Of course the parallels run even deeper when you read Eatough's assertion that part of procurement's bigger recognition problem is their *unproductive fixation on cutting costs*.[14] The irony here is that in talking about how decreased spending (whether through reduced prices, increased efficiency, or rationalized demand) has little or nothing to do with increasing shareholder value, Eatough, while on the mark, is simply confirming the findings from the May 4, 2006 article "How to Speak Like a CFO."[15] In the article, which preceded Eatough's by just short of a decade, Paul E. Teague wrote, "Finance executives in Corporate America simply don't believe that purchasing departments are really bringing in the savings they claim. That may be because finance and purchasing don't speak the same language." It would seem that Teague, Rae, and Eatough are all in agreement about procurement's credibility problem.

In fact, the following additional findings from a 2007 Aberdeen study "The CFO's View of Procurement: Same Page, Different Language"[16] and shown in Figure 2.2 are equally telling in terms of how CFOs and, by proxy, other C-suite executives, view procurement.

- Less than 20% of CFOs consider the work of CPOs and their staffs as having a very positive impact on competitiveness.
- On average, only 46% of CFOs feel that the procurement team has contributed to enterprise growth.
- Only 57% of CFOs feel that procurement contributes to enterprise profitability.

Bridging the Communications Divide

Perhaps the disconnect between procurement and the C-suite can, at least in part, be explained by the Robert Rudzki book *Straight to the*

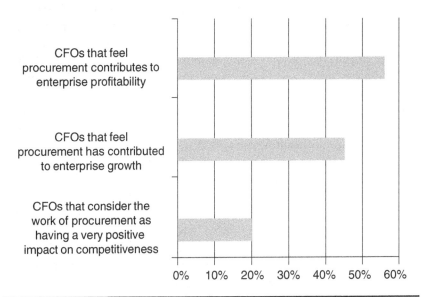

Figure 2.2   The CFO's View of Procurement: Same Page, Different Language (Data Source: Aberdeen Group, 2007)

Bottom Line: An Executive's Roadmap to World Class Supply Management. Here we find even more agreement with the already mentioned procurement thought leaders. Like Teague, Rudzki and his coauthors concluded that procurement and finance do not speak the same language. Since they describe finance as the language of the entire executive suite, not speaking finance prevents procurement from communicating well with all C-level executives, although it may be most obvious and detrimental in our dealings with finance. Rudzki provides direction for procurement professionals in terms of the five critical finance areas we should become fluent in if we want to communicate better with executive leadership. "The way to do that is to speak the language of the executive suite—that is, the *financial language* of the CEO and the CFO. In my experience, learning to *speak like a* CFO is particularly important."[17]

Rudzki's five key financial terms are:

1. ROIC (return on invested capital): Earnings divided by the total capital invested in the business (long-term debt plus stockholder equity).
2. Cost of capital: The weighted average *cost* of debt and equity. It represents what you must earn to minimally cover the expectations of your debt holders and stockholders.
3. EVA (economic value added): If ROIC is greater than cost of capital, then EVA is positive (you are adding value to the organization). If ROIC is less than cost of capital, then value is being destroyed and—absent substantial corrective action—the demise of the enterprise is just a matter of time.
4. EPS (earnings per share): The net income divided by the number of common shares outstanding. Typically calculated on a quarterly and annual basis.
5. P/E (price/earnings) ratio: The ratio of the common stock price to the annual EPS. Companies/industries typically *enjoy* certain P/E ratios, therefore, increasing the earnings often directly equates to a higher stock price.

The redirection of focus Rudzki champions aligns perfectly with Eatough and Teague's positions as to what needs to be done to bridge both the communication divide and the perceived value gap between procurement and executive leadership. The only difference between what we read in 2006-2007 and what we read and hear today is that the procurement profession has made some meaningful progress in elevating our organizational value, as reflected in Toshiba's appointment of its long-time manager of procurement and manufacturing to the CEO position. The only question is whether the Toshiba example is the exception to the rule or whether it is the start of a real and sustainable trend. As noted by *Procurement Leaders* at the time, "Mr. Tanaka's appointment surprised some people at Toshiba because he has taken behind-the-scenes roles, such as supervising supply chain management and heading the corporate-strategy office."[18] It is nonetheless a noteworthy milestone in purchasing if for no other reason than to demonstrate that being a purchasing (or procurement) professional is no longer an automatic black mark on your resume.

The fact is that purchasing or procurement professionals (or whatever other moniker you want to use) have by and large been the ones left standing outside in the *functional* cold, waiting for the executive bouncers to let us in to the *strategizing* club. With the Tanaka elevation to CEO, we may just have gained a foot in the proverbial club door. If we are to see ascensions such as the one at Toshiba become commonplace, we must first and foremost relinquish our long held belief that procurement is somehow a functional exercise in which *buyers* are little more than administrative order-takers whose performance can be rated on their ability to achieve the lowest cost. In this regard, we are our own worst enemies. We cannot change the minds of others if we continue in a role of subjugated anonymity based on maximizing transactional throughput as opposed to building and centralizing strategic influence.

As Kate Vitasek intimates in her March 3, 2015 *Forbes* article "Procurement Departments Negotiating 'Too Aggressively'", old habits die hard. This is especially true given the fact that aggressive procurement practices are still getting short-term wins along the lines being used to measure and track our performance by the executive team. Those familiar, old practices allow us to negotiate savings and increase spend under management relatively quickly. The question is, at what cost do we continue down the current road? After all, we can be sure that we will be the ones left to foot the bill for that cost, not any other function or the organization as a whole. Procurement is driven to reduce costs and demonstrate realized savings. But we are left alone to bear the blame if and when the actions required to make all that possible reflect negatively on the enterprise.

The following excerpt from the Vitasek article is telling of the responsibility that procurement must bear: "Professor John Henke's pioneering research on Chrysler's procurement practices show a direct link in aggressive procurement practices and Chrysler's profitability. Henke calculates Chrysler lost up to $24 billion in profit in the past 12 years due to 'lost supplier trust' associated with adversarial procurement practices. University of California's (Berkeley) Professor Oliver Williamson has shown that overall transaction costs increase when buyers do not act in a credible manner. Williamson says, 'The muscular approach to outsourcing goods and services is myopic and inefficient.'"[19]

Concerns like Vitasek's *lost supplier trust* and Eatough's *unproductive fixation on cutting costs* are not relegated to any one industry or vertical. In March 2015, *Supply Management* explored similar concerns in the supermarket or grocery retail industry. In the article titled "News focus: Supermarket supply chain 'bullying' harming procurement's reputation," we read about the negative consequences of overly savings-driven procurement organizations.[20] Two very critical and equally illuminating ideas about responsibility and credibility were offered up as quotes in the article.

> "The ultimate responsibility must be with boards and CEOs of companies to interrogate their supply chains and understand what exactly is happening and who is responsible and accountable."
>
> —David Noble, group CEO at CIPS

> "'We might need a new generation of buyers to bring about wholesale change."
>
> —Groceries Code Adjudicator (GCA) Christine Tacon

When you consider these two quotes in combination, it becomes clear that, while procurement is often blamed for a company's poor relationships with suppliers, we are not acting in a vacuum. We receive metrics and other prioritizing objectives from the highest levels of the organization. Replacing procurement for the sake of improving supplier relations addresses the symptoms of the problem rather than curing the cause. And, as we explored in the first chapter of this book, counting on Generation Next to automatically repair such reputational issues comes with uncertainty and too long of a lead time.

That being said, it is worth noting that GCA Tacon (quoted previously) is the same adjudicator that was involved in the investigation into Tesco's supplier management and accounting practices that were discussed in Chapter 1. She has clearly seen enough examples and consequences of antiquated, hard-nosed procurement practices to believe that a full changing of the guard is required to bring about new attitudes and approaches, particularly in low margin industries such as retail.

The overly cost-conscious procurement mind-set along with the behaviors and priorities that result from it are pervasive in low margin companies and industries. Expressions like *watch the pennies* are often repeated in meetings or displayed in conference rooms. Thin margins require aggressive cost management. In many cases, these companies have their procurement teams to thank for their success—or possibly even their survival—to this point. If a company wants their mode of supply operation to change significantly, shifts in perspective and priorities must change far beyond procurement.

It is absolutely possible to run a business on higher margins than are traditionally seen in low margin industries. In these cases, consumers need to be drawn by a value proposition beyond just return for their money. The Whole Foods chain is a perfect example. They have managed to preserve much higher margins than other supermarket chains because they trade on identity and culture rather than just food and merchandise sales. "Whole Foods' net profit margin clocks in at 4.1%, better than 85% of its competitors," wrote The Motley Fool's Justin Loiseau in June 2014. "On the other end of the spectrum, the Kroger Co. ends up with just 1.6% of sales."[21] It is safe to assume that the procurement team at Whole Foods is not pinching every penny out of their direct and indirect suppliers, but they are acting on the basis of established organizational priorities, not attempting to change the way the company works from the inside.

Whole Foods' impressive feat would not be possible without a strategy that encompasses every part of the company. Further evidence of this was provided in their April 2015 announcement that they would be launching a new chain based on the same value proposition and cultural appeal. Disappointing earnings numbers forced the company to find a new way to serve more of a growing market—younger shoppers. Millennials, while enticed by the organic, sustainable, natural Whole Foods brand, simply cannot afford to shop there.

The Whole Foods management team has announced that the new chain—365 by Whole Foods—will appeal to younger customers in that it combines the quality they expect while being more affordable. And yet someone, or more specifically, some group of people, internally have to make that possible. This new arm of Whole Foods will need to reduce their prices without sacrificing quality. As author and business journalist Bryce Hoffman wrote in *Forbes* just after the announcement,

"If properly executed, this new strategy will allow Whole Foods to take customers away from the Walmarts and Krogers of the world. That is a far better option than watering down the company's core brand just to meet short-term growth targets set by people who don't really understand Whole Foods' business in the first place."[22] Even though lowering costs is key to the success of this new endeavor, it will be handled top to bottom by a team focused on the stand-alone business model and its target customers—not by procurement alone. From operations to technology, store planning to procurement, it will take a cross-functional effort to pull this off, and Whole Foods knows it.

Not all procurement teams are qualified to be part of such a holistic effort. But while some procurement professionals take their cost-cutting duties to an extreme, we can't be on the hook alone to create or preserve large margins. Nor can we be left to shoulder the entire blame when we take the steps our performance metrics clearly emphasize, and someone doesn't like the outcome. You can't manage what you don't measure, but you also get more of what you reward. Measure on savings and you get active cost-cutting measures. Marketing, business development, and the executive-level team must lead the way by making a change of their own before procurement can shift from penny pinching to value creation.

Procurement's Transformation Imperative

Chrysler and Tesco are prime examples of how the metrics by which procurement's performance is measured have wide-ranging implications. In some cases, they have hurt the organization we intend to serve, as well as the profession itself. We need to find a way to perform in accordance with these metrics without resorting to tactics that are detrimental in the long term. It will be a challenge for many procurement professionals to adjust their thinking to reflect this new reality. The best advice on this subject may have come from Dr. Tom DePaoli, author of *Common Sense Supply Management*. He wrote, "The traditional procurement environment dies hard. My advice is to change everything. ... Get everyone completely out of their comfort zone and starting to do the tough work of relationship building."[23] The difficulty for procurement is therefore twofold: making a change is hard in and of itself, but so is the new work we are moving on to address.

Many of us still function in a business world where companies view negotiation as a winner-take-all adversarial proposition. It is important that the progression of a procurement professional's thinking runs parallel to progressive thinking within the enterprise where they work. If it doesn't, then change is necessary—including seeking employment with an organization that has advanced beyond more archaic and destructive views of the buyer-supplier relationship.

The reason that a move is likely necessary with the latter scenario is that the misalignment between business strategy and the new procurement strategy will persist, ultimately holding back the procurement professional's development and eventual adaptation to this brave new world. A procurement professional ready to come of age and take actions that are based on mutual benefit, long-term strategy, and collaboration will be acting against not only their own performance metrics, but also the executive team itself. In this regard, Handfield and Chick's suggestion that change is a collective effort that must be undertaken by everyone within and external to the enterprise rings true.

As a result, and as stressed by Andy Akrouche in his February 4, 2015 post "Strategic Sourcing and the Road to Transformational Leadership," "leadership talent must synthesize the best [...] and discard the obsolete to create something new. In my experience the 'new' to which the reader referred must be centered more on mind-set or rather organizational culture, and the related change in approach it can bring about in terms of strategic relationships."[24] In this context, companies must become strategically relational as a whole, rather than through a procurement-run initiative. Given this requirement, what does it mean to become strategically relational along the lines of what both Henke and Williamson suggested in Vitasek's Forbes article? In the following excerpt from the same post cited previously, Akrouche answers this question:

> "Being strategic has taken on an added new dimension of importance. However, most people who have made or are making the transition to *strategic procurement*, have done so within the framework of the very same adversarial models that have undermined supplier relationships in the past. So, just because there is a new awareness of importance, does not mean that one becomes strategic from a practical execution standpoint.
>
> The same can be said when it comes to relationships, or being relational. To become truly relational, an organization has to do more than talk about it. It has to extend itself beyond the T&C's of a contractual enforcement model. When one is relational, the usually inward focused strategic thinking is actually extended to include the vendor or vendor community through a continuous

system of relational governance. Unfortunately, this type of engagement has been limited to a select few.

If we are to see real traction in terms of the transformation of the overall procurement practice to one that is based on being truly strategic, the catalyst for change has to go beyond a response to exceptional circumstances or rare *one of* scenarios. In other words, the procurement practice has to become relational."

While there are many points to consider in the Akrouche excerpt, what stands out the most is the underlying need for scalable improvement beyond *exceptional circumstances or rare one off scenarios.* It is this pivotal revelation upon which the question of coming-of-age takes on real meaning. If procurement cannot come of age because the mind-set or strategy of the executive team is blocking the way, their collective maturation will be stymied until new leadership has been brought in or until the best and brightest procurement talent in the organization moves on to greener pastures, leaving behind only the individuals who see no problem with the approaches of the past.

A BRAVE NEW TOMORROW FOR PROCUREMENT

When we think of what it means to *come of age,* as described in the opening of this chapter, we are not talking about a single event or the arrival at a specific destination or point of time. This is particularly true in coming-of-age journeys aimed at reaching or maximizing relevance. Procurement must embark on a continuously progressive journey in which our ability to adapt to real-time, real-world circumstances becomes the objective—albeit a perpetually changing or shifting one. To put it another way, no one ever arrives at a permanent point of relevance. One must actively pursue and reestablish relevance over time. Procurement's coming-of-age is similar to a marathon of indeterminable length, in which we must keep pace with leaders who have traditionally come from the ranks of the CFO and CIO offices. Our lack of consistent inclusion in their ranks becomes an advantage rather than a liability in an environment of fluidity.

Leading industry experts such as Handfield, Chick, and Vitasek have long been lone voices in the proverbial wilderness, heralding changes everyone knew was necessary but most were unwilling to embrace. The backbone of their message is the emergence of the relationship-driven procurement model.

In its truest and most effective form, the relationship-driven model transforms the concept of a win-win scenario between buyer and seller from one of well-intentioned lip service, to one with practical application in the real world. Once the buyer-seller relationship becomes non-adversarial in nature, the focus can shift to one of transparent engagement in which all stakeholders operate on a collaborative basis toward achieving mutually beneficial outcomes. This belief in the outcome must be shared by all parties and demonstrated by the benefits gained through the agreement. Despite the *soft* sound to relational procurement, the results must be quite tangible.

In *Negotiating for Purchasing Professionals*, Jonathan O'Brien cautions against the win/win illusion versus reality. "Perceived wins are not limited to scenarios where one party gets duped. ... The win in a negotiation is therefore subjective based upon our perception of the deal we have done. If we believe we have achieved a good result then we believe we have a win."[25] As long as we can make sure the wins are real and not illusory, there are no longer winners and losers, but instead a shared or common view of what needs to be done both individually and collectively for a successful result.

This is a primary opportunity to act on the need to continue pursuing savings and spend under management while preserving the potential for good working relationships with those outside of the organization. The end goals may be the same, but our demeanor and tactics must change. Our influence can be built after we make significant up-front investments. We need credibility, but in order for procurement to build lasting relationships, we must trust and be trusted.

Procurement Leaders Content and Community Director David Rae wrote about this critical need for trust and the role it will play in our professional trajectory in a post titled, "Trust Us, We're In Procurement." "First and foremost, procurement must earn the trust of internal stakeholders (something that comes with credibility and results). But, more importantly, procurement must earn the trust of key suppliers, if it is to bring new capability to market before the competition."[26] The fact that this trust still needs to be built, both internally and externally, should establish it as a high priority effort. It is important to note that Rae distinguishes between credibility and results. Results do not necessarily bring credibility and vice versa. Procurement must find a way to balance the two in order to make the case for influence to colleagues outside of the function, particularly to the executive we will report to.

If Not a CPO, Then Who?

Maybe procurement is not destined to have a C-level position of our own, even with the trend toward increasingly strategic priorities. If this is to be the case, then who from the traditional executive ranks should take the lead in managing this new relationship frontier with our suppliers? Should it be the CIO? How about the CFO? Perhaps it is too early to give up on the idea of a CPO.

In reality, while all of these executives have an important role to play in leading a successful enterprise, each is, to varying degrees, limited in terms of their perspective. For example, the CFO must be able to see beyond the financial view and the metrics that governed their guidance of procurement-related projects in the past. The CIO must be able to step back from a strict technology-driven viewpoint and see how to best achieve a desired value outcome for the enterprise. Although the CPO may be better positioned than the other two to take the helm in a world of relational commerce, challenges remain if the head of procurement cannot transition away from a transaction-based approach to the acquisition process.

Given these constraints, who is best equipped to corral the diverse and at times seemingly contradictory capabilities of both internal as well as external stakeholders, and set the collective track?

JON'S PERSPECTIVE: *Enter the Relationships Management Officer (RMO)*

In his January 22, 2015 post, "Why 2015 is the year of the Relationships Management Officer," Andy Akrouche writes: "It is the job of the RMO to not only understand (organizational) goals but to provide, through coaching, capacity building training and support services, the means by which organizations will establish and manage collaborative, insight-based infrastructures for delivering improved outcomes."[27]

Whether or not the RMO position will evolve under this title, or something along similar descriptive lines, remains to be seen. However, one thing is certain—the ability to both pursue and maintain relevance, or in essence, to arrive, will require a cross pollination of both new as well as existing skills that at the present time fall outside of the traditional roles of present leadership.

While rising through the ranks to the position of CFO may not run through the CFO's office, there is a persisting belief that the company's true success picture is solely in the hands of the CFO. As a result, and similar to the acquiescence of purchasing to the finance view of the world, a good many CEOs do so as well. In short, when in doubt, we look to finance for the answers. In this somewhat muddled but comfortable dynamic, the need to break away under the moniker of a new executive position that encompasses the essential and positive attributes of the CPO, CFO, and CIO will not only create distance from the old way of thinking, but it will also establish a new source dynamic and with it a new reporting hierarchy.

KELLY'S PERSPECTIVE: *It's Time for an Operational Procurement Revolution*

In a post-executive washroom business climate, it can be as limiting to be an establishment executive as not. If that is the case, the way to incorporate collaborative or relational commerce into enterprise strategy is not through the creation of a new C-level position. The executive team must be able to balance their function-specific knowledge with their understanding of what the enterprise as a whole needs to accomplish and realize that they can not do so without the right supply partners. That challenge, in my opinion, falls primarily on the desk of the CEO. As the top executive in the organization, the CEO must have a higher level, longer-term view of the business plan so that he or she can create and maintain shareholder value and succeed in spite of competitive pressures.

Just as buyers can no longer achieve success at the expense of suppliers, a CEO that does not have a broad understanding of how the company works is destined for mediocre results, quickly followed by termination—at least in a publicly traded firm. If procurement wants to relate better to the CEO, we have to understand what their background is likely to include. In 2011, Heidrick & Struggles, an executive search and leadership consulting firm, released the results of analysis they did on the careers of all of the Fortune 500 CEOs who were in place at the time. What they found provides a possible solution to the stagnant C-suite model and procurement's inability to break through to it.

Rather than coming from a background in finance, most CEOs climb the ranks through operations. "A foundation in finance is an important building block for a career. However, only about five percent of these CEOs were promoted directly from the role of CFO—more than half were appointed from the role of chief operating officer (COO) or president."[28] In other words, those who make the company operate well are the most likely to ascend to the role of CEO. If procurement wants to either join or influence the C-suite, we must reposition ourselves as operational rather than financial—a move that may require some effort but that is not a stretch in an organization with the right mind-set.

Procurement most often reports to the CFO. According to Ardent Partners' 2015 CFO Rising report, 32% of procurement organizations report to the CFO, compared to 22% who report to the CEO and 19% to the COO: "the CFO relationship has long been one of the most important and promising ones for a CPO; it has also been the most challenging. Over the last two decades, the organizational tension between the two factions kept them from becoming true allies, forced instead to peacefully coexist."[29] Reporting to finance makes complete sense for procurement in the context of our transactional past. Our job was to find sprockets that met product design needs and showed up on time, but cost $0.005 less each. Progress was measured in terms of the extended value of those half pennies. The cumulative pennies we saved appeared (at least in theory) on the bottom half of the balance sheet and increased the net profit margin. Despite the fact that we often have tense relations with our colleagues in finance, we have more or less fallen into lock step with their objectives and methods. Realized savings and spend under management are the right performance metrics for a financially driven procurement team.

My grandmother had an expression: "Show me your friends and I'll tell you who you are." Procurement may not be good friends with finance, but in many cases we sigh, shrug, and go along with their demands because we think it is what the company, and by extension the leadership team, wants us to do. By acting as finance's friends, we are the flat penny pinchers the rest of the organization thinks we are. But with friends like that, who needs enemies? I believe we are serving the wrong master. Our acquiescence to finance's requirements has prevented us from accomplishing what we want most. If we really want to change, we need new friends.

I propose that it is time for a revolution—an operational procurement revolution. Where finance is concerned with the recognition of revenue and the preservation of margins through the bottom line, operations *creates* revenue. They are tasked with accomplishing more than the competition and making sure the consumer will want it. That is no easy task. It requires imagination rooted in reality, creativity balanced by a reasonable gross margin, and sufficient demand—even if they have to create it themselves. As Rita Gunther McGrath wrote in *The End of Competitive Advantage,* "The core idea is that the starting point for innovation should be figuring out what outcome customers are really seeking and working backward into how your organization might make that happen."[30] Add any of the following words to the end of McGrath's statement and operational procurement is a no-brainer: cost effectively, collaboratively, efficiently. Procurement would be a worthy ally to operations in such an effort. Rather than trying to preserve as much margin as possible, procurement could help product development teams create new options for material fulfillment and therefore positively affect pricing models.

Lora Cecere, the founder and CEO of Supply Chain Insights—as well as an alumnus of AMR Research—describes this alignment between procurement, production, and logistics as *buy, make, deliver.* In her opinion and based on Supply Chain Insights' research, for maximum effectiveness the *buy, make, deliver* team should report into operations at a level that places them equal with sales and marketing. As Cecere wrote on the Supply Chain Shaman blog in November 2014, "… we find in our research that companies with procurement and manufacturing reporting to the supply chain organization have stronger and more reliable results on inventory, operating margin, and ROIC. Today, 60% of sourcing organizations and 45% of manufacturing organizations report through the supply chain organization."[31]

Case in point: KPMG revealed in their 2011 *Procurement Reporting Alignment* paper, that in the Fortune 500, "approximately 25 percent of Fortune 500 CPOs report to the CEO, and 22 percent report to the COO."[32] This means that in the top 500 U.S.-based revenue-grossing companies, procurement reports through someone other than finance nearly half of the time. The same research found that in the Fortune 500, procurement only reports through finance 13% of the time. When we compare this to the Ardent Partners 32% of procurement organizations reporting to finance, the difference between leaders and average performers becomes clear.

Many of the most successful companies in the world realize that procurement's contribution is not limited to pinching the enterprise's pennies, but not all companies want procurement to take on a more strategic role. "There are noticeable differences in direction and focus between these two executives [the CEO and CFO] and this impacts what is asked of procurement and the CPO," wrote Carlos Mena of his own experience in *Leading Procurement Strategy.*[33] "Reporting to the CEO works well when procurement is driving savings and strategic sourcing, and trying to make the business case for procurement work." The question about whether the CEO or CFO is a better reporting line for procurement is more closely tied to objectives than ambition. If procurement needs insight into the overall corporate agenda for the purpose of advancing value-based activities, the CEO is a better partner. On the other hand, if procurement activity is predominantly driven by cost-based activities and objectives, the CFO is a better partner due to their natural association with the budgetary process and cost controls.

It does not matter that procurement might prefer to report to the CEO over the CFO. If it is deemed that the best fit for the enterprise is for procurement to align on cost rather than value, no amount of wishing will make it otherwise. While qualified, proven procurement professionals and organizations clearly have an opportunity to spread their wings by reporting to the CEO or COO, not all of what is currently owned by procurement should move with them. The administration of buying solutions and tactical indirect spend categories should either be reassigned to a small group that stays behind with finance or be outsourced altogether, while anyone qualified to do more than endure another year of re-negotiating office supplies should head for operations.

Once we get there, we have the option of pursuing influence, training for an executive position, or both. After all, a successful executive from operations is far more likely to become the CEO than anyone from finance.

THE LATE BLOOMER ADVANTAGE

The classic coming-of-age stories we mentioned at the outset of this chapter all feature main characters that are both literally and figuratively coming-of-age. They are adolescents making the transition from childhood to adulthood, seeing and interacting with their world in a changed or different way. Procurement is by no means an adolescent function, especially when we maintain a collective view.

Procurement's organizational roots date to the 1800s and the railroad industry. "One of the earliest acknowledgments of the procurement function can be found in Charles Babage's 1832 book, *On the Economy of Machinery and Manufactures*. He points to the need for a *materials man* in the mining sector who selects, purchases, and tracks goods and services required."[34] Despite the fact that we are still on an exploratory journey to determine the optimal shape of and role for procurement, we have nearly two hundred years under our belts. That certainly disqualifies us from being considered adolescents. Fortunately, that does not also mean that our opportunity to change has slipped away.

In the March 2, 2015 issue of *Forbes* magazine, Rich Karlgaard wrote an article titled, "Late Bloomers Are In Peril." In it, he juxtaposed the overemphasis on early bloomers with the substantial potential represented by late bloomers and modern society's common dismissal of that potential. "We're right to celebrate early success. [...] But the unintended result is that the late bloomer is getting crowded out. He/she is vanishing in the American imagination, especially with regard to business and, in particular, technology. America is in danger of losing a valuable narrative about itself, and the consequences are not trivial."[35] Just as we pointed out the possibility that exists for second career procurement professionals in the first chapter, procurement should leverage the opportunity to become a late-bloomer success story. While rising to meteoric success at a young age seems like the ideal scenario, success is not always lasting, and it is not always accompanied by influence. A late bloomer has a wealth of knowledge and expertise that can be channeled and grown moving forward.

Just as procurement is not the only team in the organization facing change, we are also not the only ones attempting to increase our influence. Nick Nanton and JW Hicks addressed this idea in a 2013 *Fast Company* article. "In the last two decades, traditional signifiers of power—such as status and position—have eroded, while the weight that *influence* carries has only increased. In fact, there are those who would argue that today, influence is even more important than traditional branding techniques."[36] Building one's individual or collective brand is as important today as building a reputation for excellence might have been in the past. In an increasingly visual, virtual networking environment, the most recognizable traits of any person have to create a lasting memory that competes with others vying for the same attention as well as all of the other available streams of content. It is not enough to be a brilliant procurement professional. We also need to know how to market and communicate our expertise, an idea Nanton and Hicks also agreed with. "Whatever your expertise might be, it doesn't do you any good if you lack the ability to influence others. To achieve true influence, your crowd has to (a) know who you are, (b) like who you are, and (c) trust who you are."[37]

Procurement has had challenges in all three of the requisites for influence listed above. We have not always clearly defined our role; there are certainly people and teams in the organization that would prefer not to work with us, and many of them definitely don't trust us. We must address the challenges in that order. First we must define our role in the enterprise—a direct outcome of the coming-of-age process. Only then can we win others over to our value proposition and gain their trust.

CONCLUSION

Arriving at a yes or no answer to the question of whether procurement has come of age (yet) is not as simple as we might like. One of the challenges of the influence-driven approach is that it is harder to see through concrete accomplishments and recognitions whether we are making progress toward our goal. There is no title, rank, or position that can prove beyond a doubt that procurement is influential. Instead, we need to act from a reciprocal position of influence—making recommendations about the direction the organization should take and seeing that our perspective is appreciated, respected, and incorporated into planning and strategy.

Until others in leadership positions recognize the value of procurement and see the benefit of having procurement teams led by those with experience in the field, we cannot hope to hold influence. We need to embrace the changes facing us, and expect to continue changing in ways that reflect the dynamics in the enterprise we serve and the markets we function in.

REFERENCES

1. Pete Spiller, Nicholas Reineke, Drew Ungerman, Henrique Teixeira, *Procurement 20/20: Supply Entrepreneurship in a Changing World*, (New Jersey: Wiley, 2013), 22.
2. "Bildungsroman," *Wikipedia*, Accessed March 21, 2015, http://en.wikipedia.org/wiki/Bildungsroman.
3. "Coming-of-Age Story," *Wikipedia*, Accessed March 21, 2015, http://en.wikipedia.org/wiki/Coming-of-age story.
4. Charles Dominick and Soehila Lunney, Ph.D., *The Procurement Game Plan*, (Fort Lauderdale: J. Ross, 2012), 49.
5. Carlos Mena, Remko Van Hoek, and Martin Christopher, *Leading Procurement Strategy: Driving Value Through the Supply Chain*, (Philadelphia: Kogan Page, 2014), 13.

6. Gerard Chick and Robert Handfield, *The Procurement Value Proposition: The Rise of Supply Management,* (Philadelphia: Kogan Page, 2015), xii.

7. "Jean-Baptiste Alphonse Karr," *Wikipedia,* Accessed March 23, 2015, http://en.wikipedia.org/wiki/Jean-Baptiste_Alphonse_Karr.

8. Mena, Van Hoek, Christopher, *Leading,* xviii.

9. Matthew Eatough, "Leaders Can No Longer Afford to Downplay Procurement," *Harvard Business Review,* March 27, 2014, https://hbr.org/2014/03/leaders-can-no-longer-afford-to-downplay-procurement.

10. Jon Hansen, "Procurement's Expanding Role and the Executive of the Future," *Procurement Insights,* August 3, 2007, https://procureinsights.wordpress.com/2007/08/03/procurement%E2%80%99s-expanding-role-and-the-executive-of-the-future/.

11. Ibid.

12. "Are there any limits to procurement's role?" *Supply Business,* Accessed March 12, 2015, http://www.supplybusiness.com/previous-articles/winter-2006-7/features/executive-debate/.

13. *Supply Business,* http://www.supplybusiness.com/previous-articles/winter-2006-7/features/executive-debate/.

14. Matthew Eatough, https://hbr.org/2014/03/leaders-can-no-longer-afford-to-downplay-procurement.

15. "How to Speak Like a CFO," *TechZone 360,* May 11, 2006, http://www.techzone360.com/news/2006/05/11/1646976.htm.

16. Andrew Bartolini, "The CFO's View of Procurement: Same Page, Different Language," *Aberdeen Group,* November 2007.

17. Robert A. Rudzki, "How to Put the 'Strategic' Back in Supply Management," *Supply Chain Quarterly,* 4th Quarter 2010, Accessed April 23, 2015, http://www.supplychainquarterly.com/print/scq201004strategic/.

18. "Toshiba Procurement Chief Makes CEO," *Procurement Leaders,* 28 February, 2013, http://www.procurementleaders.com/news-archive/news-archive/toshiba-procurement-chief-makes-ceo1.

19. Kate Vitasek, "Procurement Departments Negotiating 'Too Aggressively,' *Forbes,* March 3, 2015, http://www.forbes.com/sites/katevitasek/2015/03/03/procurement-departments-negotiating-too-aggressively/.

20. Will Green, "News Focus: Supermarket Supply Chain 'Bullying' Harming Procurement's Reputation," *Supply Management,* March 10, 2015, http://www.supplymanagement.com/news/2015/news

-focus-supermarket-supply-chain-bullying-harming-procurements
-reputation.

21. Justin Loiseau, "1 Ridiculously Simple Solution to Maximize
Whole Foods Market's Margins," *The Motley Fool*, June 29, 2014,
http://www.fool.com/investing/general/2014/06/29/1-ridiculously
-simple-solution-to-maximize-whole-f.aspx.

22. Bryce Hoffman, "Whole Foods Spinoff Plan Makes A Whole Lot Of
Sense," *Forbes*, May 9, 2015, http://www.forbes.com/sites/ ｀
brycehoffman/2015/05/09/whole-foods-spinoff-plan-makes-a
-whole-lot-of-sense/.

23. Dr. Tom DePaoli, *Common Sense Supply Management: Tales from
the Supply Chain Trenches*, North Charleston: CreateSpace, 2012),
57-58.

24. Andy Akrouche, Strategic Sourcing and the Road to Transformational Leadership," *Strategic Relationships Solutions*, February 4,
2015, http://www.srscan.com/strategic-sourcing-and-the-road
-to-transformational-leadership/.

25. Jonathan O'Brien, *Negotiation for Purchasing Professionals*, (Philadelphia: Kogan Page, 2013), 7.

26. David Rae, "Trust Us, We're In Procurement," *Procurement Leaders*, April 23, 2015, http://www.procurementleaders.com/blog/
my-blog--david-rae/2015/04/23/trust-us-were-in-procurement.

27. Andy Akrouche, "Why 2015 is the year of the Relationships
Management Officer," *Contract IQ*, January 22, 2015, https://
contractiq.wordpress.com/2015/01/22/why-2015-is-the-year-of
-the-relationships-management-officer/.

28. Jeffrey S. Sanders, "The Path To Becoming A Fortune 500
CEO," *Forbes*, December 5, 2011, http://www.forbes.com/sites/
ciocentral/2011/12/05/the-path-to-becoming-a-fortune-500-ceo/.

29. Andrew Bartolini, *CPO Rising: The Agility Agenda*, (Ardent Partners, March 31, 2015), 8.

30. Rita Gunther McGrath, *The End of Competitive Advantage*, (Boston:
Harvard Business Review, 2013), 106.

31. Lora Cecere, "Misnomer," *Supply Chain Shaman*, November 9,
2014, http://www.supplychainshaman.com/demand/misnomer/.

32. "Procurement Reporting Alignment," *KPMG*, Accessed March 28,
2015, https://www.kpmg.com/US/en/IssuesAndInsights/Articles
Publications/Documents/procurement-reporting-alignment.pdf.

33. Carlos Mena, Remko Van Hoek, Martin Christopher, *Leading Procurement Strategy: Driving Value Through the Supply Chain*, (Kogan
Page: Philadelphia, 2014), 23.

34. Mike Nolan, "The History of Procurement: Past, Present, and Future," *SourceSuite*, Accessed March 27, 2015, http://www.sourcesuite .com/procurement-learning/purchasing-articles/history-of -procurement-past-present-future.jsp.
35. Rich Karlgaard, "Late Bloomers are in Peril," *Forbes*, February 11, 2015, http://www.forbes.com/sites/richkarlgaard/2015/02/11/ late-bloomers-are-in-peril/.
36. Nick Nanton and JW Hicks, "Without Influence, Knowledge and Skill are Not Enough to Build Your Brand," *Fast Company*, July 23, 2013, http://www.fastcompany.com/3014584/how-to-be-a -success-at-everything/without-influence-knowledge-and-skill -are-not-enough-to-bu.
37. Ibid.

WAV Web
Added
Value™

This book has free material available for download from the
Web Added Value™ resource center at *www.jrosspub.com*

3

Is Procurement Strategic?

"The fundamental problem is that deeply ingrained structures and systems designed to extract maximum value from a competitive advantage become a liability when the environment requires instead the capacity to surf through waves of short-lived opportunities." The End of Competitive Advantage, Rita Gunther McGrath[1]

Although the procurement function evolved out of tactical purchasing through the adoption of new technology and increased emphasis on strategic talent, procurement is no longer simply about buying goods and services in an improved way. We are driven to extract maximum value from every dollar spent by the enterprise, out of every supply relationship, and through the full term of every executed contract. At one time, savings were primarily negotiated through efficiency gains due to supply base consolidation: leveraging projected volume to achieve maximum economies of scale.

While we met our short-term objectives using this approach, we created difficulties for our future selves by inadvertently embedding unseen pockets of risk and dependency within the supply chain. Relationships with key suppliers were few and far between, in some cases resulting in little more than animosity. We also created the impression that procurement is a tactical function, more likely to muscle than think our way through a problem. The seeming intelligence vacuum created as a result of operating within that tactical bubble now requires us to play catch-up in terms of understanding the needs of those with whom we must work, and breaking free from the confining capability framework of the past.

1

As Dr. H. Thomas Johnson, an American accounting historian and professor of business administration at Portland State University, wrote, "Perhaps what you measure is what you get. More likely, what you measure is all you'll get. What you don't (or can't) measure is lost."[2] In the face of the desire (and pressure) to become more strategic, procurement is still measured by performance metrics that seem to hold us back rather than propel us forward. We follow processes that are supposedly strategic as though they were checklists. We hold internal and external contacts at arm's length, claiming that the need to preserve our objectivity requires distance. In other words, our actions belie our aspirations.

There are many opportunities for procurement to take a more strategic approach. Unfortunately, we are so focused on holding up the frameworks we have built for ourselves that many of them never come to pass. Procurement often struggles to move beyond the narrowly defined scope of our performance metrics and processes. These frameworks are centered around objectives such as achieving best price or maximizing proper governance, but we should also be able to see the connections between the potential future of our supply partners and our own ability to succeed. This is particularly true as investing in supplier *futures* gives us an opportunity to improve the field of choices before the next time we must renegotiate a contract. Until procurement finds a way to reconcile the seeming differences between the way we are measured and what we actually want to accomplish, we will find a strategic identity elusive.

INTO THE LOOKING GLASS

Perhaps if we want to chart a course to strategic procurement it would be helpful to consider another function that has completely quantitative performance metrics yet is considered a strategic contributor: business development. Salespeople have excruciatingly quantitative metrics: how many dollars did they sell on what date of each product or service the company offers? Despite such structured metrics, they must work in diverse and strategic ways. They have to build relationships with people outside of the organization with whom they often find themselves at odds. They are responsible for many activities that do not contribute directly to their quotas, yet they complete them to the best of their ability, understanding that as long as it all works out in the end, the time and effort invested are worthwhile.

Procurement stands to learn a lot from our sales counterparts, including how to successfully interact with everyone from the executive team to individual budget holders. It is important to communicate clearly and directly, to see every conversation as a sales opportunity, and to be open-minded to any approach or technique that allows us to achieve our desired end. Do we have to like it all? Absolutely not. But we do need to succeed and be able to represent that success through the metrics the enterprise has set out for us. Sales professionals have not been prevented from creating value because they have quantitative metrics—and procurement should be no different.

The 20-Second Rule

All that being said—buyers beware! It is as simple as that. In our last chapter we indulged the need for procurement professionals to individually and collectively observe the changes that are coming, along with those that have already arrived. We (hopefully) pondered, internalized, and matured as a result. The time for contemplation is over. We need to get a move on if we are going to be the authors of our own destiny. Part of what has held procurement back from the transition to strategic is that we are unable to articulate what that means. Concepts such as strategy, transformation, and value are so abstract that they require clear vision and communication in order to catch on. The less definition these ideas have, the more difficult it is to demonstrate our ability to achieve them.

In the spirit of improving procurement communications effectiveness, we recommend what has been referred to as *the 20-second rule*. As bloggers, interviewers, and social media networkers in the commentary sector of procurement, we have learned to read quickly, digest fast, and summarize abstract meaning in less than 140 characters. Blink and an opportunity is lost. Pause too long and the moment is over. Our practitioner colleagues must employ the same sense of timing. We do not advocate recklessness or thoughtlessness, but rather the straightforward simplicity that is the savior of anyone short on time and long on to-dos—namely, the executives whose attention we seek. We must think and speak at the same speed and depth as the C-suite before we can begin to get traction.

When considering any new subject matter, always look to gain an understanding as quickly as possible, and sum it up in a simple statement. For many, this may sound reminiscent of the *dot com* boom days and the purported logic behind the proverbial elevator pitch. Specifically, if you cannot clearly demonstrate or explain to me the value of what you have to offer in 20 seconds or less, you either do not know what you are talking about, or what you have is of no interest to me.

Back then, of course, everything was moving at light speed, as anyone and everyone was jumping on the rocket to Internet riches—both real and imagined. There was no time for discussion or lengthy debate, just action. If you didn't rise to meet the challenge, someone else did. Despite the inherent risks and shortcomings, we still like the 20-second rule—even with today's somewhat pedestrian pace and the more cautious, risk-averse attitudes found in and around procurement. After all, that pace and those attitudes may be what are holding us back.

We are often asked to review content or ideas and provide feedback for individuals and organizations. Anyone who has been in the position of having a valued opinion is likely to want to demonstrate respect by giving each person and their question and/or idea proper consideration *on a timely basis.* However, in order to give everyone a fair ear, it is unreasonable to go down each proverbial rabbit hole based upon vague concepts and random thoughts of perceived brilliance. No matter how complex or abstract an idea, its core meaning must be captured succinctly before it can catch on. In the spirit of the old adage of being prepared before seeking someone's advice or input, we suggest taking the 20-second test before approaching anyone with thoughts about procurement's strategic journey. Can the core of the idea and its value be presented in 20 seconds?

Here is why the 20-second rule remains a valuable approach:

1. If explaining your value proposition requires a long and winding *Of Human Bondage*-type journey, no one will have the time to listen or be willing to invest the time to hear you out. This is the reason why the majority of PowerPoint graphics and charts are a waste of time. [Note: Check out Jon's Procurement Insights post on *PowerPoint Failures* for more details on how not to make presentations.]

2. If it takes you a long time to explain what you provide, it will take even longer for you to implement it, and time is money. This is the compounded conversion effect, in which the length of time it takes for me to understand your solution or service's value is multiplied tenfold in terms of implementation time and investment.

3. If the situation is too new or too fluid, your message may be broad and convoluted as you search to find the right combination of words and ideas to get the desired reaction from your

audience. Organizations and ideas have to be stable before they can fully mature and cannot be sold or communicated well before then. [Note: We have seen this dynamic with companies such as eProcurement vendors who are trying to either gain scalable traction beyond an initial one-account success or create inroads into new markets.]

4. Respectful expedience is a gate that swings both ways. The daily stream of calls, e-mails, and social network messages brings story ideas, interview requests, career advice questions, and vendor inquiries. Demonstrating respect through timely responses requires good judgment about which topics are worth the time they will require.

To reinforce our point about the importance of brief, clear expression, each of the above reasons for using the 20-second rule also follows it. It takes a reasonable 20 seconds to speak each of the four justifications out loud (minus any notes). If you cannot be equally brief and clear in your own delivery, there is still more work to be done before you pursue or address an executive audience. And while the elevator pitch approach has traditionally been geared to selling a product or service, the underlying principle of the 20-second rule is ideally suited to the procurement world for its effectiveness in introducing new ideas. When we hold ourselves to the same standard set for external pitches and propositions, we act strategically and prove our strategic potential at the same time.

Procurement Must Learn to Sell

The 20-second rule, or elevator pitch, is not the only trick procurement should learn from sales. It would be easy to see salespeople as little more than ambitious, troublesome professionals compensated for closing deals. But contracts are a side effect of an effective sales process. The core of a successful sales process is quickly and accurately diagnosing opportunities for improvement and then winning over prospects to the recommended solution by using an approach that is a good cultural fit. It also requires a keen sense of awareness about the reactions and impressions of decision makers. Listening, not speaking, is what makes for an effective pitch.

In a December 2014 HBR.org post, former magician and current corporate communications consultant Tim David offered the following advice: "If you get the sense that it's turning into a commercial instead of a conversation, then you're doing it wrong. Stop pitching and ask another question. You should only be doing between 15-20% of the talking."[3] In fact, David advocates for a single sentence pitch, rather than the 20-second approach. Regardless of the exact length of the pitch, the message is clear—less is more. We speak so that we can listen, rather than the other way around. Every statement should be made for the response it elicits as much as the information it imparts.

When we think about it in those terms, procurement sells all the time, often without realizing it. Until we accept this idea, we won't be able to get any better at it. Believe it or not, the shortest path from tactical to strategic procurement is a well-delivered sales pitch to the right executive at the right time. We *sell* finance on new opportunities to drive efficiency. We *sell* the executive team on the strategic advantage we represent as an in-house dedicated function. We *sell* internal stakeholders on the merits of a new supplier or an alternate material that offers unique value. Just as negotiating no longer needs to be an archaic grudge match, selling does not need to be carried out using a confrontational or pushy approach. We can lead, rather than shove someone forward and still end up in the same place. The difference is the attitude they have about working with us after that point in time.

The key to delivering a strategic message is to be a quick study, sometimes adapting mid-meeting, in response to organizational requirements or customer interests. We must prove we understand the challenges at hand, even when we are working with colleagues that do not have a clear grasp of the situation themselves. Once procurement accurately articulates a problem, brainstorming can begin to reach the best solution. Our combined ability to listen, comprehend, and empathize will either open the door to our success or bar us from entry. Just as a salesperson without those skills is unlikely to get much of a bonus, procurement professionals and teams without them will be trapped forever in the tactical realm.

The other advantage of learning to think and speak like sales is that the executive team usually holds a business development-oriented view of the enterprise. In many companies, business development encompasses both sales and marketing. This combination of revenue generation and demonstrated understanding of the current and potential addressable market plays well to the executive team's desire to hear more about the next great market opportunity. Procurement, on the other hand, may come across as overly focused on yesterday's opportunities— including what was wrong with the company's execution of them. Even though it is critical to the company to have such a view of operations, it is less naturally palatable to the C-suite and business development teams alike.

Sales people often see procurement professionals as a cold, steely bunch. A sales side webinar participant commented once that procurement conference rooms are the coldest places on earth. Our poker faces have apparently had the desired effect, because many sales people would apparently like to check our backs for control panels to make sure we are human. While this may have offered an advantage in the cost cutting days of the past, it does little more than make us look out of place in the warm, collaborative dynamics created by today's relational business climate. It also does little to endear us to an executive team that is already more closely aligned with business development. This is an important, if not painful, pill to swallow if we truly want to become strategic. After all, we will be unable to succeed without the support of the executive team. If they don't want to work with us, they are unlikely to encourage our ascension to any position of influence, whether with a C-level title or not.

A New Paradigm Requires a New Approach

We know that negotiating cost savings is no longer enough for procurement to be considered a success by the people who matter, but it also has almost nothing to do with being strategic. In order to make the leap to a strategic designation, we need to create value for the organization. We hear this from executives, associations, publications, and thought-leaders. Knowing how to get started is a challenge because every situation and opportunity is so different.

Successful sales organizations evolved in response to the need for value creation a long time ago, forced to do so by new approaches to procurement. Strategic sourcing brought with it apples to apples comparisons based on price. Suppliers couldn't refuse to provide pricing, at least if they wanted a chance at winning the business, so they tried to influence the decision-making process by proving themselves so valuable that they rose above the rest of the field. In many cases, they were motivated purely by compensation, a powerful driver that we should not forget when we are addressing any executive with clear financial or operational objectives in their compensation package. If a sales representative can do their homework and increase their understanding of our executives' compensation objectives or targets, so can we. There are cost implications to any objective, so if procurement can unlock the connection between their capabilities and the events that will improve executive compensation, everybody wins.

Attempting to take a new approach to our results will also require us to modify some of the processes we have in place. It is in the best interests of the enterprise to allow each supplier to offer up their best recommendations in the bid process. As a result, the time has come for procurement to better recognize supplier innovation in sourcing and negotiation. The increased focus on value by our corporate leadership, and the ability of sales to speak their language will either open a door for procurement or clear a path right past us. If a sales person sees an opportunity to bypass procurement and reach the right executives, they will take it. Likewise, if the C-suite perceives that a worthy supplier is being blocked out by an overly structured bid process, they will sign the deal without procurement's blessing and consider us ill-suited for projects requiring judgment in the future. Capturing value does not mean surrendering in the battle over price, just balancing costs and benefits in better proportion. If we are to weigh multiple factors more evenly in the future, procurement should want to be the ones holding the scale.

We also need to recognize that the procurement/sales relationship is not about us versus them, but about all of us and what we can accomplish together. Sales professionals feel the same stresses we do, if not more, and they often see us in the driver's seat when we think we are running behind their cars. They aren't terrible people any more than we are bloodless, cost-reduction zombies. We can't (and shouldn't) fully collaborate with sales in every spend category, but when the conditions are right, joining forces with a supply partner may be the only way to a better solution. It goes against most of what we know about creating competition and harnessing the forces of capitalism, but recognizing opportunities for collaboration can be the difference between tactical and strategic procurement. Having the vision to see a long-term opportunity past a short-term objective will set capable procurement professionals and organizations apart from the pack.

Of course, it is quite a bit easier to be an effective salesperson if what you are offering is desirable to your intended consumers. And, just as many modern supply chain leaders are finding, demand is both unpredictable and transient. *The End of Competitive Advantage* by Columbia Business School Professor Rita Gunther McGrath, whom we quoted at the beginning of this chapter, provides a perspective on the way businesses should develop and maintain their strategy to remain competitive. Gone are the days when companies could achieve a leadership position in a market and then continue to dominate for decades without making significant changes. Innovative companies develop products across traditional sector lines, making the industry-based model of competition assessment obsolete. McGrath advises defining competitive strategies based on arenas, which she defines as smaller market segments defined by consumer behavior and geography as well as the product or service being sold.

When we start to think about how this concept applies to procurement, one key takeaway is finding the right mix of acquisition models: "… access to assets, rather than ownership provides flexibility and scalability without having to commit to a particular path and that the ready ability to access assets eliminates the advantage of actually owning them, in many cases."[4] The ability to be an opportunistic organization is tied directly to the level of potential flexibility: contracts included. If capital is tied up in resources, whether equipment or people, it takes longer to change direction and proves more costly to the organization. Building disengagement plans into contracts at a contained cost becomes a strategic advantage—one that a capable procurement team can orchestrate. Much like the wins associated with getting rid of nonbeneficial evergreen contracts, minimizing costs while also maximizing future options will change traditional strategies where savings are predominantly based on larger volume commitments and longer contract terms.

In fact, much of what supply management professionals have relied upon in the past may be more of a hindrance to competitiveness if flexibility becomes a priority. In most cases, sourcing projects are based on accurately anticipating volume, requirements, and service expectations for the lifetime of a contract in order to negotiate optimal pricing. If predicting future consumption doesn't create value, we must develop the ability to manage the costs of requirements and volumes we expect to change. "In an exploitation-oriented firm (the traditional approach to competition that McGrath argues is no longer optimal), reliable performance, scale, and replication of processes from one place to another make a lot of sense because you can operate more efficiently and gain the benefits of scale."[5] As a result, the whole basis of the procurement function must shift—including our skills and solutions.

No one in any part of the organization should expect a strategy based on transient advantage to be easy or comfortable. Given the amount of airtime being dedicated to *procurement transformation* and the performance expectations that go along with it, it seems clear based on McGrath's model that the process will take a toll on all of us. Significant changes in results require equally significant changes in methodology. The inherent risks will cause some professionals to consciously hold back and prove others unequal to the task.

Transformation is also not a process that we should expect to carry out overnight. It can take years to shift a team from activity types that range from tactical to strategic to one that only has strategic contributors on the direct payroll. Under these circumstances, it isn't just the tactical workers whose positions are eliminated who have to adjust to change. Strategic procurement professionals who have been part of a more traditional organization in the past will need time to acclimate to having a smaller team assigned to manage longer term, higher pressure initiatives. Acknowledging the inherent risk and articulating the anticipated return becomes a critical role for leaders of transformation procurement efforts.

IS IT POSSIBLE TO STANDARDIZE STRATEGY?

From the earliest days of procurement, we have been defined by the structures put in place to guide our efforts. The common six-step (or five- or seven-step) process, and all of its sub-steps, may have been revolutionary concepts in their earliest days, but over time have become a cumbersome approach that our internal stakeholders and suppliers seek to bypass. In the push to maximize savings and spend under management, procurement prioritized efficiency and consolidation over critical thought and net impact. The promised benefits of technology solutions often gave us further incentives to put even more governance and structure in place. The more frameworks we established in an effort to increase the scope of our coverage and guarantee the results, the more rigid we became. The end result of all this is that anyone who advocated for putting those structures in place is looked at as unsuited for leading procurement into the next phase of our evolution.

JON'S PERSPECTIVE: *Buyers Need Not Apply*

I offer the following *interesting* take on what I believe will mark the transformation of the profession from functional buyers to strategic professionals. Warning, some who are reading this might be offended, angry, and perhaps even ready to toss the book in the burning fireplace. My only suggestion would be to hold off on turning the pages into kindling—especially if you are reading this on your iPad, in which case you definitely do not want to toss it into the fire—and look beyond your initial reaction to what are compelling observations that are in line with what many other industry pundits are saying.

Going forward, functional procurement processes such as indirect material operational resource management (ORM) and maintenance, repair, and operations (MRO) spend will be outsourced, while more complex acquisitions will evolve into virtual teams or entities consisting of project-specific experts from participating stakeholders—both internal and external to the buying organization—who are skilled in the areas of relational governance. These virtual entities, while recognizing the interests of individual stakeholder organizations, will have a joint mandate or objective focused on a shared mutual gain or outcome.

With indirect material acquisitions, technology's role will evolve into one of streamlined fulfillment, while more complex acquisitions will leverage *socialized* platforms to manage relationship output as opposed to transactional throughput.

Case Study: Department of National Defense (DND)

In an effort to boost service level agreement (SLA) performance from a 57% next-day delivery capability to the contractually required 90%, the service organization providing support for the DND's information technology (IT) infrastructure outsourced their MRO acquisition process to a third party.

Within 3 months, SLA performance improved to 97%. The purchasing department head count of the service organization that had previously managed MRO purchases was reduced from a pre-outsourced 23, down to 3. The remaining 3 were more administrative—a function that would not be required with cloud-based P2P solutions.

Even though a 2007 CPO Agenda Roundtable made up of senior executives from major global corporations such as Nestlé, Danone, British Airways, and Merrill Lynch concluded that "there is going to be a continuing need for what was referred to as low-level buyers," their conclusion that "one strategic business thinker with the right skills and capabilities is worth 10 or 12 of your normal, run-of-the-mill purchasing people,"[6] speaks directly to the evolution of the procurement professional and the emergence of the project specific expert.

In terms of the *low-level buyers* reference, we must remember that in 2007, cloud-based P2P solutions were not on the collective horizon, nor were they understood relative to the extent of their impact on the market. Like other advancements, these new solutions render the low-level buyer position utterly dispensable.

The functional aspects of what we presently do will be outsourced, while complex acquisitions will require a strategic approach that is centered around a relational governance model that facilitates communication, collaboration, and shared mutual gain. Strategic thinking along these lines was reflected in a Forbes article by Kate Vitasek titled "Procurement Departments Negotiating Too Aggressively."[7]

In the article, which has rightly received considerable attention, Vitasek talks about the need to move beyond the adversarial practices that have led to short-term wins in favor of a relational approach that takes a longer term view of the procurement process. This shift in practice sensibilities reflects the strategic thinking that is needed in a rapidly changing global economy where factors such as regional industrial benefits, sustainability, economic development, and innovation as well as fair trade accountability become the basis for measuring procurement's contribution.

While some may not like to hear it, one's ability or inability (or unwillingness) to adapt to this new reality, will determine if they are going to be a part of the big organizational picture going forward. If you fall into the latter group—at which point you can feel free to toss this book into your fireplace now—then you will likely become part of the 47% of all purchasing professionals who will, according to International Association for Contract and Commerical Management (IACCM) CEO Tim Cummins, become redundant. By the way, hold off on sending Cummins any nasty notes of protestation, as he was referencing the results of an Aberdeen study when he made the statement at the Commonwealth of Virginia's 2014 Forum.

KELLY'S PERSPECTIVE: *The Extinction Paradigm Is Not Unique to Procurement*

Many of the pressures and trends previously described are more organizational than procurement-specific. Procurement has been encouraged to remove the burden of tactical employees from the payroll. In some cases, the answer was outsourcing, in others it was automation. At the end of the day you have a smaller head count managing the same scope of work, but at a lower fixed cost.

It is that fixed cost that will cause this trend of eliminating low-level workers to expand into other functions—sales included. Just as dedicated buyers are becoming a thing of the past, traditional sales *order takers* are being phased out or replaced by new distribution channels. While high-value enterprise customers will always be managed by an elite (meaning: expensive) team of sales executives, small- to medium-sized enterprises can have their needs addressed in a far more cost-effective way through channel partners.

The importance of the math behind the decision to serve a total market differently by relevant segment divisions is that it is value-oriented. Elite sales teams expect to be compensated for their effort, including the risk they take on by having their compensation tied to the decisions of others. For the enterprise taking such an approach, the staffing investment is worthwhile because of the value of what they get in return. A high fixed-cost headcount requires both high upside accounts and a long-term, sometimes global, perspective. Allowing channel partners to address less profitable customers may mean leaving a few *dollars on the table* (to use an old procurement expression), but they get a percent of the generated revenue with no fixed cost whatsoever, something that has value in itself, as we learned from McGrath.

Sales is not the only other function forced to face the inevitability of natural selection. As procurement professionals, we are so focused on our objectives and challenges that we do not realize how the changes we are seeing affect other functions in the enterprise. Less work being completed by direct hires means less work for human resources (HR) organizations. Even when this work is completed through contingent workforce programs, rather than full outsourcing arrangements, the management of the services and spend either requires HR professionals with different skills, or a transfer of responsibility to procurement.

In March 2015, The Outsourcing Institute and Alsbridge shared the results of research into vendor management and outsourcing models. Since all corporate decisions ultimately come down to the numbers, they looked at the ability of different processes and efforts to positively impact the financials of a company. Based on the research done by Alsbridge, "vendor management has a six times greater impact on earnings before interest, taxes, depreciation, and amortization (EBITDA) than focusing solely on labor cost reductions."[8] Translation: even when HR is able to reduce the cost of labor done in-house, they still can't make the contribution to financial health that a well-managed supplier program can. So while it may be hard to be in procurement, or in sales, it may be even harder to be in HR.

Once we accept that the extinction paradigm applies to the value equation of any high fixed-cost function in the enterprise, we may be able to take a different attitude towards it. As the saying goes, *it's not personal.* There is no need for procurement to be defensive, acting as though the outsourcing or automation of our tactical work is a slippery slope that will eventually lead to the elimination of all in-house procurement talent. It is instead an opportunity to be elevated to a higher level of influence and regard.

Becoming Strategic Is Not an Option—It's a Requirement

Now that we have explored what it means to be strategic, including what the experts think and how management views procurement's role, both historically as well as going forward, it is reasonable to make the assertion that in most cases procurement is *not* strategic today. But the door is not shut on the opportunity to become strategic in the future. In fact, becoming strategic is no longer an option, it is now, more than ever, a necessity.

The million-dollar question is: how does one become strategic? If you have to walk the talk, what is the talk you are supposed to be walking—and in what direction?

In Andy Akrouche's post "Strategic Sourcing and the Road to Transformational Leadership" that we referred to in the last chapter, he wrote the following:

> "Being strategic has taken on an added new dimension of importance. However, most people who have made or are making the transition to 'strategic procurement,' have done so within the framework of the very same adversarial models that have undermined supplier relationships in the past. So, just because there is a new awareness of importance, does not mean that one becomes strategic from a practical execution standpoint.
>
> The same can be said when it comes to relationships, or being relational.
>
> To become truly relational, an organization has to do more than talk about it. It has to extend itself beyond the T&C's of a contractual enforcement model. When one is relational, the usually inward focused strategic thinking is actually extended to include the vendor or vendor community through a continuous system of relational governance. Unfortunately, this type of engagement has been limited to a select few.
>
> If we are to see real traction in terms of the transformation of the overall procurement practice to one that is based on being

truly strategic, the catalyst for change has to go beyond a response to exceptional circumstances or rare 'one of' scenarios. In other words, the procurement practice has to become relational."[9]

In reading and absorbing the above, one of the points that becomes immediately evident is that becoming strategic is not a journey one takes alone or in isolation from their organization. It requires a fully interconnected *team* approach. The organization, in cooperation with procurement, must recognize the need for and work toward a new model of enlightened engagement with internal and external stakeholders.

This is the critical factor that was highlighted by Dr. Robert Handfield and Gerard Chick when they wrote that the "… integration of procurement across the business is not the responsibility of a few but rather a challenge that must be embraced company-wide."[10] Outside of this collaborative foundation, becoming strategic is impossible.

If your organization talks about the importance of being strategic in the same context of the win-win buzz terminology that is long on sentiment but short on actual practice and implementation, the odds of your becoming strategic are remote, at best. Talk is perhaps the least strategic option of all. While collaboration is undoubtedly a critical component of strategic action, critical thought will ultimately have a greater impact on procurement's strategic potential than discussion. One or more of the leading members of the procurement organization must be an effective strategic thinker, and they must connect with the C-suite on a strategic level in order for the right activities and outcomes to result. If the C-suite is either not strategic or is not open to the need for increased strategy in procurement, little can be done to effect change within procurement.

The question you then have to ask yourself is not what does it mean to be strategic, or how do I become strategic, but where can I go to become strategic?

IS IT TIME TO MOVE ON?

A daily part of the LinkedIn experience is the *Influencers* update, featuring insights and advice from some of the world's most recognized thought leaders. The list includes Richard Branson, CNBC host Suze Orman, and former GE bigwig Jack Welch, just to name a few. While these luminaries of the business world often have something worthwhile or memorable to say, sometimes the most poignant reflections come from relative unknowns. In this category of surprising sources of wisdom was a March 2015 open call for advice with the title, "I Quit! Everything You Ever Wanted to Know About (Gracefully) Leaving a Job" written by Amy Chen, an editor at LinkedIn.

In what can only be described as being a panoply of timely wisdom given the focus of this book and in particular this section of this particular chapter, the responses to Chen's post make it clear that this is not our fathers' world. The days in which maturity and stability were equated with having a cradle-to-grave position with a single company no longer apply. The time of the *lifer*, if not already over, is coming to an end. Not because of a lack of corporate loyalty, or uncertain economic times (although both of those are present factors today), but because it is no longer the optimal route to stay at the same company for one's whole career. Robert Herjavec, chief executive officer (CEO) of Herjavec Group and a *shark* on the ABC show *Shark Tank*, offered up this advice, "We can't win at everything we do and in my experience, those who achieve greatness learn what they are good at, understand what they are passionate about, and find a way to pursue both in combination."[11] The only way to achieve such self-knowledge is by pushing ourselves out of our comfort zone and fully accepting the possibility of failure. Once we are beyond the boundaries of that comfort zone, a whole new range of possibilities arise, some more expected than others.

As an increasing number of companies are considering outsourcing or contingent workforce models to meet their productivity needs, procurement professionals should keep their minds open to alternate paths as well. In a 2010 conversation with IACCM CEO Tim Cummins regarding the general effectiveness of outsourcing as a viable vehicle to enable companies to compete in the ever emerging global marketplace, overall economic impact, as well as the numerous challenges of maintaining an adequate level of security in the cloud, one particular point stood out. Cummins' stated that outsourcing is in reality, and in the context of history, a *return to a position of normalcy*.[12]

Referencing the British Economist Ronald Coase, whose seminal works include "The Nature of the Firm" (1937) and "The Problem of Social Cost" (1960), Cummins indicated that other than a relatively brief period in history, the concept of long-term or cradle-to-grave employment is, or at least was, by and large a short-lived concept. A blip on the proverbial radar screen if you will.

Why is this important? One of the main issues toward which the detractors of outsourcing—including those who might not agree with the

Buyers Need Not Apply perspective—will point, is the likelihood of job displacement. Now would be a good time to remember Tim Cummins' point regarding the 47% redundancy findings we referred to earlier in this chapter. Although we may talk about this redundancy as though it is one thing, there are a variety of causes. Some procurement professionals will become redundant because responsibility for their spend has been outsourced, automated, or sourced to the point of diminishing returns. As new skills are added to the list of requisite skills for procurement and the overall profile changes, professionals that do not have these skills and cannot learn them will have to be phased out.

Depending on your age and in particular for those over 50, you will recall a time when changing one's job more than once or twice over the course of a career was a rarity. In today's world, being in the same position with the same company for more than three years is considered an oddity and to some a sign of a clear lack of motivation and ambition. Even compensation trends indicate the benefits associated with changing companies. In their 2015 annual procurement salary survey, the Next Level Purchasing Association found that changing companies is a reliable way to increase one's paycheck. Their findings, based on the responses of 1,300 procurement and supply management professionals around the world led them to the observation that "purchasing and supply management professionals who were recruited from other organizations made an average of 15.3% more than those that were promoted from within!"[13] In Figure 3.1, you can see the responses broken down by gender and location. This observation held true even after controlling for the gender and location of survey participants, making it a transcendent way to increase salary potential.

This trend is something that younger procurement professionals have instinctively figured out and which matches their instinctive desire to

Gender (Managers & Above)	Average Salary Promoted, Overall	Average Salary Recruited, Overall	Average Salary Promoted, North America	Average Salary Recruited, North America	Average Salary Promoted, Outside of North America	Average Salary Recruited, Outside of North America
Female	$61,259	$71,006	$78,853	$83,380	$36,961	$45,487
Male	$67,274	$76,865	$101,728	$108,727	$48,839	$55,624
OVERALL	**$65,832**	**$75,927**	**$93,361**	**$100,278**	**$47,640**	**$54,707**

© Next Level Purchasing, Inc. Purchasing & Supply Management Salaries in 2015 Report. Released 3/31/2015.

Figure 3.1 Purchasing and supply management salaries by point of entry

broaden their horizons. At the conclusion of procurement seminars, it is not uncommon for young procurement professionals to come forward and indicate that their strategy for career and income advancement is tied directly to a nomadic mind-set in which they would move on to the highest bidder every two to three years. While the frequency of change is in and of itself an interesting discussion—particularly relating to the impact such movement has on the procurement profession, including the organizations for which these young professionals work—the point is simple. To become strategic, change is necessary. And in a recognition of that change, Cummins more recently referenced Coase in an IACCM post on "Redefining Trading Relationships." "It is time for a new Ronald Coase to emerge and define the business model of the 21st century—because it is this that determines the means of supply and the consequent need for trading relationships and how they are formed and managed."[14] Any one of the young professionals moving *on* in order to be able to move *up* in the profession could be the one to rewrite the expectations for successful relationships between star performers, suppliers, and employers. One thing's for sure—if an organization is truly looking for a change in procurement that the more established members of the team are unwilling or unable to execute, the combination of younger professionals who are open to such change and who expect to cycle in and out every three years or so will make that change a reality.

Are you prepared to stay with your present organization even if they continue to adhere to the old ways of doing things where *might is right* in terms of supplier negotiations and job performance is based on cost savings alone? Interestingly enough, your answer to this question will determine—not just for yourself, but for your organization—if procurement is (or can become) strategic within the confines of your present situation.

KELLY'S PERSPECTIVE: *Quitting Is Hard*

Knowing when it is time to make a move is a difficult decision. I found myself thinking about this at the end of 2014 after listening to a Proxima Group webinar featuring Jon, as well as Tim Cummins from IACCM; Robin Shahani, the Managing Director and CPO at TD Ameritrade; and Jonathan Cooper-Bagnall, the Head of Commercial Strategy at Proxima Group.[15] The event built on a previous webinar that presented the idea of corporate virtualization—a Proxima Group term for the increased reliance by corporations on suppliers to meet product and service requirements that have historically been addressed in-house. This particular panel was tasked with extending the implications of corporate virtualization forward into the procurement organizations and practitioners of the future.

In my opinion, the absolute high point of the event was precisely eight minutes in (I know this because I listened to that part of the webinar on demand at least six times), when Cummins made the following statement: "To be blunt, too often procurement as a function is actually seen as a barrier to commercial innovation, not its source." I completely agree with Cummins on this. I believe we are at a point in our collective professional evolution where bluntness is required. We do ourselves no favors by sugar-coating the truth, especially since it is validated by what we have already discussed about the differences between procurement, business development, and the executive team.

There are actually two intertwined truths in Cummins' statement: that procurement is a barrier to innovation—and that procurement is *seen* as a barrier to innovation. In some ways, it makes no difference which is actually the case. Perception is reality. If we do not make fundamental changes to the way procurement works and is seen, either one is just as likely to serve as an impenetrable barrier to our aspirations.

I didn't have to face the reality of the possible implications of such a barrier until Cooper-Bagnall brought up the topic of supply base innovation. He posed a rhetorical question about who in the organization is responsible for making supply base innovation possible. He pointed out the difference between the respective rigor applied to direct and indirect spend and noted that most innovation has historically been seen in direct spend categories—spend that is often not managed or even touched by centralized procurement. Add to that his apt observation that some companies are unsure whether procurement needs to evolve into a strategic function at all, and we are left in a somewhat uncomfortable position as professionals trying to build a career in a seemingly stunted function.

If the organization wants more innovation from the supply base than procurement is either willing or able to deliver, and since procurement has a track record of being out-performed by nonprocurement approaches to spend management, I'm not sure that elevating procurement is the answer for all organizations. The idea that procurement may have *maxed out* makes me sad because I really enjoy this profession; I always have. If my organization came to me and said, "We need your skills, experience, and knowledge to help better manage the commercial requirements of the enterprise, but, in order to have the desired effect, you'll need to leave procurement." Would I go?

I can answer without hesitation that I would. The opportunity to continue the work at hand in an elevated fashion would be too appealing to resist. I am equally confident that I would not be suited to the task or the opportunity being presented without the time I had spent in procurement. There is immediate value in the procurement perspective. Unfortunately, that potential is being held back by the infrastructure, baggage, and reputation of the procurement institution. I do not think procurement is doomed. There is no way that professionals as impressive as the ones participating in the Proxima Group panel, or who write the articles and books quoted elsewhere in this book, would dedicate their careers to a terminal function. I also don't think there is one answer to the challenges and opportunities we face today. The only certainty in this scenario is change—the change we are willing to bring about and how we respond to the changes thrust upon us.

Facing the Dip

Before trying to answer the *would I go?* rhetorical question for yourself, consider the perspective of Seth Godin, an author, innovator, and thought leader often brought in to address companies, and their sales organizations in particular, about making tough but smart business decisions. He wrote a little book called simply, *The Dip*.

The central theme of the book is that you must be able to discern which projects are worth continued investment of time and energy and which ones you need to find the courage to quit. According to Godin, you have reached a *dip* when you start to feel like you are spinning your wheels or your enjoyment of tasks is no longer what it once was, or even if you find yourself being typecast in the role you currently fill. Any of those situations should be a signal that it is time to selectively quit what you are working on so that you can make a change by taking on something new.

In these times, the exercise Godin recommends is looking at the project, relationship, task, etc., and assessing whether you are on the path to becoming the best in the world. Fortunately, the scope of your world domination can be very specific. You don't have to aim to take down Google in order to put his advice into use. If you can define your quest, then you are on the right track and you can keep moving toward your goal. The fact that it is not easy to become the best makes the effort all that much more worthwhile. As Godin states in his book, "The Dip creates scarcity; scarcity creates value."[16] And what is it that procurement individuals and organizations want to do more than anything else? They want to create value. In order to do this, at least according to Godin's philosophy, we also need scarcity.

Scarcity can be something that others in the organization are not able to do, but it can also be something they are not willing to do. Procurement professionals should think of unmet requirements or unfulfilled demand as an opportunity to set themselves apart from the pack. As long as there is the realistic potential for return, the fact that a task is difficult or *messy* should make it all that appealing to procurement. This could include everything from data cleansing to cost modeling to serving as the interface for difficult suppliers. Even the management of tail spend, the bottom 20% of a corporation's spend that is usually associated with 80% of the suppliers or transactions, may serve as an opportunity.

But the challenges and associated opportunities described in *The Dip* are not just good and bad, there is some grey area as well. The key distinction in the book is between a dip and a cul-de-sac. A dip is a temporary setback that you can push through with continued effort and creativity. A cul-de-sac is a lull that feels temporary but there is no way out—regardless of how much energy you invest. While at times they will feel the same, the primary difference is in the future potential associated with your current efforts. Anything that has become a cul-de-sac should be quit immediately in favor of something that has the potential of rewarding your efforts.

If we take this philosophy and apply it to procurement, here are some examples of dips that come to mind:

- You've been trying to break into the marketing category for over 18 months without success.
- The business unit based in Memphis has a notoriously poor compliance record.
- A long time incumbent supplier is refusing your request for more immediate insight into their financial records.

And a few cul-de-sacs as well:

- The current chief financial officer will not budge on his position that *cost avoidance* is malarkey (and possibly hogwash as well).
- The internal stakeholder team responsible for final award decisions refuses to consider switching to a new supplier.

- An incumbent supplier continues to miss quality/delivery targets no matter how many performance management meetings you force them to attend.

With any of the above cul-de-sacs, the point is not that they aren't worth your continued investment of time, but rather that something else is a better use of that effort. The best approach may be considering what activities or responsibilities your procurement group is positioned to be the best in the world at and then looking at your plate to see what you can eliminate to make room for them. If, as we have suggested a number of times previously, the dip or cul-de-sac is one that cannot be escaped because the C-suite does not agree with the changes procurement wants to make, the decision is hard, but clear. It is time to go—out of procurement or out of the company.

This decision, and the resulting move, requires a great deal of courage. It sounds simple and logical enough to leave a situation where the return is diminishing to move on to one with endless potential. The reality, however, is that a person who makes this choice is accepting a great deal of uncertainty, and potentially taking a step back in the short term to move forward in the long term. Nothing worth having comes easily, and coming to the realization that the procurement team you are part of has come to the end of their development while you have more growing to do is no exception. Every day spent in indecision is a lost opportunity under such circumstances. Having the vision and conviction to embrace uncertainty and make a move anyway is the final confirmation that staying put was a professional death sentence.

PajaS: Procurement as Just Another Service?

As hard as the decision to stay or go may be for each of us who have to face it, we are empowered in that *we own* the decision. Moving on does not have to mean a lateral or upward move from one traditionally structured procurement team to another. There are brave new forms of procurement capability being built all the time. We increase the number of options for staying in procurement *and* becoming more strategic by freeing ourselves from conventional expectations and organizational frameworks. An option that defies the standard view was described in a March 15, 2015, *Procurement Leaders* guest post by our oft quoted colleague Gerard Chick: "Has the Procurement-as-a-Service Era Dawned?"

In the post, which he wrote at Procurement Leaders' request (a sure sign that procurement outsourcing is a model or trend to be taken seriously), Chick combined the idea of outsourcing procurement with the changes that have been seen in outsourcing as a business model. It would seem that the outsourcing idea is a bit ahead of procurement, in that it has already made the leap to strategic—at least in some cases. If outsourcing is no longer relegated to managing tactical, transactional work, then more complex functions like strategic procurement become candidates for outsourcing. "Procurement is a business; and the business of procurement is to deliver 'customer' satisfaction. For procurement to succeed and remain relevant to the modern enterprise, it needs to become a combination of a strategic M&A department scouring the supply market for disruptive technologies, and a strategic marketing department seeing beyond the traditional boundaries of what the customer wants because often they have no idea what they might want in the future."[17]

One of the most common discussions in procurement is terminology-based; what exactly is the difference between purchasing and procurement? Is there actually a difference between the two? This precise hair has been split so many times that we will not address it again directly in this book. If we wanted to, we could write a book about the books and articles that have gone into the topic at length. Instead, we will consider the constant need for new terminology in procurement, regardless of what the popular term of the moment seems to be.

Procurement grew from the roots of established corporate purchasing departments. These groups were unquestionably tactical, as most predated the idea of supply management being able to contribute to competitive advantage. From there, purchasing achieved the elevated title of procurement by layering strategic sourcing and possibly spend analysis on top of the purchasing knowledge and know how that was already in place. As the strength of this centralized team and the improvement of available technology made it feasible to support an increased amount of distributed buying activity, eProcurement solutions were put in place. Although it may have been part of conscious strategy at the time, the end result is that procurement has ended up close to where purchasing began. Procurement is now often considered to describe buying activity rather than anything more strategic. The result is something like a family tree that does not fork. No matter how hard we try, procurement keeps returning to tactical buying while the more strategic pieces are stripped off.

CONCLUSION

The simplest answer to the question posed in the title of this chapter—is procurement strategic?—is no. Sure, there are some companies or industries or individual teams that have reached the strategic plateau, but this is not the common scenario. For the most part, procurement organizations are still struggling to get a foothold in the strategic door, partly because the desired changes have not been well defined and partly because we are not ready to act the part. We still have a lot to learn, from our colleagues in sales and from others in procurement. The best move is to have a no-holds-barred dialogue where stereotypes are aired and overcome before working collaboratively to develop a credible business approach for the future. And once we have increased our knowledge base and self-awareness, we must be prepared to make decisions, even hard decisions, to move in the right direction.

REFERENCES

1. Rita Gunther McGrath, *The End of Competitive Advantage: How to Keep Your Strategy Moving as Fast as Your Business*, (Boston: Harvard Business Review Press, 2013), 5.
2. James Considine, "What You Measure is What You Get?" *iSixSigma.com*, Accessed on April 6, 2015, www.isixsigma.com/community/blogs/what-you-measure-what-you-get/.
3. Tim David, "Your Elevator Pitch Needs an Elevator Pitch," *Harvard Business Review*, December 30, 2014, https://hbr.org/2014/12/your-elevator-pitch-needs-an-elevator-pitch.
4. Rita Gunther McGrath, *The End of Competitive Advantage*, (Boston: Harvard Business Review, 2013), 76.
5. Ibid., 75.
6. Jon Hansen, "Procurement's Expanding Role and the Executive of the Future," *Procurement Insights*, August 3, 2007, https://procureinsights.wordpress.com/2007/08/03/procurement%E2%80%99s-expanding-role-and-the-executive-of-the-future/.
7. Kate Vitasek, "Procurement Departments Negotiating 'Too Aggressively,'" *Forbes.com*, March 3, 2015, http://www.forbes.com/sites/katevitasek/2015/03/03/procurement-departments-negotiating-too-aggressively/.
8. Kelly Barner, "Webinar Notes: Why Vendor Management Must Change: 3 Most Common Dysfunctional Aspects of the Current Model," *The Point*, March 27, 2015, http://buyersmeetingpoint.com/blogs/bmps-qthe-pointq/entry/webinar-notes-why-vendor-management-must-change-3-most-common-dysfunctional-aspects-of-the-current-model.

9. Andy Akrouche, "Strategic Sourcing and the Road to Transformational Leadership," *Strategic Relationships Solutions*, February 4, 2015, http://www.srscan.com/strategic-sourcing-and -the-road-to-transformational-leadership/.

10. Gerard Chick and Robert Handfield, *The Procurement Value Proposition: The Rise of Supply Management*, (Philadelphia: Kogan Page, 2015), xii.

11. Amy Chen, "I Quit! Everything You Ever Wanted to Know About (Gracefully) Leaving a Job," LinkedIn, March 10, 2015, https:// www.linkedin.com/pulse/i-quit-everything-you-ever-wanted -know-gracefully-leaving-amy-chen.

12. Jon Hansen, "Outsourcing ... A Return to a Position of Normalcy," *Procurement Insights*, August 5, 2010, https://procureinsights .wordpress.com/2010/08/05/oustourcing-a-return-to-a-position -of-normalcy/.

13. "Purchasing and Supply Management Salaries in 2015," *Next Level Purchasing Association*, March 31, 2015.

14. Tim Cummins, "Redefining Trading Relationships," *IACCM.com*, December 11, 2014, https://www.iaccm.com/resources/ ?id=8315&print.

15. "The Procurement Team of the Future," *Proxima Group*, Accessed April 16, 2015, http://insight.proximagroup.com/the-procurement -team-of-the-future.

16. Seth Godin, *The Dip*, (New York: The Penguin Group, 2007), 21.

17. Gerard Chick, "Has the Procurement-as-a-Service Era Dawned?" *Procurement Leaders*, Accessed April 16, 2015, http://www .procurementleaders.com/blog/my-blog--guest-blog/2015/03/10/ has-the-procurement-as-a-service-era-dawned.

This book has free material available for download from the
Web Added Value™ resource center at *www.jrosspub.com*

4

Is There Truth Behind the Numbers?

"Almost all data analysis is about crunching numbers from the past and extrapolating these numbers into the future. For obvious reasons, the past does not include data on things that haven't happened or ideas that have not yet been imagined. As a result, data analysis of the future tends to underestimate or even ignore past events or conditions that can't be measured while overestimating those that can." The Moment of Clarity, Christian Madsbjerg and Mikkel B. Rasmussen[1]

In 2005, the commencement speaker at Stanford University addressed many of the topics that you might expect to find in such a speech. He talked about facing obstacles and learning from them. He talked about finding what you love to do and sticking to it, even when the going gets tough. He even talked about life and death. In a completely unexpected story, he talked about taking a break from his core class work in college to take (of all things) a calligraphy course and how important that ended up being later in his professional life. "It was beautiful, historical, artistically subtle in a way that science can't capture, and I found it fascinating," he said in recognition of calligraphy. He stated that it taught him to respect the balance between art and science, and to recognize that that balance is required for anything to be both impactful and lasting.[2]

He also spoke about the challenge of learning from your past while leaning toward your future. "Again, you can't connect the dots looking forward; you can only connect them looking backward. So you have to trust that the dots will somehow connect in your future. You have to trust in something—your gut, destiny, life, karma, whatever." The commencement speaker at Stanford that year was the late Steve Jobs, then CEO of Apple, and one of the greatest innovators of all time. He was only able to take that class in calligraphy because he had dropped out of college at the time, which freed him up to take noncore classes. He could not possibly have known it then, but what he learned in that class led him to emphasize typography when he was designing the Mac years later, a style decision that carried out the recognized need for balance between art and science.

Upon first consideration, the excerpt from *The Moment of Clarity* that opens this chapter seems to contradict Jobs' words about connecting the dots in retrospect. Although it requires a little more reflection to realize it, the two quotes actually say very much the same thing. The resulting lesson is an important one for anyone trying to use historical data to prepare for and make decisions about uncertain future events. Christian Madsbjerg and Mikkel B. Rasmussen, the authors of *The Moment of Clarity*, talk about the role that uncertainty needs to play in data analysis. Regardless of how thorough we are with our analytics, it is impossible to factor in changes and forces that we do not know will affect future trends and events. Jobs said a similar thing, albeit from a hypothetical future perspective. He said that connections between past and future events only have meaning when we look at them in retrospect. Like Madsbjerg and Rasmussen, he indirectly agreed the events that end up being significant receive a larger portion of our focus in retrospect, while the events that did not are overlooked. It is possible that Jobs also took classes in cooking, basket weaving, or architecture, but they were not included in his commencement address because what he learned in those classes did not end up having a role in the design of the Mac or some other major milestone in his much-discussed professional endeavors.

Yet, and in line with the old axiom—or perhaps lament would be the better word—about *generals always fighting the last war*, focusing strictly on what has already happened as opposed to what will happen is sheer folly. The only generals that get the opportunity to fight future wars (even using the tactics and strategies of the last) are the ones who have come away victorious. As Winston Churchill told us, "History is written by the victors." In order to emerge as victors, we have to understand the past without being defined by it.

The problem is that in the procurement world, and perhaps even beyond the realms of our profession, we ultimately suffer from a data myopia brought about by increasing access to information. In what can only be described as a *can't see the forest for the trees* scenario, we do not have a balanced perspective that enables us to tie the past to the present ... and extrapolate it to get a peek at the future. In other words, we treat what has happened and what will happen as two separate and distinct realms. The resulting tension for procurement comes from being trapped between those two worlds while being neither resident nor master of either.

The other challenge procurement faces when it comes to data and analytics is a combination of managing the sheer volume of available information and taking wise but artistic license. There is a reason why the opening question of this chapter isn't, *do the numbers represent the truth?* We ask if there is truth *behind* the numbers because there is still a quest to be had when it comes to applying data in a beneficial way. Advancements such as *big data* and the Internet of Things (IoT) ensure that there will be no shortage of raw data to cleanse and analyze any time soon. But the skills and aptitudes required to manage data and those needed to creatively apply it are not often found in the same people. As technology improves and the role it plays in the overall process expands, the line where humans must pick up the torch and carry it forward from machines continues to move.

ANALYSIS VERSUS ANALYTICS

Using data for differentiation and competitive advantage requires a firm understanding of concrete facts and the application of the notions and trends culled from it. For procurement, data and its application often meet in spend analysis solutions. Spend analysis has long been a critical enabler of procurement organizations. Over the last couple of years, however, the term analysis has gradually been replaced by analytics. According to BigDataCraft.com, "Analysis is the examination process itself where analytics is the supporting technology and associated tools."[3]

The above definitions place the division between analytics and analysis at the point where the technology's capabilities end and human interpretation and application begin. In other words, it is not a question of whether analytics or analysis will best be able to accomplish the task at hand. The combination of both is required in order to meet data actionability expectations. Although it is common for procurement to discuss the shift from analysis to analytics in the context of spend management, the accepted definitions and the line between them apply to all of our analytical efforts. As corporate data becomes *big*, and the IoT begins to deluge us with information, the line between analysis and analytics becomes even more critical because spend data will be joined with demand and usage details, external enrichment, and trends. The context this additional information adds to the spend allows us to be more effective in our existing tasks and also to take on new ones.

Since specific definitions can be given for both analysis and analytics, we must consider why there has been a transition from analysis to analytics in spend management. The line between the two has not always been as clear as it is now. The natural maturation process and increased competition have driven improvement in spend solutions as well as the professionals who implement and use them. In fact, advancements on both fronts have contributed to procurement's ability to differentiate between analytics and analysis and select the most appropriate solution (and term) for each context.

Analytics: Improvement in Technology

In the past, the implementation and maintenance of spend solutions was highly labor intensive, resulting in solutions that were web-accessible but involved little to no automation under the hood. The time required to process data took long enough that refreshes were only feasible on a quarterly basis. With improved automation, cleansing and categorization can be completed faster and refreshes can easily be done on a monthly rather than quarterly basis, and are sometimes done even more frequently than that. Some solutions even allow companies to handle the entire process themselves in far less time than in the past.

Beyond advancements in the technology that automates data cleansing and refreshes, spend analytics allows users to interact with their data in such a way that they get continuous improvement in data accuracy, completeness, and turnaround time. Individual users are empowered to add their own insights and layer data on top of data using one universal tool. Insights coming from users and third-party data enrichment are captured in spend analytics, minimizing the need for further manipulation in Excel and enabling other internal users to gain direct access.

Analysis: Advancements in Talent

While spend solutions are capable of taking the data further before users interact with it, the same is true of the conclusions that can be drawn by those users in an equal allotment of time. Analysis is a manual process, and to some extent it needs to be. This should not be misinterpreted as tactical; nothing could be further from the truth. Only humans can internalize all of the relevant market forces and internal information needs, and combine them with spend data to make subjective decisions and recommendations. The competitive advantage resulting from human interpretation is made possible because procurement does not need to extensively cleanse or manipulate data before they can start their analysis.

Far from being analysis, spend work in the past amounted to little more than procurement professionals filtering data and exporting it for use early in a strategic sourcing project. Today, procurement makes more advanced use of spend solutions, including risk monitoring and compliance tracking. In addition, there are regular users far beyond procurement in the larger organization. Finance, accounts payable, and operations teams that have access to a spend solution can apply analytics capabilities in vastly diverse ways with little assistance.

The combination of progress made in technology and talent has not only differentiated analytics and analysis, it has allowed both technology and people to earn the terms they bear. What we used to know as spend analysis technology was little more than spend display, and what we used to refer to as analytics was actually just advanced cleansing. Making sure that enabling technologies are doing as much heavy lifting and enrichment as possible frees up procurement professionals to do the strategic work required to create value and competitive advantage for the organizations and colleagues they support. As a public procurement blogger, Helen MacKenzie wrote of Big Data, "There's so much potential, there's so much we can find out. The key is to make sure you have a plan to get out of Big Data and TAKE ACTION on what you find out today."[4] In the emerging world of big data and analytics, procurement should use all of our current analytics capabilities and solutions to demonstrate the value we provide on a number of fronts.

Optimization

Speaking of heavy lifting, there are few opportunities to better leverage technology in the analytical work of procurement than optimization. Optimization is like the ultimate bell or whistle in an eSourcing solution, but for every organization that requires it to be in place during the qualification and selection process—very few use it regularly or to its full potential. We most commonly think about optimization being used to analyze supplier bids and bid packages in advance of negotiation and award, but this is really just the beginning.

Any decision that procurement must either make or support that can be expressed in terms of inputs, variables, and constraints can be automated through optimization. Rather than leading procurement to one right answer, investing in optimization helps everyone on the team understand the role played by constraints. As Alan Holland, CEO of Keelvar Systems, a solution specializing in optimization for procurement wrote, "Contrary to some misconceptions, optimization can act as the bridge between the competing objectives of cost and quality because transparency increases trust and forms the basis for open dialogue."[5] By exploring the cost, flexibility, and availability implications of any given constraint, organizations can make more informed decisions.

Despite what some may think, making use of optimization does not require that all of the inputs or variables in a scenario be cost-based or even numeric. As Holland wrote in the same previously quoted post, "The key to realizing a collaborative agreement is to have certainty on trade-offs between cost and non-cost objectives."[6] What the variables do need to be is logical. *Non-cost* does not necessarily equate to *subjective*, and the more work procurement can do to capture information related to the non-cost needs and wants of the enterprise, the more we can make use of advancements in optimization. The real benefit is improved decision making accuracy and efficiency. Seeing the difference in results—on all fronts, cost and otherwise—based on one set of constraints and variables versus another, does more to help us understand the role those variables play in connecting our qualified options and the objectives for the category.

ACHIEVING BALANCE

In analyzing the data that results from past transactions, we need to think not in the context of what will happen next based upon that data; instead, we need to look at data from the standpoint of what we had hoped would happen and what ultimately did. There are a whole range of processes and behaviors that feed into a given data set. Making data analytically relevant requires as much work outside of the numbers as within. Were we able to make the right decisions or set the optimal priorities based on the available information and our interpretation of it? If not, we must ask ourselves whether the problem was an unpredictable glitch in the turn of events or whether we did not interpret that data correctly.

Data is a tangible reflection of the processes and strategies utilized in pursuit of past objectives and goals. If we failed to achieve those goals, then the problem is in the processes and strategies, and not the numbers themselves. Another way to think of this is in terms of a doctor treating a patient's symptoms without trying to understand the underlying illness. While the prescription may alleviate the symptoms, at least for a time, it may not eliminate the cause. In time, either the symptoms may return, or new ones could appear, but this does not mean the prescription was the problem. It was the doctor's understanding of the illness—their analysis, if you will—that failed the patient, not the medicine.

In much the same way, we have to learn to push beyond our view of the *symptoms*, looking beyond historical numbers to measure real time practical outcomes. Otherwise, similar to looking down at your feet while you are walking, we will always be able to see our next couple of steps, but will ultimately lose sight of where we are headed.

This latter point was clearly demonstrated at the 2014 Virginia Public Procurement Forum in a session titled "The ABCs of Spend Analysis," (see Figure 4.1). Focused on finding the truth behind the numbers, the results from a case study in which there was an $800 million gap between the projected and actual spend was discussed with the audience. A project with an original budget of $900 million eventually resulted in a cost of only $100 million to the supplier. Unfortunately, the big picture consequences of this large change were no less problematic than they would have been if the situation had been the reverse (i.e., the

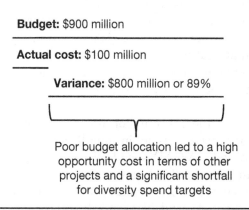

Figure 4.1   The ABC's of spend analysis

project being over rather than under budget by $800 million). The obvious impact included the loss of access to allocated funds for other areas that had pressing needs. The deeper, more pressing concern for the state of Virginia was identifying the actual problem they needed to solve. Do you, for example, focus on the immediate urgency of having to deal with the adjusted spend and its consequences, or do you focus on the budgeting and contracting process associated with the original budget?

Ultimately, and to their full credit, the state did not blindly view coming in under budget as a success story. Conventional thinking would suggest that any project that comes in less expensive than expected is cause for celebration. *Great job purchasing department!*—with handshakes and back slaps all around. This is a critical point because a *numbers only* view is good news even as it obfuscates the bigger issue. The bigger issue in this case was getting to the bottom of how it happened and why the estimate was so far off. Was the problem a misunderstanding of the market or were the original requirements misrepresented? How deeply ingrained were the errors that led to the variance? This sort of deep, introspective approach is the first step toward looking beyond the numbers for the truth.

The truth of the matter in this case is that there was a disconnect between projected, budgeted, or billed spend and what was actually owed. Adding to the complexity was a delay in *when* each type of spend was recognized by supporting systems. The state had a process for capturing spend data and budgeting funds that recognized costs in the month they were billed, while any future adjustments to the original expenditure were applied in a later month. This created a feast or famine situation with winners, losers, and a great deal of data instability where the actual operational or acquisition activity did not match the spend transactions. The anticipated $900 million in spend, $800 million of which was not needed, was not available to other areas in the state that may have needed additional financing, thereby delaying potentially important projects and eliminating an opportunistic, agile use of funds. This was a famine that later turned into a feast when the money became available again.

Conversely, when the $800 million was eventually freed up, the reversal meant that the state was not in compliance with its small, women, and minority-owned (SWAM) spend allocation requirements for the original purchase period. A feast that ultimately turned into a famine, in that SWAM targets that were originally met—even exceeded, now fell far short of the targeted spend. Not until all of the transactions and their associated positive and negative consequences had a chance to work their way through all related systems did the numbers even come close to matching the truth of the situation—resulting in a delay between events and decisions and being able to quantify the results.

Going forward, and looking at the numbers in the context of both individual and collective goals, the state of Virginia was able to identify the points of breakdown in the acquisition process and the severe disconnect between the actual situation and what the data would have indicated—both at the time and in retrospect. Fortunately, they were also able to institute the necessary changes to ensure that this would not occur again in the future, but it was a tough lesson to learn. Do you see how the state was able to eventually link the numbers from the past to improve the processes that would ultimately have an impact on the future? They looked beyond the numbers to diagnose the cause and understand the changes and activities actually taking place.

JON'S PERSPECTIVE: *Looking Beyond Procurement*

Back in 2008 when I first started to investigate the obvious communication gap between the finance and procurement departments within organizations, there were telltale indicators that such a breakdown existed. The most ominous was the fact that the vast majority of savings claimed by procurement, such as cost avoidance, was discounted as being irrelevant by the company bean counters.

Largely the product of the artificially created silos of historic functionality, these gaps, many experts propose, could only be bridged by a shift in procurement focus. This included what Robert Rudzki, president of Greybeard Advisors and coauthor of *Straight to the Bottom Line*, identified as the five critical finance terms every purchaser should know. The terms (which we covered in more detail in Chapter 2) are:

- Return on invested capital (ROIC)
- Cost of capital
- Economic value add (EVA)
- Earnings per share (EPS)
- Profit/Earnings (P/E) ratio

As Rudzki wrote in a 2010 article for *Supply Chain Quarterly*, "Procurement and supply managers who understand the CFO's perspective and can present their ideas in that context are heading to the top of the profession. Those who don't—or won't—master this skill seem to end up perpetually carrying out tactical directives and are unable to gain control of their careers."[7]

While technically sound and quite relevant when they were penned a decade ago, Rudzki's guideposts for effecting better internal communication between procurement and finance are now somewhat outdated in terms of their scope.

We are no longer looking at the now myopic breakdown in the singular communication channel between finance and procurement, but instead multiple areas within the global enterprise including information technology (IT). All of which, it should be noted, are currently influenced by as many as four different generations simultaneously employed within the same organization.

There will be those who will question the true impact of a multi-generational workforce on a company's ability to communicate internally and ultimately to perform. Regardless of your thinking, one thing is for certain—it is a variable that complicates, rather than clarifies, the indigenous breakdowns to which Rudzki had originally referred. In fact, as newer generations of procurement professionals—who have actually *chosen* (versus falling into) their field of work—graduate from schools in which finance is now as much a part of the curriculum as are the all too familiar purchasing basics, the range of expertise becomes less of a question. This shift toward a more holistic enterprise awareness and knowledge means that the very nature or make-up of the aforementioned gaps have also changed to one of dissemination and practical application.

Collectively, these additional elements dramatically change how we do business, especially as we enter into the complicated realms of the governance of global supply chains. While still noteworthy, Rudzki's determination that there is a need for procurement professionals to expand both their view and understanding of the role they play in their organization's success, including how said contributions are quantified by other stakeholders, no longer goes far enough. Today's procurement professionals must comfortably embody many different attributes to establish and maintain meaningful relevance in a world that is no longer one dimensional.

Or, to put it another way, the numbers or business intelligence, or whatever other name you give it, must ultimately be converted into action before they can be meaningful.

USING DATA TO FIND THE TRUTH

Assuming there is truth behind the numbers and other data that procurement has access to, procurement must determine what form that truth will take. The truth, at least in the context of procurement's journey to better understand and interpret the internal and external conditions we operate in, must include perspective. The truth, in this case, ends up being the observations that are acknowledged as the foundation for any resulting strategy.

How do we cut through the noise and transform raw data into actionable insights? This is an interesting question that was recently posed through one of a myriad of social media seminars proclaiming the promise of *big data*. Even as our common approaches and relevant technologies change, there is still an underlying process that must be applied to data that has changed little in concept. We get raw data from one or more systems. We cleanse and categorize it, and if we have the funds and access to relevant information, we enrich the data with solutions from third parties. Next we apply the analytical functionality of our solutions before we go *human hands-on* and perform our own applied analysis. Constraints and variables are modeled and their relative impact is weighed. We may even make use of optimization to improve our decision making.

To the extent that procurement is a data-driven discipline, we are closely linked to the capabilities of our technology for visibility and insight. And while quality data is an essential foundation for all of procurement's efforts, the time required to make it actionable comes with a high opportunity cost. In many cases, we are slaves to data cleansing and report creation. Our solutions, despite how they are characterized, often serve as no more than accessible, segmented storage. Making sure that enabling technologies are doing as much heavy lifting and enrichment as possible frees up procurement professionals to do the strategic work required to create value and competitive advantage for the organizations and colleagues we support.

This point was driven home by Nipendo's Eran Livneh's post "What is the Internet of Things and What Does It Mean to the P2P World?" In writing about the Internet of Things and Humans (IoTH) in relation to the P2P process, Livneh states that, "we should preserve the genius of Humans to focus on where it's really needed: strategic thinking, process design, and management by exception. The day-to-day is better left for 'Things': an invoice comes in, automatically validated against internal rules and external data sources (e.g., tax rates), reconciled to the ERP system of record, and approved for payment. When Humans do a good job designing the processes and system to support them, over 90% of the invoices can be handled by Things without any Human touch."[8]

What improved analytics really provides us with is the opportunity to be discretionary about where human touch is employed—an optimization scenario in and of itself. The value proposition associated with management by exception is defined by the percentage of exceptions to total data. Even after resolving the issues that led to exceptions, we must determine why those exceptions occurred and what can be done to resolve a greater number of them via automation in the future. In the age of data collection and analytical automation, it is the people that provide differentiation and represent subjectivity in decision-making models. The more our machines are able to *learn* from humans, and the more humans are able to see the trends and systematic causes of exceptions, the more collective progress we will make. As Tim O'Reilly, founder and CEO of O'Reilly Media, put it, "… so many of the most interesting applications of the Internet of Things involve new ways of thinking about how humans and things cooperate differently when the things get smarter. It really ought to be called the Internet of Things and Humans—#IoTH, not just #IoT!"[9]

Both Livneh and O'Reilly's well-made points about the combination of man and machine extend beyond the functional P2P process to encompass all of the elements of a modern, global procurement practice—including the capture, structure, and utilization of data. This brings us back full circle to the break between data resulting from past transactions and strategies looking to maximize the potential of the present and future. Having access to data that we can apply on a practical, realistic basis going forward represents the bridge between what has happened, what will (or can) happen, and how ready we will be for it.

This need for a bridge applies to the internal and external data we analyze as well as the data output from our own reporting of spend, savings, and suppliers. We have evolved in our use of data, in part because solutions are now faster, less expensive, and more intelligent. But there is a human growth element to this as well; procurement recognizes that the more types of data we pull into our analysis, the more well-rounded and enabling our resulting conclusions will be. Of course, while our capabilities and solutions were maturing, other enterprise solutions were improving as well.

Procurement is now competing with other functions in the enterprise for the ownership of data and systems as well as for recognition as experienced analysts. Despite the fact that we are dependent upon data to meet our objectives, we are also increasingly aware that no data set can tell the full story of procurement's value, at least not in the short term. We often find ourselves in the precarious position of arguing for our mastery of data while also emphasizing that our *numbers* do not fully capture what we are capable of, and may even constrain our ability to contribute to competitive advantage. This is a dichotomy that we must resolve. Data will never fully represent the totality of a complex situation and yet it will never be replaced as the foundation for our understanding of reality and as the basis for recommendations.

Case Study: GE Jet Engines and Data Analytics

Procurement is not alone in our uphill battle in the face of increased access to data. GE Research uses the data collected and reported by their jet engines to manage the costs of maintenance. As Bill Ruh, Vice President of Software at GE Research, explained, "The airline industry spends $200 billion on fuel per year so a 2% savings is $4 billion."[10] Those numbers would turn the heads of most procurement professionals. In order to have a positive impact on those costs, GE's engines generate and communicate huge volumes of data. One engine sensor generates over six times as much data as Twitter does in a day, and each engine can have as many as twenty sensors in it. With all that being said, GE is not solely focused on analysis skills in their recruiting and staff development programs. "Ruh is looking not merely for great mathematicians or engineers, but for people who can understand the meaning of the data sets when applied to a machine operating in the real world."[11] And that is the piece that is such a challenge, both because it is not easy and because it is always changing—the meaning of those data sets change with every other relevant variable: from fuel prices, to security requirements, to the weather.

In addition to the immense challenges of collecting and harnessing all of that data and all of those variables, any commercial enterprise naturally wants to find a way to convert that investment into a revenue stream. This is another way that procurement can serve a valuable role with regard to data and top line growth. Procurement can apply knowledge and systems to create analysis or analyzed content that customers will pay to receive. There is no sense in collecting all of this data unless someone can assist clients in applying it to their own requirements and circumstances. Making the connection between data, observations, and operational application is a role we are used to serving in.

With access to new data types and voluminous new data comes an incredible opportunity to accomplish something unique and distinguishing. But, just like the challenge of creating supply market intelligence has become both easier and harder with the expansion of the Internet and the proliferation of *free* content, the challenge shifts from being one of location and application to one of quality assurance and filtering. Having said that, for the right person with the right skills in the right circumstances, the opportunity could be career defining. "The enormous breadth, depth, and raw amount of data sets like these create opportunities to analyze multiple dynamic variables," wrote the McKinsey team of authors behind *Procurement 20/20: Supply Entrepreneurship in a Changing World.* "The ability to translate the trove of information into actionable insights will increasingly be a source of competitive advantage."[12]

What is particularly important about their point is that the translation of data into intelligence or insight is a requirement for seizing a potential competitive advantage. We have become accustomed to thinking of *transformation* in procurement as an advanced initiative to be pursued when the *low-hanging fruit* is all dried up. In this case, the transformation—or translation—is a prerequisite for action. Data by itself has very little value. It is the process it goes through and the solutions we use to view and analyze it, that make it a valuable asset.

Procurement's Three Truths: Spend, Supplier, Social

It would be easy to spend this entire chapter delving deeper and deeper into analytics, analysis, and data. In fact, if any of the observations and generalizations we have made about the typical procurement persona ring true, that would be our natural inclination. But there is a second (and equal) part to the question that guides this chapter. It is the truth. When we ask if there is truth behind the numbers, we cannot just focus on the numbers and other data that procurement has to work with. We must also consider what form (or forms) the truth takes. But before we can set out to locate that truth, we have to have some concept of what it is we seek. What is truth?

There are two relevant definitions of truth that we can juxtapose, hopefully without getting too abstract, in our quest for a better understanding of the term *truth*:

1. *The body of real things, events, and facts*
2. *A judgment, proposition, or idea that is true or accepted as true*[13]

When you combine procurement's approach to data and the actionable insights we pull from it, both of the aforementioned definitions are incorporated. The data we work with, whether in the form of numbers or otherwise, belongs to the first definition of truth. Data is made up of facts that result from real things and events. But, as we have established, procurement cannot act on data alone. We have to extend and extrapolate data to support recommendations, observations, and applications for it to have any operational meaning or value. This is where the second definition of truth becomes relevant.

To be able to find truth behind the numbers implies that the numbers and the truth are not one in the same. Although we can be very thorough and careful in our analysis, all of our interpretation and perspective add just as much variability as they do value. As Robert Rudzki wrote in *Straight to the Bottom Line*, "Your own numbers shouldn't lie."[14] His point was made in the context of ensuring that procurement uses valid benchmarks and justifications for the contributions we claim. We have an imperfect knowledge of the conditions we work in, both internally and externally. The truth we act upon in our application of data is an accepted truth, not an actual truth. At any given time, we have to act on the best available truth, but that truth is always changing—at least if we are doing our jobs well. Time passes, new information becomes available, and priorities and objectives change. The variables that are reflected in the transformation of data into intelligence are as much our business as the inputs or outputs from our process. As such, they need to be as documented and justified as the recommendations we ultimately make.

There are three primary categories of truth that procurement has experience working with: spend, supplier, and social. Each starts with one or more sets of data and goes through the analysis and application process to become a truth unique to that moment, team, and context (see Figure 4.2).

The Spend Truth

Historically, procurement only had ownership of spend and other transaction-based data. Any enrichment that was done to that data was rudimentary. In fact, although it was billed as *enrichment* at the time, what was really happening was more like cleansing. Supplier parent and child relationships were established and a taxonomy was applied based on a combination of supplier name and location. That approach, while critical, added more clarity than context to the data.

Figure 4.2   Procurement's Three Truths: Spend, Supplier, and Social

Once that was done, what we had was a solution that allowed us to see how much money had been spent, when, by whom, with whom, and (roughly) on what they spent it. Although this combination of facts was a truth, it told us very little that we could use to manage that spend along lines that are more strategic than leveraging economies of scale. Taking a more strategic approach requires building an understanding of why the money was spent, how much value was created in return, and whether the stated objectives were achieved.

In order to move from a factual spend truth to an accepted spend truth, we need to incorporate more data enrichment (diversity status, risk level, financial information) to elevate our view of the data. We also need to accept that before any analysis can begin, we need to get the rest of the story from internal and external stakeholders. This requires that naturally analytical procurement professionals take a leap of faith—that in order to get closer to the accepted truth, we have to move away from facts and data. It seems contradictory, but learning to work with accepted rather than factual truth makes us far more action oriented, more likely to get results, and more likely to provide insight—as imperfect as it might be.

In response to demand for more functionality and greater visibility, today's spend analysis solutions must differentiate themselves on how quickly and easily they can be updated and how much context they offer for data. We also have the option of pushing for greater independence. Putting users in the driver's seat is an advantage because it allows procurement to have greater control over their own data and how it is categorized. And when the majority of the cleansing, categorization, and enrichment takes place in the spend analysis solution rather than afterwards, the inherent reliability grows because the process of reaching the same numbers—the same truth—can be repeated by different team members.

The difference between a mediocre spend analysis solution and a robust one is like the difference between a circle and a sphere. It is true that a circle goes all the way around a given center point, and it is the same basic shape, but it is still flat. A sphere, on the other hand, also goes all the way around the center point, but in all three dimensions. It leaves no perspective of the center point unseen. As procurement learns to leverage this new expanded view, we not only improve our management of known opportunities, but we uncover opportunities that have been sitting unseen, waiting for someone to monetize them.

The accepted truths that we need to be able to pull from spend today are far from the *how much, when, with whom, and for what* approach of the past. Creating strategic value requires that procurement also seek to determine whether the money should have been spent, if it was spent with the right supplier, and if there was a better way to reach the desired end result. We will always have to directly engage with stakeholders and suppliers in order to fully understand the meaning of the spend and what is received in exchange, but the more we can incorporate into analytics, the more visibility we will have in-hand before those conversations.

The Supplier Truth

If spend is the primary source of procurement's data, suppliers are a close second. We collect basic information, such as location, annual revenues, and employee count, but we also keep records on their legal background, qualifications, and growth plans. To the extent that procurement has taken responsibility for enterprise resource planning (ERP) systems and supplier or vendor masters, we now also own the factual truth about our suppliers. We know where they are, who manages them, if we have any sell-side business with them, what their diversity status is, and what their performance has been. Just as third-party enrichment expanded the potential of spend analysis, supplier relationship management and supplier performance management result in information that, once applied to more factual truths, creates an accepted truth specific to the buying company and category of spend.

Just as we have discussed with the factual truth about spend, the factual truth about suppliers can be as limiting as it is accurate, particularly with the growing prevalence of relational and collaborative supply partnerships. A vendor master no more captures the truth about a supplier than an invoice total and date represents the full story of a dollar spent. In *Supplier Relationship Management*, Jonathan O'Brien wrote about the need to expand procurement's perspective when it comes to the information we include in our assessment of supplier effectiveness. "There are many things we could measure and many different sources of information. ... It is important, too, to look beyond the obvious measures."[15] The accepted truth about our suppliers must be a representation of their total potential for value creation. Visualizing this potential may be where data and numbers fail us most. When it comes to our dealings with suppliers, the numbers *make a better door than a window* because our performance metrics and targets obscure the clarity of our vision.

When we are dealing with suppliers, procurement is usually in one of a few modes. If we are preparing a bid, we are focused on specifications, demand quantities, and costs. Once we move on to negotiation, it is hard to pull our eyes away from the potential for savings. During the term of the contract, we measure total spend and compliance rates. While all of these measures are important and represent a piece of the truth in their own way, they all miss the point. When we focus on what is, it becomes harder to see what can be. Any effort our suppliers make to engage with us in a more subjective way is often viewed by procurement as an inappropriate attempt to subvert the objectivity of our process. When working with suppliers, particularly those with the potential to become collaborative partners, procurement must remember that they, too, must accept the truth we arrive at through data and insight.

The Social Truth

Last but not least, procurement is often faced with corporate social responsibility, environmental, and diversity targets that have almost no root in our data at all. The truth paradigm in this case works in the opposite direction of the other two we have just considered. Spend and supplier truths start as factual truths and must be adapted to become accepted (interpreted, actionable) truths. Social truth, on the other hand, often starts as accepted truth, and we have to find some way to back into the facts to support it. The acceptance in this case is on the part of stakeholders, shareholders, and consumers. Companies hear their message loud and clear, and act on the message they get from these important voices for the sake of public relations and brand risk mitigation if for no other reason.

In a 2015 *Procurement Insights* guest post, Nick Ford addressed head-on the challenges of converting social or sustainably motivated impact into financial impact, whether through procurement's efforts or otherwise. "The main challenge with sustainable procurement is that the benefits are all in the long-term, whereas in the short-term, companies see nothing but additional costs. That initial set-up that I mentioned earlier comes at a cost. There will also be an increase to the cost of most goods as price is no longer the primary determining factor when sourcing. In an ideal world, corporations would look past the implementation costs and the reality that they will now be paying more for the same goods, and rejoice in the fact that they are helping the world. Peace and love, man. Sadly, companies don't think like that."[16] The fact that companies don't take a more altruistic approach without being encouraged by their constituents is an indication that corporate strategy naturally flows *from* data, not *to* it. In the case of corporate social responsibility, we are working against the natural flow.

Whether you see social supply initiatives as an important opportunity for procurement to create value or a frustrating distraction from the primary business of spend management, we have to find a way to incorporate them in our plans and in our understanding of the truth in the categories they affect. In *Green Purchasing and Sustainability*, Robert Menard wrote, "The reality is that a combination of pressure from society, government, and even customers will sooner or later force us to turn our attention to CSR [corporate social responsibility] concerns. More importantly, it is purchasing's responsibility to manage the more practical and tangible aspects of sustainability because they all relate to cost savings."[17] The fact that, as Menard suggests, sustainability has practical and tangible *aspects*, also indicates that a significant portion of the justification is neither practical nor tangible. This is a difficult rational obstacle for analytically minded professionals to overcome.

Can Procurement Own the Truth?

At the end of the day, all of the effort required to transform data into actionable intelligence leaves us with a stand-alone asset of considerable value. If procurement's role with regard to data is seen as being limited to ownership, once it is cleansed and enriched and available in an accessible format, we are no longer needed. If, on the other hand, procurement is seen as having a deeper understanding of the data and how it can be mined for insights, we demonstrate the value of keeping us involved.

By repositioning ourselves as the owners of that asset without holding others at arm's length, we reposition ourselves relative to data, to intelligence, and to both the factual and accepted versions of the truth. Trying to keep nonprocurement colleagues in the dark in order to preserve this role is an ill-fated short-term strategy. We work with smart people, and in order to deserve the opportunity to work with them, we have to know something they do not.

KELLY'S PERSPECTIVE: *Prove How Hard Data Maintenance Is by Making It Look Easy*

My sense is that procurement falls into a common human trap when it comes to data and all of the associated cleansing, categorization, enrichment, analytics, etc. In order to prove how hard we are working (because let's face it, despite all of the advancements in technology, we are still working incredibly hard to make data usable) we often spend too much time talking about it. The conversation probably goes something like this:

> CEO: How is it that we don't know exactly how much we are spending on X component across all of the suppliers that are approved to provide us with what we need?

> PROCUREMENT: Well, you see, the supplier we buy the most from bills us in a consolidated format. We only have access to that line item detail if we ask them to send us an alternate reporting format. The problem is, those reports don't sync well with the spend data we pull for our analytics solution because they are dated by order date rather than payment date. Often the amounts and quantities we paid for cross into different order date periods, and those are what the managers base their budgets on. So you have to decide if you want to see what we spend rolled up and accurate with our payment dates or on a detailed level that aligns with orders and budget planning.

> CEO: *Silently looking down.*

> PROCUREMENT: Sir?

> CEO: Oh, I'm sorry. Were you talking? I apologize for cutting you short, but I have to get off to an operational planning session with the VP team. Thanks for the information.

The plain and honest truth of the matter is that executives do not care how hard or messy it is to get the data into a useable state. All of the activity and effort associated with that is considered a means to an end—period. The C-suite wants to see results, applications, and (ideally) visuals. With a few exceptions, they are more interested in seeing the insights drawn from data than the numbers themselves.

In this way, data and analytics are like modern art. If we employ the right level of elegant simplicity, there is a chance someone else in the organization will look at the data and either say or think, *I could have done that*. Think of a picture you might see hanging in a modern art gallery that looks like your seven-year-old painted it with their lunch. It is easy to laugh and say, *my kid could have painted that*, but the fact of the matter is—they did not. The very talented people in the art museum who know all about such things can see the difference between your messy art wall at home and the canvas on the wall in their museum. Smart executives are similar in that they can tell the difference between a good data manager or analyst and a poor substitute even if a snarky colleague cannot.

In the long run, we are better off doing that sort of work in dedicated silence and then moving on to the value-added activity of drawing conclusions and making recommendations. A smart executive will know that it was not possible to arrive at those insights without procurement also being able to handle the grunt work that preceded it. There is no need to waste their time or divert their focus to demonstrate just how dirty and hard the grunt work was (because they probably wouldn't be listening anyway). That approach is more likely to be interpreted as a lack of procurement's confidence in the quality or validity of conclusions and recommendations. So let Joe in facilities maintenance be snarky all he wants; if he was really better at it, he would have been given the responsibility, rather than procurement.

THE TRUTH ABOUT PREDICTIVE ANALYTICS

Now that we have extensively explored the concept of truth and how it applies to procurement and the data we work with, we must address the complex topic of predictive analytics. By definition, predictive analytics cannot be truth, as the resulting (anticipated) events and data have not yet transpired. In this case, it is the path, or the correct interpretation of data and all of the contextual factors surrounding it, that substitute for truth.

The goal for many procurement teams is to reach the point where analytical efforts can support predictive strategy development. In the ultimate reversal of the *driving while looking through the rear view mirror* stereotype, this advancement would allow procurement to combine and enrich data sets and perform analysis in support of forward-looking recommendations—thus, putting plans in place for trends that are coming but which have not yet happened. Predictive analytics is more like driving with your eyes closed while listening to yesterday's news on the radio and yet never hitting anything, arriving safely, and ahead of schedule. In order to make this possible, we have to be able to visualize and follow the trail that joins the two.

As Lora Cecere, founder and CEO of Supply Chain Insights and former AMR Research analyst, wrote in her 2015 book *Supply Chain Metrics that Matter* about the challenge of navigating complex conditions using historical data, "Closing this gap requires descriptive, predictive, and prescriptive analytics. While descriptive analytics enable reporting and data analysis, predictive and prescriptive analytics enable the management of operational flows. In contrast, predictive analytics enable operational alerting while prescriptive technologies recommend actions to take."[18] Even when we are predicting future events, we cannot allow ourselves to become abstract. Every recommendation and observation must be connected to the operational reality of the here and now.

The Break Between Operational and Predictive

Part of the operational reality we must accept is that our data cannot lead us to a predictive view of the world unless we find a way to represent the *forces* within it. Spend transactions are pure history. Supplier data is flat fact. The forces are what caused us to spend money and the priorities are what caused us to select certain suppliers who actually offer predictive value.

In some cases, such as with seasonality, we simply need to obtain a sufficiently representative demand or spend pattern to understand and prepare for expected trends. In other cases, we may have the more ambitious goal of predicting less cyclical or completely unexpected events. Each piece of information and source of insight should be considered for whether or not it holds predictive value. This is another example of where art meets science, as it did for Steve Jobs in his design of the Mac. In retrospect, the calligraphy class held predictive value that his other elective classes did not. The trouble is that, in the moment, they all would have appeared equally likely to be connected to his future success.

Douglas Laney, a Research Vice President at Gartner, presented a webinar on predictive analytics in early 2015 called *Use Predictive Analytics to Help You Capitalize on Business Moments*.[19] His presentation was interesting partly because he was so straightforward in his explanations—going so far as to describe himself as not much of a Magic Quadrant guy, in reference to Gartner's well-known matrix of solution evaluation. He was a compelling speaker on this particular topic because of the clash of topic and style. Laney addressed an abstract idea in a concrete way. While illustrating the value of predictive analytics through case examples, he cautioned against getting swept up in the trendiness of the idea. It is hard enough to pull in a complete internal data set and enrich it with external information so we should always remember that predictive analytics is only one type of approach to using data for the creation of value and competitive advantage.

To that point, it is useless to try to invest in predictive analytics for its own sake. It is not a broad effort, where a dataset is examined for traces of evidence about the future. Attempting to use predictive analytics requires a defined scope of inquiry so that the analysis can be deep and detailed—something not possible with a larger data set. Predictive analytics is better applied as a micro-correction to a macro-direction that has already been determined.

Even in the case of trying to predict and prepare for supply chain disruption, some sense of focus is usually determined in advance. This focus comes less from the data itself than a company's read of supply markets, trade routes, and suppliers. The data can then be used to pinpoint weak points, time frames, and available alternatives. As Richard Waugh, Vice President of Corporate Development at Zycus, wrote for the International Associationf or Contract and Commerical Management (IACCM), "Leading procurement organizations will increasingly be able to anticipate future spending patterns, rather than just analyzing historical spending, and will be able to prevent supply risk failures, such as supply chain disruptions, before they occur."[20] While our goal is commonly stated in the way Waugh presented it, to prevent supply risk failures and supply chain disruptions, the actual goal is to keep disruptions from affecting our organization. Many disruptions are unstoppable. The plan must be to move away from the weaknesses that are most likely to strike.

Although it is wise to be cautious, and some risk mitigation activities may be taken unnecessarily, we can never eliminate risk altogether.

It would simply be too costly. In the most extreme example of this, companies have the option of vertically integrating so that they have complete visibility into all tiers of production along with control over the choices that are made and the flows of information—it would be an inefficient approach. Working with suppliers allows us to take costs out of the supply chain and to benefit from specialist expertise.

Sunil Chopra and ManMohan S. Sodhi addressed the need for balance between risk and cost in the MIT Sloan Management Review, "Today's managers know that they need to protect their supply chains from serious and costly disruptions, but the most obvious solutions—increasing inventory, adding capacity at different locations, and having multiple suppliers—undermine efforts to improve supply chain cost efficiency."[21] At the end of the day, each link in the chain must position itself as more efficient than the competition. Overemphasizing risk avoidance will increase costs without adding value and price a solution out of competition. Ideally, predictive analytics help us see where taking on additional cost will add value in the long run, by remaining operational or controlling input costs when our competitors are unprepared.

Data and Behavior

It is common to consider *the numbers*—as we have been discussing them in the chapter—as the trail left by operational performance and transactions. While that is not a perfect match by any means, data is even less well-suited to serve as an indication of the behaviors and behavioral motivators in an enterprise.

As procurement professionals, we chafe at the idea that savings or spend under management captures the contributions we make. Every other function should be regarded in the same way. While numbers and data are convenient in that they can stand alone and are facts, they do not tell the whole story. As Aubrey Daniels, an internationally recognized expert on management, leadership, safety, and workplace issues, as well as an authority on human behavior in the workplace, reminds us of the danger of assuming numbers represent the whole truth: "never reward a result without understanding the behavior that created it."[22]

The poignant reminder in this simple quote is that data is neither good nor bad. Just as data without action has no value, numbers without an understanding of the underlying activity mean nothing. Numbers are not good news or bad news, but they may indicate both depending on the circumstances and understanding of the people viewing them. In the best case, having quantitative benchmarks gives managers and teams a focal point for their efforts. In the worst, they motivate the wrong behaviors or unscrupulous choices. Daniels explained this in yet another post on the relationship between behaviors and results. "In a results-only culture, managers do whatever is necessary to achieve the desired outcomes. That can include doing things that are illegal or unsafe, such as at GM, or, as at the VA—changing numbers to boost results while endangering the lives of veterans."[23]

While we naturally assume that predictive analytics is a numbers-based activity, there is a behavioral aspect to it as well. We may not be able to extrapolate current data sets to predict future conditions, no matter how enriched they are, because there is an inherent delay working against us. It takes time to get the numbers in a form where we can access and work with them. Even if it is a small delay, it puts us at a disadvantage for predictive activities. Behavior, on the other hand, which leads to the data we would eventually get, is happening now, right in front of us. Observing and tracking behavior, and connecting it with desired results, is a much more direct way of trying to positively impact the future than through straight data.

CONCLUSION

The greatest challenge ultimately faced by procurement professionals, in fact all professionals, is that access to data, whether big or small, does not necessarily result in increased knowledge or useful intelligence. It is the ability to look behind the numbers to understand their true meaning at a practical level that must be the primary focus if this learning is to be applied—with value—moving forward. Focusing on data for its own sake is a mistake because only through translation and application do the enterprise and the decision makers within see the potential for value. If we lose sight of the need for application, procurement may lose the opportunity to position ourselves as reliable stewards of data. Data, in the modern enterprise, results from what are rapidly becoming complex, extended global supply networks. Perhaps the best answer to the question opening this chapter is that there are always numbers in the truth, but not always truth in the numbers.

REFERENCES

1. Christian Madsbjerg and Mikkel B. Rasmussen, *The Moment of Clarity: Using the Human Sciences to Solve Your Toughest Business Problems*, (Boston: Harvard Business Review Press, 2014), 43.
2. "'You've got to find what you love,' Jobs says," *Stanford Review*, June 15, 2005, http://news.stanford.edu/news/2005/june15/jobs -061505.html.
3. "Terminology: Analysis vs. analytics and more…" *Big Data Craft*, October 27, 2010, http://45.55.186.118/?p=62.
4. Helen MacKenzie, "Warning: Once You've Plunged Into Your Big Data You Might Never Come Up For Air!" *Helen-MacKenzie.com*, February 18, 2015, http://www.helen-mackenzie.com/procurius/ warning-once-youve-plunged-into-your-big-data-you-might-never -come-up-for-air/.
5. Alan Holland, "Logistics Vs Procurement," *Keelvar*, February 24, 2015, http://keelvar.com/2015/02/24/logistics-vs-procurement/.
6. Ibid.
7. Robert A. Rudzki, "How to put the 'strategic' back in supply man- agement," *Supply Chain Quarterly*, 4th Quarter 2010, Accessed April 23, 2015, http://www.supplychainquarterly.com/print/ scq201004strategic/.
8. Eran Livneh, "What is the Internet of Things and What Does It Mean to the P2P World," *Nipendo*, April 22, 2014, http://www .nipendo.com/blog/what-is-the-internet-of-things-and-what-does -it-mean-to-the-p2p-world/.
9. Tim O'Reilly, "#IoTH: The Internet of Things and Humans," *Forbes*, April 14, 2014, http://www.forbes.com/sites/oreillymedia/2014/ 04/18/ioth-the-internet-of-things-and-humans/.
10. Cliff Saran, "GE Uses Big Data to Power Machine Services Business," *Computer Weekly*, January 2013, http://www.computerweekly .com/news/2240176248/GE-uses-big-data-to-power-machine -services-business.
11. Ibid.
12. Peter Spiller, Nicolas Reinecke, Drew Ungerman, Henrique Teix- eira, *Procurement 20/20: Supply Entrepreneurship in a Changing World*, (New Jersey: John Wiley & Sons, 2014), 89–90.
13. "Truth" *Merriam-Webster.com*, Accessed April 22, 2015, http:// www.merriam-webster.com/dictionary/truth.
14. Robert A. Rudzki, Douglas A. Smock, Michael Katzorke, Shelley Stewart, Jr, *Straight to the Bottom Line: An Executive's Roadmap to*

World Class Supply Management, (Fort Lauderdale: J. Ross, 2006), 69.

15. Jonathan O'Brien, *Supplier Relationship Management: Unlocking the Hidden Value in Your Supply Base*, (Philadelphia: Kogan Page, 2014), 121.

16. Nick Ford, "Sustainable Procurement: Converting Environmental Impact into Financial Impact," *Procurement Insights*, March 23, 2015, https://procureinsights.wordpress.com/2015/03/23/sustainable -procurement-converting-environmental-impact-into-financial -impact-by-nick-ford/.

17. Robert Menard, *Green Purchasing and Sustainability: How Green Purchasing Saves Money and Creates Sustainability*, (Dallas: Brigitte Media, 2011), 7.

18. Lora M. Cecere, *Supply Chain Metrics That Matter*, (New Jersey: John Wiley & Sons, 2015), 26.

19. Douglas Laney, "Use Predictive Analytics to Help You Capitalize on Business Moments," *Gartner*, Accessed May 7, 2015, http://www .gartner.com/webinar/2983218?ref=SiteSearch&sthkw=Douglas %20Laney&fnl=search&srcId=1-3478922244.

20. Richard Waugh, "Improving Procurement in 2014 - how five predictions might affect your choices!" *IACCM Contracting Excellence*, March 31, 2014, https://www.iaccm.com/ resources/?id=7478&print.

21. Sunil Chopra and ManMohan S. Sodhi, "Reducing the Risk of Supply Chain Disruptions, *MIT Sloan Management Review*, March 18, 2014, http://sloanreview.mit.edu/article/reducing-the-risk-of -supply-chain-disruptions/.

22. Dave Johnson, "ASSE Safety 2014 Speaker Q&A with Aubrey Daniels: 'Senior leaders must understand the science of behavior,'" *Industrial Safety and Hygiene News*, June 9, 2014, http://www.ishn .com/articles/98813-asse-safety-2014-speaker-qa-with-aubrey -daniels.

23. Aubrey Daniels, "Managing to Results Isn't Enough; Focus on Behaviors," *Talent Management*, August 22, 2014, http://www .talentmgt.com/blogs/5-performance-reset/post/6718-managing-to -results-isnt-enough-focus-on-behaviors.

This book has free material available for download from the
Web Added Value™ resource center at *www.jrosspub.com*

5

Are Win-Win Collaborations Really Possible?

"As with any relationship, it cannot just be turned on, it needs to be courted, pursued, built, and reinforced with consistency and persistence. Both sides need to want it and need to invest in making it happen." Supplier Relationship Management, Jonathan O'Brien[1]

Your palms grow sweaty and your heartbeat quickens. As the detective leans in closer, his knuckles turn white with the pressure of supporting his weight against the table. He glares at you for an uncomfortably long time, and when he finally speaks, you can tell from his tone that this is only going to get worse.

"The way I look at it," he says, suddenly effecting disinterest and moving back, "you have two choices. You can tell me exactly what you and your friend over there did, or you can keep your mouth shut and take the fall alone. He's probably already ratted you out to my partner anyway. They always do. I'm going to give you exactly sixty seconds to make up your mind, and then the deal we've offered you—which is more than you deserve in my opinion—is off the table." He turns away slightly and looks at his watch, underlining the fact that your sixty seconds are already ticking away.

56 seconds…

Things had gone so unbelievably wrong. There wasn't supposed to be anyone in the building after hours. This was going to be a quick in-and-out job. You and Joe were going to slip in the back way after making quick work of the single lock with a pair of bolt cutters, grab the copper pipe, and deliver it to a prearranged buyer for easy cash. In—out—profit—done. Now, because of an unexpected late night visit from the janitor, you're isolated in a stale-smelling interrogation room trying to figure out what to do. And while the payout from the big score seemed like a thrill earlier, now it just means grand larceny.

37 seconds...

The deal on the table isn't great, and you can't be sure how clearly the janitor saw you. How good of a case did the cops really have?

25 seconds...

You have two options. You can refuse to cooperate or try to lay the blame on Joe, which wouldn't be a complete lie. He was the one who approached you with this stupid idea in the first place. This is his fault. According to the detective, if you stay quiet and he takes the deal, you face a sentence of three years. On the other hand, if you both stay quiet, the most they can get you for is a single year on a reduced charge. But if you both flip, you both do two years. If only you had discussed this possibility before tonight. What will he do?

12 seconds...

"Tick, tick, tick," says Detective Ricker, looking impatient.

Welcome to the prisoner's dilemma.

The prisoner's dilemma is a common way of teaching game theory in negotiation training. Two prisoners are held separately as interrogators try to get one or both to confess so that they can charge them with a steeper sentence than their current evidence supports. If they stick together, they both get the best possible outcome. If both break loyalty, the charges result in the most severe punishment. If one defects and one remains silent, the one who refused to give a statement gets a harsher punishment than if both stayed quiet, while the defector goes free. "In game theory, betraying your partner, or *defecting*, is always the dominant strategy as it always has a slightly higher payoff in a simultaneous game," wrote Max Nisen in an article for *Business Insider*. "However, on an overall basis, the best outcome for both players is mutual cooperation."[2]

The question that arises in prisoner's dilemma exercises is, why would two rational human beings act separately when they would benefit more by working together? Despite this lesson and the logic behind it, individuals and organizations have a tendency to act out of self-preservation, unable to resist the temptation of the slightly higher payoff described by Nisen, along with the suspicion that the other party will fall to the same weakness and betray them.

Enter collaboration. Companies are suddenly, at least in their intent, talking about forging partnerships rather than buying from vendors or suppliers. Data exchanges are opened. Risks are borne mutually and long-term results are paramount. The appeal of collaboration seems to be almost universal, but the execution is difficult. Companies that select this path have to let go of the models they have relied upon in the past, accepting a more labor-intensive approach for seemingly amorphous benefits. While letting go of past conditioning may require help from an experienced collaboration facilitator, the mind-set of the enterprise and all individuals within it must also be open to the value of collaboration in order for it to work. While collaborative supply relationships are often entered into with rosy expectations, they are put to the test in the messy reality of modern business.

THE APPEAL OF COLLABORATION

In the opening paragraphs of this book, we made reference to Robert Handfield's statement that the "integration of procurement across the business is not the responsibility of a few but rather a challenge that must be embraced company-wide."[3] Handfield's point is crystal clear: building real and productive relationships is as much an act of will as it is intent, but intent can be so abstract that it is unlikely to be a motivating factor for the enterprise at large.

What this means from a procurement perspective, however noble the intent or pressing the need to redefine the supply process, is that both shared and individual objectives must be satisfied through any potential collaborative arrangement. This is particularly true of the buyer-supplier relationship. Evolving from transactions to relationships and partnerships requires a new level of transparency that will seem both foreign and even contradictory for many in procurement who are accustomed to the *knowledge is power*, one-sided approach to resource maximization. While adversarial relationships or simply transactional dealings with suppliers seem to come more naturally, collaboration is suddenly the more highly prized approach.

Perception: The Biggest Obstacle to the Win-Win Scenario

In a 2015 post titled "While familiarity purportedly breeds contempt, it certainly doesn't lead to procurement fraud," Andy Akrouche identified what is perceived as being one of the main obstacles to building support for truly collaborative relationships between buyers and sellers: the idea that the open dynamic required to support collaboration is directly linked to a breach in procurement ethics or vulnerability of lost leverage.

Akrouche credits *the myth of familiarity* with propagating the fear that greater exchanges of information between buyers and sellers necessarily leads to lack of independence. Specifically, how "building a close working relationship with supply partners will somehow undermine the integrity of the procurement process. In short, and in a misguided effort to ensure purported fairness, a transactional approach to business relationships is pursued."[4] In response to this, most buyers have adopted a transactional mind-set that limits their engagement with supply partners to a narrowly defined series of activities and exchanges in which the deliverables are governed, not by reason and open communication, but by onerous terms and conditions that serve to partition stakeholders from one another. In other words, it is seen as preferable to limit the potential of a supply relationship than to risk creating (or appearing to create) an untoward arrangement.

Akrouche also references an earlier article by Colin Cram that highlighted how fraud and corruption are badly damaging the economies of many African countries. In Cram's article, titled "Combating Fraud in Africa and Beyond," he makes the point that while there has been particular emphasis on driving out fraud and corruption in Africa, all nations are vulnerable to varying degrees. In addition, they are not immune to the negative consequences of a procurement function that does not operate independently and in the best interests of the organization "because fragmentation and a lack of independence of procurement organizations are a recipe for bad practice and corruption."[5] His point about lack of independence is valid, and it applies to poor decision making and inefficient management of supply just as much as corruption.

And buyers are not the only ones with concerns to hold them back from forming deeper relationships. Suppliers may be afraid that an overly close relationship with one customer will create the appearance of favoring their product and service needs before those of their other customers. If anything is going to cause a supplier to hesitate, it is the potential for negative impact on their revenue stream or market share.

The problem with both of these perspectives is that buyers and suppliers are already inextricably linked together, just by the fact that they are dependent upon each other for survival. A buyer must acquire the products and services their company needs to support the operation and produce offerings for sale. Suppliers fill that need while also securing their own revenue stream, part of which is invested in the development of new products and services. Neither is acting altruistically, because it isn't necessary. While mutual dependence might look like weakness at first, it is actually what helps prevent fraud and corruption in procurement. If two parties can find an arrangement where acting out of self-interest benefits them and another, the conditions are ripe for collaboration. In an increasing number of cases, supply relationships are not just about supply, but also about product refinement, improved implementation, regulatory compliance, and increased results. Both sides should come to the table with the value they want to receive in return for some additional investment of time and effort.

In this context, and with the addition of the Internet and social media connectivity to inter-company communication, Akrouche's social or relational outsourcing model makes a great deal of sense. As he wrote in 2012, "What is especially encouraging about the socially oriented approach is that it creates an environment of trust between key stakeholders. This means that potential problems can be recognized, acknowledged, and dealt with effectively as opposed to remaining either hidden or alternatively justified, which ultimately results in little if any meaningful action being taken to remedy the situation."[6]

Fearing closer working conditions would leave problems such as the ones Akrouche described unaddressed. Looking back to the points made by Cram, the same potential for corruption exists in every transaction or relationship because they are all based on the decisions and motivating factors that appeal to naturally flawed human beings. As a result, it is better to increase transparency and discuss concerns openly than to attempt to avoid temptation through the imitation of what would otherwise be very productive interactions.

The main obstacles to successful collaboration seem to be a combination of a company's ability to trust its suppliers with greater insight and information, its ability to trust that procurement can take a step forward without crossing the line marking the end of propriety, and trust in the fact that the opportunity for return outweighs the potential risks of supporting greater interaction. The shared issue is trust. Our response should be to foster trust through substantiated benefits, to provide proof. We certainly have the option of working to improve the mind-set that bars sharing with suppliers by demonstrating procurement's ability to collaborate without colluding. It is likely to be more effective, however, if we can either prove how significant the opportunity is or show the cost of not pursuing a collaborative path.

Once our methods of approaching spend management align with the values that make collaboration possible, even necessary, we are able to demonstrate that we can be trusted to engage without prioritizing Nisen's slightly higher (but individual) payoff over the collective advantage for the organization and that suppliers have equal incentive to do the same.

JON'S PERSPECTIVE: *Peace, Love, and Collaboration*

In the book *e-Procurement: From Strategy to Implementation*, Dale Neef referred to the *closed door meeting* mentality as being the greatest impediment to true internal collaboration.[7] More than 15 years later, his observation still rings true. This confinement of strategy to a select few experts reflects a lack of confidence with the overall level of internal expertise, resulting in poor or ineffectual external collaboration.

Collaboration is, as it turns out, an act of will. In other words, there has to be a deliberate and focused intent to communicate as opposed to dictating or abdicating. Yet far too many senior executives seem to choose the latter options.

For example, most eProcurement initiatives are—at least in the recent past—based upon a *pass the buck* mind-set. In these instances, the end-user client attempts to divest themselves of responsibility for an initiative's success by incorporating onerous performance terms and conditions into a vendor's contract. Even though the vendor recognizes that the terms are unrealistic, they adopt a *let's win the business first and worry about making it work later* approach.

This is why there is so much media hoopla when a contract is first signed, but virtually little, if any, follow-up down the road. Think about it for a moment—how many times have you read a press release about a contract win a year or two down the road, announcing that the promised outcome had been achieved. Your answer, if it is like mine, is telling—*never*.

As an aside, and as we discuss in Chapter 9 regarding procurement media coverage, this is where the journalists, analysts, and bloggers have failed miserably. It is also the reason why the cycle of eProcurement initiative futility churned and burned for so long. No one knew the outcomes of much-heralded contract wins. We were disproportionately bombarded with positive news while being left in the dark on the actual results. Communication and collaboration, it is safe to conclude, usually start and finish with the preliminary sales cycle. Of course, recognizing that communication and collaboration are a problem is one thing—knowing how to fix them is another. The starting point has to be based upon trust and transparency.

When you seek to find the right strategic partners to work with in pursuit of a desired outcome, you have to create an engagement mechanism that promotes an open and honest dialogue. Otherwise, you fall into the liar's trap that International Association for Contract and Commercial Management (IACCM) chief executive officer (CEO) Tim Cummins wrote about in a 2010 post. In "The Power of Negotiation," Cummins identified "the 'conspiracy' that leads executives on both sides of the table to 'lie' to their trading partners and to create a combined version of 'the truth' that leads to mutual delusion over what they can achieve, by when, and for how much."[8]

Cummins adeptly points out that such fabrication is not limited to a few by following up with the question, "How truthful are any of us when we are seeking to impress someone with whom we want a deal or a relationship?"[9]

The key takeaway from his article "The Power of Negotiation" is that there is too great of an emphasis on winning contracts as opposed to actually laying the groundwork for success. When you are focused on winning, there is no time for any real or truthful collaboration between buyer and seller. Prospective supply partners will usually say whatever is necessary to win the business, hence Cummins' liar's trap. So what is the answer?

Forget everything you learned from Vince Lombardi when he said, "Winning isn't everything, it's the only thing."[10] Those creating tenders have to stop using methods and models that perpetuate the competitive elements associated with static outcomes. Instead, they have to focus on a shared journey approach, in which the greater emphasis is placed on the ability of partners to work together to leverage each other's strengths and address any weaknesses. This is what will empower and enable them to collectively work toward achieving a mutually beneficial outcome.

Shared journeys acknowledge strengths *and* weaknesses. And yet, the Chester Karrass mantra that, "In business as in life, you don't get what you deserve, you get what you negotiate,"[11] still (sadly) has a dominant presence in procurement today. As a result, it is understandable that suggestions such as the one previously mentioned about shared journeys will (for some) conjure up images of peace, love, and psychedelically painted VW vans.

To this I have just one response—with 85% of all eProcurement, or for that matter, all complex contract initiatives failing to achieve the expected results, how is the old method working out for you? Like deeds, results speak volumes. Given that the outcomes related to the old way of doing business speak volumes—and not in a good way—it is time for a change. How will you make a change?

Start by making open and honest collaboration part of the bid process itself, as opposed to being an afterthought that is more lip service than practice. If you want an example of how well this approach works, read the I35 Minnesota Bridge case study in Kate Vitasek's *Vested: How P&G, McDonalds, and Microsoft are Redefining Winning in Business Relationships* or Andy Akrouche's *Relationships First: The New Relationship Paradigm in Contracting.*

If you are looking for the full peace, love, and collaboration experience, don't forget to listen to an Iron Butterfly album when you read Vitasek or Akrouche. (Joan Baez is also good.)

THE END OF THE EFFICIENCY PARADIGM

In earlier days in our field, when purchasing teams were *upskilled* to become procurement through strategic sourcing etc., the basic strategy was simple. Our mission was to take an unruly, and in some cases largely unknown, supply base and consolidate it. We leveraged economies of scale, centralized demand, and standardized specifications in order to bring down the cost of each unit and standardize contract and payment terms. The addition of eSourcing technology made it possible to undertake the same strategy faster and (at least in theory) with less hands-on time. Spend efficiency became the ultimate goal, and procurement embraced the idea that each supplier's solution should be captured, compared, and analyzed in the same set of boxes as all of the other suppliers offering the same things.

Supplier presentations, when permitted at all, were more of an afterthought. They were often one-sided inquisitions where internal stakeholders and executives peppered supplier teams with questions while offering up little additional information about how the product or service would eventually fit into the operation. In more devious cases, supplier presentations became dramatically staged events, where the timing of one session ending and the next one beginning was deliberately orchestrated so that the two closest competitors would be forced to face each other—albeit only in passing—in the lobby, hallway, or elevator. This was intended to reinforce the notion that procurement was in charge and communicated to both (unfortunate) suppliers that the contract was far from secure.

Sir Isaac Newton figured out in the seventeenth century that there are certain laws of motion that the universe must abide by. One of them applies directly here: "When one body exerts a force on a second body, the second body simultaneously exerts a force equal in magnitude and opposite in direction on the first body."[12] It is easy to forget this sometimes when you are dealing with people rather than Newton's Cradle or the little desk model with the suspended silver balls that click into each other. For every demonstration of procurement's power, we cause some reaction in our suppliers—whether we recognize it or not. The supplier presentation charade is likely to cause suppliers to keep critical and useful information under wraps, for fear that a competing supplier will be given that information in an effort to have them *match* it. It prevents the openness that is critical to collaboration, but is also key in making a fully informed decision about which supplier is the best match.

Unintentional (if Efficient) Commoditization of Supply

Whether through sourcing or negotiation, the early days of procurement were all about a sort of deliberate commoditization. Procurement would labor over detailed specifications with the intent of forcing participating suppliers to provide the requested information—and *only* the requested information. Anything submitted above and beyond was often viewed as an attempt to skirt the process by subversively appealing to stakeholders' desire for a more value-oriented or even emotional connection to their suppliers. If an attempt to seize such an opportunity didn't lead to the supplier being disqualified, it was certainly a mark against them.

The result of all this suffocating standardization and one-way communication was that very little differentiating value ever made it onto procurement's radar screen. Sometimes this led to underperforming or underwhelming supplier performance. In other cases it led to a poor cultural fit between the two organizations. When a supplier's sales team had an existing connection other than procurement, or was particularly spunky, they might end-run the procurement process to get their message across directly to decision makers. After all, sales is far more interested in closing a deal than in following procurement regulations.

When you look up antonyms for collaboration in a thesaurus, two of the terms that appear are separation and division.[13] There can hardly be two better words for the effect most traditional strategic sourcing (and therefore procurement teams) had on buyer-supplier relations. While we may have engaged in this approach with the very best of intentions, we still diminished our potential and capped the value created for the organization. It is the *effect* and not the *intention* of our approaches that we need to revisit. As we try to transition to a more open approach, we need to be on guard against the separatist elements in our processes and in our thinking. Some are more obvious than others, and these lingering remnants of days past threaten to spoil our future efforts.

Whether because of legacy frameworks or just because they are so challenging, many collaboration programs fall short of reaching their goals. In 2013, Boston Consulting Group (BCG) and the Procurement Leaders Network surveyed senior purchasing executives and found "that while most companies pursue some sort of collaboration with their suppliers, only about two in every five programs follow standardized approaches. As a result, most programs focus narrowly on operational efficiency, leaving opportunities like shared innovation, speed to market, and improved quality unexplored and their associated benefits unrealized."[14] In fact, according to the same survey, even the broadly labeled *operational efficiency* comes mostly from reduced costs. Seventy-seven percent of the responding executives identified cost savings as their highest priority for investing in collaboration. From these findings we can conclude that even after the benefits of collaboration are recognized, somehow procurement is unable to break beyond the efficiency paradigm, the need for scalability, and a limited view of what the potential impact could be.

This disconnect prevents procurement's attempts to become more collaborative from progressing beyond mere lip service. Why engage in a new approach to supply management (collaboration) just to get more of the same kinds of results (savings)? It would seem that if you just want more of the same, the simplest approach would be to continue working as you have been. The additional complexity of taking a new path to reach the same end seems inefficient.

Sometimes, additional benefits are lost because the processes we have in place are not designed to uncover them. The fact that procurement is likely to continue using processes already in place, even when a more collaborative or strategic approach is being taken, does not give these unique forms of value the opportunity to present themselves. An example of this is early access to new products and services. Despite the fact that they offer a competitive advantage to the buying organization, procurement must be opportunity driven rather than process driven to take advantage of them. The framework for communication with suppliers needs to be regular and extend beyond the sourcing and contract negotiation processes. A standardized 90 or 180 day check-in model is not opportunistic enough. While it may be characterized as proactive, because we are holding meetings without necessarily having a reason to, this is one time when procurement should strive to be reactionary. Setting up an environment where supplier partners provide us with the circumstances to react to should be the driving force behind investment in collaboration.

While taking a collaborative approach to existing processes may generate better results, the improvement will be measured in terms of existing performance indicator categories rather than adding new categories of value realization. A procurement approach driven solely by cost—or our traditional processes—can only improve below the line performance, while interactions driven by the buyer-supplier relationship itself open the door to above the line improvements in revenue as well as increased profit margin.

Leaving Scalability Behind

If procurement wants to move beyond models and mind-sets that are driven solely by efficiency, we need to find new approaches to take their place. While scalable activities are based on the value associated with managing more with less people/effort, less cost, less suppliers, and less time, truly collaborative approaches are practically artisan in nature. Far from being a commoditization of what we can do or of the finished product, collaboration requires us to seek out unique opportunities and relationships. Find a problem and solve it. Find a need and fill it. While the time and effort required are far more substantial than working through a conventional transactional approach, so is the potential for return.

Artisans or craftsmen work over the course of a lifetime to hone their skills. Each effort is a work of art, whether in the traditional sense or not. In addition to the extra time and resources required to complete a project, there is a sense that the final creation is special and that it is truly one of a kind. That uniqueness assigns value to the creation as well as the creator. The process and end result are far more personal, customized in a way that requires an understanding of the need as well as the skill associated with fulfilling it. According to Marcus Starke, a Global Marketing Executive at SAP, the artisan mind-set is focused on quality as well as opportunities for the artist to develop a new skill. "The artisan views each new customer as an opportunity to improve their craft and produce an even better product for their customer. While the core of what they produce remains relatively unchanged, each new generation of artisans uses new tools and techniques to improve the product they create."[15]

In procurement, this concept may translate to a particularly complex business problem or supply need to fulfill, one that cannot be addressed using a mass market or production line approach. The partnerships required to achieve a lofty goal require as much investment as the time required to reach the finish line once they have been forged. Working relationships have to be built up, trust has to be established on both sides, and the opportunities for mutual gain need to be articulated. Collaboration is a perfect example of where we can apply our supplier segmentation skills to identify a select few companies or categories for a high investment, high impact approach. It is not sustainable to apply this approach in a larger percentage of cases, nor would the potential for benefits justify it.

The other takeaway for procurement is that an artisan views the process of adding to their skills as equal in importance to the item produced as a result. Some artists would say that the process of creation is the actual point of their efforts. This mind-set is the complete opposite of how procurement has thought in the past and how most of us still think today. After acknowledging this reality, the best way for procurement organizations to embed collaborative potential in their ranks is to focus on finding people with the right mind-sets rather than the right skills.

Sprint versus Marathon

Just as it is not worth applying a highly collaborative approach in all categories of spend or with all suppliers, it is not necessary for everyone in procurement to be successful under collaborative supply conditions.

There will always be multiple kinds of spend to address through different approaches, and the skills of the procurement team must reflect this diversity of requirements.

One set of personalities, aptitudes, or skill sets positions a professional to be an artisan collaborator, while another is better suited to a scalable, high volume approach. Being collectively good at both as needs arise means having both kinds of professionals on staff. The challenge for managers and leaders is to have the right balance of skills or perspectives on the team and to assign them appropriately.

This balancing of personalities and timing is much like what is required to take an idea from a fledgling business concept to a large sustainable organization. Most founders are like sprinters. They have energy, vision, passion, and drive in enormous proportions. Founders have the conviction to build something new from the ground up in highly uncertain conditions and without a trail to follow. But while they are essential for the first leg of the race, they are not usually the best leaders for the long run. They often struggle with the decision to move on, even when it has become clear to others that it is time for the organization to become more stable and set a pace that positions them for success in the long term. Both founders and those who take over from them need to be entrepreneurial and have vision. The team has to continue to pursue new ideas while balancing the practicality to test, build traction, and gain buy-in that leads to sustained momentum.

Any founder that is more than a *one-hit wonder* will move on from each idea, whether it is ultimately successful or not, and start again. A new idea requiring different specialization and fresh energy will consume them until the time comes once again to hand it off. Like the artisan, cultivating opportunities is about the process for these entrepreneurs, not the enterprise(s) that may result. While there is some repetition to the entrepreneurial process, it is not focused on churn for the sake of efficiency.

The leader who succeeds the founder must be able to establish a scalable model that preserves the energy and appeal of the launch. How many cycles can the organization execute at a minimal (or optimal) cost per cycle without detracting from the value proposition that secured their early success? There is an expectation that they will be able to replicate any early successes at a lower cost, perfecting a process or methodology so that new hires can be trained to carry out what was organic from the initial team. These leaders are training and pacing for a marathon rather than a sprint. There is less tolerance for errors because there are fewer unknowns. This creates the requirement for standards and frameworks that guarantee some sort of a result that the business development part of the organization can use to sign contracts and generate revenue.

If procurement is able to hire professionals that embody the sprinter or founder mind-set, they will be positioned to succeed in a collaborative arrangement. They don't need to make the effort repeatable so it can be executed again with another supplier. They need to get the current situation right, giving no thought to the future application of what they are learning. As Dave Henshall wrote on Purchasing Practice, "If procurement is to reach the pinnacle to which it aspires it must demonstrate entrepreneurial behavior which enables their organizations to capitalize on market opportunities and to manage the associated risk. In the future powerful ideas will be generated from almost anywhere."[16] Founders are motivated by the idea of ideas. They create as a primary function, not as a secondary effort on top of their other tasks.

There is also a place for collaborative marathon runners in procurement. While they may not get the ball rolling or blaze new trails, they take what the sprinter/founder has learned or accomplished and overlay it on a larger team and larger scope of work for improved results. Once procurement has successfully carried out one or two collaborative efforts, it is well worth looking at the transferable learning that will improve all of procurement's activities, not just those that are deliberately collaborative in focus.

The planning and hiring process is much like sourcing pipeline management. Procurement needs to know in advance how many collaborative efforts the organization wants to manage simultaneously and what is required to make that possible. Like sourcing projects, there are effects beyond the core team. Collaborative relationships are likely to require significant investment from high-level executives as they are, by definition, core to enterprise success. In other words, there are constraints beyond skill sets and procurement headcount that have to be taken into consideration up front to collaborate successfully.

A TALE OF TWO BRIDGES

On August 1, 2007, the St. Anthony Falls Bridge collapsed into the Mississippi River during rush hour traffic, killing 13 people and injuring 145. In an effort to reopen the critical I-35W transportation thruway as soon as possible, the Minnesota Department of Transportation

(MnDOT) worked with a number of suppliers using the collaborative Vested Outsourcing model to rebuild both infrastructure and public confidence.

The work to rebuild began only 18 hours after the collapse. For this particular effort, time really was money. Without the vital transportation link the bridge provided, there was a significant daily cost to motorists, businesses, and local communities. The target completion date was ambitiously set for December 24, 2008. Each day of early completion offered the suppliers a $200,000 incentive and each day late was assessed as a penalty in the same amount. In the end, the new bridge opened one year and seventeen days after the collapse. Perhaps more impressively, it reopened three months ahead of schedule and on budget. MnDOT didn't manage this amazing feat by mercilessly driving suppliers or by holding them to an aggressive schedule with detailed service level agreements. They did it by setting a collaborative tone from the outset for the entire project team and sticking to it until the effort was complete.

Kate Vitasek and Karl Manrodt described the St. Anthony Falls Bridge project in their book *Vested: How P&G, McDonald's, and Microsoft are Redefining Winning in Business Relationships*. Part of what elevates their appreciation of the construction project is the recognition of how many *against the grain* decisions and unique circumstances had to coincide for the effort to be a success. "After researching dozens of supplier relationships, we begin to see a common theme emerge. Simply put, companies actually tend to get what they ask for and what they pay for. The problem is that what they ask for and pay for is not necessarily what they really want."[17] MnDOT and their team managed to resist the urge to tightly control their suppliers. Part of the key for companies that want to take a more collaborative approach is that they shouldn't expect to tell their suppliers exactly what to do. Like the St. Anthony's Bridge team, they need to focus on the desired end result and accept that there will be some variability in how they reach that point. There has to be give-and-take as well as openness to alternatives. Trust did not completely eclipse oversight, but it did change the form that oversight took.

In this particular project, the importance and cost of time was evident to all parties involved, but so was the solemn responsibility of rebuilding the bridge. Not only did each supplier have to work collaboratively with MnDOT, they had to work equally well with the other suppliers and with the community as a whole. Reaching the end result—a new bridge that supported traffic needs and memorialized the lives that were lost—became everyone's focus and sole purpose. The collaboration was driven by that end result rather than the other way around. All of the involved parties had to pull together and communicate to solve each problem. MnDOT chose partners that had the qualifications to do the work, but they also selected companies they were comfortable working with in close quarters. MnDOT moved away from the typical contract management approach that transfers all risk to their suppliers. They shared in the risk, which ultimately meant that they shared in the credit for the project's success.

Collaborator as Bridge

There is no question that having a methodology or philosophy, such as the Vested model, helped the team on the St. Anthony Falls bridge project. There may have even been someone on the team whose job it was to make sure that the overall collaboration went well. There are plenty of professionals with the knowledge and experience required to be a facilitator of such efforts: Kate Vitasek and Andy Akrouche are just two who come to mind. The circumstances of a given project play a large part in determining if a collaborative approach is the right one, but the people involved play an integral role in determining whether collaboration is possible.

What companies often need is a collaborative *bridge*—someone with the ability to make sure everything is going as planned. They will help to accelerate the process, but they cannot be a replacement for ownership in-house—ownership of both the results and the outcome. The company trying to collaborate must already have the internal willingness to make the requisite changes—even when they are uncomfortable. It is not enough to hire someone with the right experience to lead the project. Everyone involved in the effort must be willing to collaborate in thought and deed.

If we apply this back to our first *bridge* in Minnesota, MnDOT effectively had to plan the project backward. They started by defining the desired outcome and used it to model the right people and mechanisms needed to achieve it. In so many cases, procurement projects are founded on the belief that if we pick the right supplier, that will result in the right outcome. That is not usually the case with collaboration because partnership is such a critical element. And yet this should not to be taken to suggest that all procurement projects should be so focused on the outcome that all variability and flexibility is driven out. That comes with its own challenges.

In the past, the systems and processes we used alienated suppliers and limited the potential for relationships, but they also somehow failed to prevent what you might call preferential decision making. In extreme examples, even our standard processes were counterproductive. In a 2011 video interview with Jon Hansen, Al Gordon, the CEO and Chairman of National Strategies who spent time as a senior aide to former New York State Governor Mario Cuomo, said, "Over 90% of requests for proposals (RFPs) in the United States in the government market are already predetermined by the time the RFP comes out. In other words, it's the company that gets involved really early on in the process who helps create the RFP who gets the deal."[18] He reminds us that our mindset and actions must match if our processes and systems are to function as designed.

We may have thought we were objective because we ran a good RFP process, but in many cases we had already made up our minds before the process began. While it is completely reasonable to want to work with a supplier with whom procurement has built rapport, it is critical to understand the impact that has on decision making. Suppliers have their own habits to break. Sales people will look for opportunities to advise procurement or technical representatives during the development of the RFP so that it favors their solution. Even worse than having our minds made up before the process began, these skewed RFPs resulted in us having our minds made up for us by people who were more interested in their own gain than the success of their customers. Legacy practices on both sides have to be recognized and culled out where they still exist.

CAREER CONDITIONING AND THE CHANGING OF THE GUARD

As we have now done many times in this book, we must consider the collaborative shift that needs to be made in the context of whether current procurement professionals can adjust or whether they need to be replaced. It certainly looks like the advantage goes to the Generation Next procurement professionals. They are more worldly in terms of their perspective. Many of them have better suited qualifications and skills because they chose careers in procurement or supply chain rather than being placed there for headcount reasons. Young professionals are also more accustomed to sharing information about themselves online on social networks. They do so despite being warned repeatedly to contain and control their digital footprint. This serves as evidence of the fact that they think differently, and see the world differently, than their more established colleagues. And, as we have proposed, it is manner of thinking rather than skills or experience that positions someone for success in a collaborative economy.

In his book of essays, *The Second Curve: Thoughts on Reinventing Society*, philosopher and economist Charles Handy wrote, "New thinking is not the prerogative of those in authority. They are often too wedded to their accustomed ways, to that first curve, to conceive that another way might be possible."[19] It is one thing to learn a new skill, it is entirely another to see the world in a new way and think about it in a different light. This is much harder to learn. If Handy is right about the blind spot that those in positions of authority have toward new approaches, there is a silver lining in procurement's current inertia. It means that the ideas of the future, the solutions procurement is so desperately waiting for, may already have been conceived. They just have not reached acceptance among those who have the influence to spread and support them.

In a May 2015 article written for *In-Procurement Magazine*, Gerard Chick questioned the potential rise of this mind-set shift directly. He asked whether "an alternative, innovative procurement mind-set is starting to emerge; one that recognizes the enduring need for functional legitimacy and authenticity (i.e., there is no substitute for having deep procurement skills) together with a sense of ambition, accountability, and self-responsibility—accepting that senior roles sometimes trade responsibility for influence."[20] What this statement brings to the discussion of the bridge from past to future is some clarity about what procurement's current leaders lend to its future potential. The word *legitimacy* is well-chosen by Chick. Young professionals may bring new thinking and fresh energy, but they do not have the legitimacy of their more experienced colleagues—yet.

The trade of *responsibility for influence* is an important consideration as well—particularly within the context of collaboration. While traditional spend management approaches come with great responsibility, especially in the functional sense, collaboration requires influence as well as the traits that allowed that influence to be built in the first place. Accumulating and using influence is less about knowing how to execute a process than it is being able to read and respond to a new and complex situation in a way that leads to a favorable outcome for all parties—and that is the key at the heart of collaboration.

KELLY'S PERSPECTIVE: *Collaboration Can Be Hard to 'Read'*

One of the things that can be difficult about any professional role requiring subjective judgment is that you have to be able to read people. Just as analysis is based on facts and numbers, a solid collaborative relationship is based on your ability to pick up on the unspoken intentions and motivations of people you don't know very well. And if reading someone's emotions isn't hard enough, in order for that information to be useful, you have to be able to reason out why they feel the way they do. If you read tension in the body language or tone of a supplier, it could be because they are under pressure to close the deal with you, because they are waiting for a call from a buyer at your main competitor, or because lunch isn't agreeing with them. All three are plausible explanations. Every communication carries meaning in the words spoken, the tone in which it is spoken, and in the body language of the speaker—assuming you are speaking in person.

Taking in all of that information while also communicating through your own practiced words, tone, and body language is absolutely exhausting. But nobody ever said we should expect collaboration to be easy. I consider myself to be a very good *people reader*—both personally and professionally—but one of the tricks I have learned over time is that you don't need to play all roles in a meeting. I like to strike a balance between heavy involvement in the planning for a strategy session and less of a speaking role in the session itself. I find that I can *read* the room much better when I'm not trying to speak at the same time. Knowing that that approach works for me gives me a reason to watch any other *second chair* players in the room besides myself. Just because someone isn't doing most of the talking doesn't mean they aren't in charge.

There are a few other complexities to overcome even if you have the ability to read people and can translate your observations into an effective approach. Most communication is now done via e-mail or phone, meaning that the body language element is lost, which is very hard. And of course, since procurement is most often trying to read the body language of suppliers, we have to be aware that some skilled communicators will give you a false sense of optimism about the potential for a collaborative relationship. Telling the difference between someone who is ready to pursue a win-win relationship and someone who doesn't want to jeopardize a contract by saying no, can be hard.

Being able to communicate well on all levels with a supplier is essential for collaboration. While we talk about relationships with suppliers, at an execution level we're talking about the people who work for that company. Corporate culture is one thing, but if the right people aren't assigned to your account, the potential will be severely limited. Getting it right from the start is critical, even if it means taking the tough step of asking for a different account manager to step in—before the contract is signed. Otherwise, the extra effort required to communicate effectively will detract from the energy left over to create value.

Varying Attitudes toward Risk

In order to truly fear risk, you have to have known stability. Recent college graduates and entrants into the workforce have never known anything but lean economic times. This makes jobs harder to come by and forces professionals to learn to live with a constant level of uncertainty. When you do not expect smooth sailing, rough waters are far less intimidating. While this most directly applies to the economy and job market, there is an associated conditioning that makes up-and-coming professionals less susceptible to the potential for risk. The question for them is not stability versus risk, but how much risk of what kind? If there is always going to be some level of risk present in the equation, that changes the math on any given individual's risk-versus-reward logic.

Acceptance of risk also alters the priorities of any ambitious individual looking to build a career. Since the security of any situation is limited at best, professionals have to invest in something that transcends a job or role. Roz Usheroff, an expert in personal and professional branding, addresses the role that uncertainty plays in the choices of successful, risk-tolerant individuals: "In today's global marketplace, the ability to adapt to different situations and requirements—oftentimes with different companies—is the key to your ongoing success."[21] This adaptive skill plays well in a project-oriented, collaborative business climate where each effort is addressed as unique and where there is no expectation that it will be replicated later. In other words, we are back to the idea of needing entrepreneurship and artisan craftsmanship in procurement to fulfill our collaborative potential.

IN COLLABORATION, CLOSE DOES NOT ALWAYS EQUAL GOOD

Most organizations accept the fact that some sort of spend or supplier segmentation needs to be done before investing in collaborative relationships. As we have discussed, the difference between a scalable model and an artisan model comes with very different levels of commitment and hands-on effort. But collaborative relationships are not automatically a good thing. In fact, establishing a close relationship can lead to as many problems as opportunities if it is not managed right.

In their article, "The Dark Side of Close Relationships," which ran in the Spring 2005 edition of the *MIT Sloan Management Review*, Professors Erin Anderson and Sandy D. Jap talked about the perils of not making enough of an investment in tending to a relationship once it is established. "Relationships that appear to be doing well are often the most vulnerable to the forces of destruction that are quietly building beneath the surface of the relationship. In other words, close relationships that seem the most stable can also be the most vulnerable to decline and destruction."[22] One of the interesting points made in the article is how one party in a close relationship tends to respond when they feel they have been wronged by another. According to Anderson and Jap, the otherwise positive presence of increased trust often turns into carte blanche benefit of the doubt—even when it isn't appropriate. A wronged party may explain away the incident, finding it hard to believe that the company they formed a tight bond with would knowingly do them harm.

The difference between collaboration in theory and collaboration in reality is huge. Just ask anyone who's ever made the mistake of basing a relationship on the Erich Segal or *Love means never having to say you're sorry* philosophy of relationship management. Not only does being in a close, valued relationship require constant compromise—and sometimes apologies—but not wanting to put things right after inevitable missteps invalidates the premise on which the relationship is supposed to be based. An organization should not enter into a collaborative relationship with a company they do not respect as an equal, nor should they accept less than above-board treatment once in a relationship.

This brings us back to the difference between acting collaboratively and being truly collaborative. It can be very hard to tell the difference between the two based only on execution models, but when the going gets tough, or when external conditions shift, people in relationships that are not truly collaborative will find it very difficult not to revert to their leveraged-based, self-preservation focused practices of the past.

In a 2004 *Harvard Business Review* article on "Building Supplier Relationships," Professors Jeffrey Liker and Thomas Choi compared the supplier management practices of Japanese automakers to the American automakers who tried to emulate their approach. After seeing the successes of their Japanese competitors, American automakers tried to form closer relationships with their suppliers, and they made some real progress. "However, while these American companies created supply chains that superficially resembled those of their Japanese competitors, they didn't alter the fundamental nature of their relationships with suppliers. It wasn't long into the partnering movement before manufacturers and suppliers were fighting bitterly over the implementation of best practices..."[23] The American companies made the mistake of thinking that by adopting the practices of the Japanese companies without also adopting their mind-set, or *fundamental nature*, that they could get—and more importantly, sustain—all of the benefits of meaningful supplier relationships.

The very nature of those relationships and the results that can be derived from them starts with what having a relationship means to both parties. Not all agreements lead to relationships, nor should they. Throwing around the term relationship carelessly demeans it and makes it harder to tell which interactions are actually associated with relationships and which are simply transactions.

A collaborative supplier relationship is also not necessarily forever. Circumstances do change, as do market conditions, and when this is the case, it is advisable to either terminate or phase out a close relationship. This may mean reverting to a transactional relationship or ceasing relations altogether. The fact that this reality exists reminds us of another fact about supplier relationships—they are not personal. By using the word relationship we imply that there is something about the dynamic that exists between the two companies that transcends a typical exchange. Over time, the representatives of the parties may build up a personal rapport in addition to the professional relationship they have been assigned to carry out. That is a natural byproduct of having regular contact with someone and is no different than the relationships that are built up over time between coworkers. But just as coworker relationships should not hold individuals back from accepting new positions, relationships that are built up between buyers and suppliers cannot become impediments to the value they have been tasked with creating.

CONCLUSION

We started this chapter with one illustrative story about a prisoner, and we will conclude with another. This reference to the *Spanish prisoner's story* comes to us in a quote from Sir Winston Churchill:

> Remember the story of the Spanish Prisoner.
> For many years he was confined in a dungeon.
> One day it occurred to him to push the door of his cell.
> It was open; and it had never been locked.[24]

In any situation where we compare the relative advantages of experience and fresh perspective, we have to consider how much of the difficulty of changing is real and how much is self-imposed. In many cases we will find that the more difficult obstacles to overcome are the ones we have created in our own minds. Is it that the *dinosaurs*, as Kate Vitasek described them, can't evolve to thrive under new conditions or is it really that they would just rather not? If the latter is the case, they may be in a situation like the Spanish prisoner, self-held captives. This is not to suggest that these professionals are lazy or disagreeable, but they may be giving in to the temptation to stay where they feel safe and comfortable, consoling themselves with the idea that they are the victims of circumstances outside of their control.

Not to enable that school of thought, but there is a component of it that has to do with their personal and professional evolution to this point and the kind of environment in which that evolution happened. In many cases, procurement professionals have been conditioned not to test the jail door. Executives who sent people to procurement because they didn't want to have to deal with them any more certainly did not do so with the expectation that they would spark a revolution once they got here. No, they were sent to procurement because it was a way to contain them and continue to keep a firm hold on the direction of the function. Now that we are ready to become more collaborative in our dealings with suppliers, it is officially time to break free from any and all prisons we find ourselves constrained by.

REFERENCES

1. Jonathan O'Brien, *Supplier Relationship Management: Unlocking the Hidden Value in Your Supply Base*, (Philadelphia: Kogan Page, 2014), 319.
2. Max Nisen, "They Finally Tested The 'Prisoner's Dilemma' On Actual Prisoners—And The Results Were Not What You Would Expect," *Business Insider*, July 21, 2013, http://www.businessinsider.com/prisoners-dilemma-in-real-life-2013-7.

3. Gerard Chick and Robert Handfield, *The Procurement Value Proposition: The Rise of Supply Management*, (Philadelphia: Kogan Page, 2015), xii.
4. Andy Akrouche, "While familiarity purportedly breeds contempt, it certainly doesn't lead to procurement fraud," *SRS Can*, March 19, 2015, http://www.srscan.com/while-familiarity-purportedly -breeds-contempt-it-certainly-doesnt-lead-to-procurement-fraud/.
5. Colin Cram, "Combating procurement fraud in Africa and beyond," *The Guardian*, June 8, 2012, http://www.theguardian.com/public -leaders-network/2012/jun/08/combating-procurement-fraud -africa.
6. Andy Akrouche, "Relational Outsourcing and The Role of Service Level Agreements (Part 3)," *SRS Can*, April 18, 2012, http://www .srscan.com/relational-outsourcing-and-the-role-of-service-level -agreements-part-3/.
7. Dale Neef, *e-Procurement: From Strategy to Implementation*, (New Jersey: FT Press, 2001).
8. Tim Cummins, "The Power of Negotiation," *Commitment Matters*, September 1, 2010, http://commitmentmatters.com/2010/09/01/ the-power-of-negotiation/.
9. Ibid.
10. "Vince Lombardi Quotes," *BrainyQuote.com*, Accessed July 18, 2015, http://www.brainyquote.com/quotes/quotes/v/vincelomba 115467.html.
11. Graham Speechley, "You Get What You Negotiate," *Leadership Quote.org*, October 25, 2012, http://leadershipquote.org/2012/ 10/25/you-get-what-you-negotiate/.
12. "Newton's Laws of Motion," *Wikipedia*, Accessed July 5, 2015, https://en.wikipedia.org/wiki/Newton%27s_laws_of_motion.
13. "Collaboration," *Thesaurus.com*, Accessed 15 May, 2015, http:// www.thesaurus.com/browse/collaboration.
14. Robert Tevelson, Jonathan Zygelman, Paul Farrell, Stefan Benett, Peter Rosenfeld, and Andreas Alsén, "Buyer-Supplier Collaboration: A Roadmap for Success," *BCG Perspectives*, August 21, 2013, https://www.bcgperspectives.com/content/articles/sourcing_ procurement_supply_chain_management_buyer_supplier_ collaboration_roadmap_for_success/.
15. Marcus Starke, "Artisan Marketing, Part 2: The Artisan's Focus on Quality," *MarcusStarke.com*, February 11, 2013, http://marcusstarke .com/marketing-all/artisan-marketing-part-2-the-artisans-focus-on -quality.

16. Dave Henshall, "Entrepreneurial Disruptors Required," *Purchasing Practice*, July 15, 2015, http://purchasingpractice.com/entrepreneurial -disruptors-required/.

17. Kate Vitasek and Karl Manrodt, *Vested: How P&G, McDonalds, and Microsoft are Redefining Winning in Business Relationships*, (New York: Palgrave MacMillan, 2012), 38.

18. Jon Hansen, "The winning bidder in government tenders are selected before the RFP is actually issued 90% of the time…" *Procurement Insights*, April 7, 2011, https://procureinsights.wordpress .com/2011/04/07/the-winning-bidder-in-government-tenders-are -selectedbefore-the-rfp-is-actually-issued-90-of-the-time/.

19. Charles Handy, *The Second Curve, Thoughts on Reinventing Society*, (London: Random House, 2015).

20. Gerard Chick, "Procurement in the Future? This is Tomorrow Calling; What Have I to Lose?" *Optimum Procurement*, May 29, 2015, http://www.optimumprocurement.co.uk/news-article/optimum -press/10/procurement-in-the-future-this-is-tomorrow-calling -what-have-i-to-lose/199.

21. Roz Usheroff, *The Future of You: Creating Your Remarkable Brand*, (Palm Beach: Usheroff Institute, 2013), 20.

22. Erin Anderson and Sandy D. Jap, "The Dark Side of Close Relationships," *MIT Sloan Management Review*, April 15, 2005, http:// sloanreview.mit.edu/article/the-dark-side-of-close-relationships/.

23. Jeffrey Liker and Thomas Choi, "Building Supplier Relationships," *Harvard Business Review*, September 2004, https://hbr.org/2004/ 12/building-deep-supplier-relationships.

24. K. J. Roberts, *Motivational Phrases for All of Life's Challenges!*, (Bloomington: Trafford Publishing, 2011).

This book has free material available for download from the
Web Added Value™ resource center at *www.jrosspub.com*

6

Do We Really Need Another Chapter about Finance?

"Procurement does not just work in a vacuum where we only negotiate with suppliers. A CPO needs to work well with the rest of the executive team so that they will accept that procurement deserves to have a decision-making role." The CPO, Christina Schuh, Michael F. Strohmer, Stephen Easton, Armin Scharlach, and Peter Scharbert[1]

When we were blocking out the chapters for this book, we had one that opened with the question, *Will Procurement and Finance ever be aligned?* It seemed reasonable—almost necessary—to have a chapter on procurement's sometimes troubled, but enduringly intertwined relationship with finance. We were happy with the idea. Our publisher was happy with the idea. Then came the time to write the chapter, and everything we came up with on the subject seemed like it had already been done, had already been *gone over*. It didn't have the kind of uniqueness that we have pushed ourselves to incorporate into the other chapters. Ironically, we ended up writing this chapter last, suggesting that the writing process has taken us on a journey that allowed us to get a fresh perspective on any of the rote topics we might have otherwise included.

The relationship between procurement and finance has been covered thoroughly and well. In fact, and not that we take issue with any of the other thought leaders that have written about procurement and finance in recent years, we question the idea that enough relevant changes have taken place since Robert Rudzki wrote *Straight to the Bottom Line* in

2005—at least in terms of justifying a rewrite by us on the topics of results generation, management, and measurement.

That doesn't mean there wasn't still a chapter to be written. In fact, the basic structure of this chapter was buried in a conversation we had about the procurement/finance relationship (as well as about a million other things). Why does procurement keep talking about finance? It is highly unlikely that they think or talk about procurement in equal measure. Sure, sometimes procurement reports to the chief financial officer (CFO), and in those cases it is just as important to keep finance happy as it is for us to keep our publisher happy. But if procurement is pushing to move away from realized savings as our primary performance metric, or at least to have it balanced by something more strategic, shouldn't we spend more of our time and effort trying to get attention from operations or marketing than complaining about finance?

What we need to do is stop fixating on finance so much and instead take a broader look at how all of the functional cogs in the enterprise machine work together. Rather than another chapter on procurement and finance, what we really need is a chapter that looks at evolving function identity, including but not restricted to procurement, and how those new identities intersect in a proper operation.

CAN YOU WALK THE WALK TOGETHER IF YOU DON'T TALK THE SAME TALK?

There is no question that procurement doesn't speak the same language as finance. We also don't speak information technology (IT) or human resources (HR)—thank goodness for small favors. There has been a lot of discussion in management circles about breaking down functional silos so that information and insight can flow freely back and forth, but for every wall we complain about or pull down, we put another up. The dual irony is that as many silo walls are built to make those inside feel *defined* as are built to keep out foreign invaders.

In this regard Vijay Govindarajan, a fellow at Harvard Business School and the author of *Reverse Innovation* perceptively wrote, "Business silos, just like agricultural silos, hold something important and make it hard to get at. ... And the bigger the company the more harmful a role silos play. Silos create an environment where sharing and collaborating for anything other than one silo's special interests is virtually impossible."[2] Govindarajan makes equally good points about how silos contain valuable resources and yet constrain the flow of ideas, information, and relationships between the silos. What procurement needs to accept is that if we want the benefits of increased interaction we need to be willing to let go of the comfortable safety of old silo walls.

In some cases, the silos have been built by C-level executives looking to stake claim to and defend their territory. Even if there are operational advantages to taking the walls down, misguided C-level executives will not only see and maintain them, they may oversee their construction based on their own backgrounds and prejudices. This is one of the reasons procurement should not necessarily lament not having a C-level procurement professional. As long as it is still possible to have influence, being free from the silo building business allows us to be more agile.

That being said, there is some comfort in definition. If we take those walls down, how much risk is there that we will be less certain of our own role? Procurement wants a transformation. We demand change. We seek improvement. Who's stopping us from getting all of these things and more? Finance? Not really. If we actually have a vision for what we want to do, we should be able to just get to work without worrying what they or anyone else (except maybe the chief executive officer) thinks about it. Someone needs to lead the corporate change that is required, and in many cases leading that change means just getting to work and making it happen. What we need to get over is the idea that finance (or anybody else for that matter) is going to give us the legitimacy we seek. We have to legitimize ourselves through vision driven action. When you have legitimacy, you're so focused on what you're doing that you aren't held back by corporate hierarchy or politics. You don't even see the silo walls that hold others back.

There are plenty of shifting elements in the modern corporate landscape that deserve our attention more than the rivalry that exists between corporate cliques—increased availability of data and shrinking lag times are among them. There is so much more data available to us today than there was in the past, and it is available so quickly—practically in real time. With that speed of availability comes an imperative for actionability—use it or lose it, baby! Historically, procurement received data long enough after the triggering event, that we had the crutch of knowing it was only accurate enough to be used as part of trending or modeling exercises. That is no longer true, unless of course, we pause so long after receiving data that we artificially diminish its potential value. Real time data should be converted to intelligence and applied in as short a time as possible.

Interestingly enough, also found within the subtleties of Govindarajan's statement is the answer to how procurement can overcome our greatest obstacle. We need to find a way to identify and distribute responsibilities without creating cumbersome infrastructure. A modular format is far more dynamic than a silo. Modules can be self-sufficient, but are also able to quickly connect and disconnect from other modules as needed. Independence is the key, especially as we need to learn to thrive in a less certain organizational structure. Any definition we create for ourselves should be based on what we are and what we do, not on a fixed relationship to another group.

JON'S PERSPECTIVE: *Show Me the Money!*

Way back when, I wrote a piece on how CFOs view the contributions made by their organization's purchasing department in relation to the things that really matter. I referenced the findings from a 2007 Aberdeen CFO survey highlighting what I believed were a number of key findings and which we shared in detail in Chapter 2 of this book. The net-net of the findings is that few CFOs see procurement as contributing to competitive advantage: roughly half think we contribute to enterprise growth, and only a few more than that see us as contributors to enterprise profitability.

As you absorb this information, add into the equation the fact that more than 80% of what purchasing people consider to be tangible savings, CFOs discount as being irrelevant to the organization's bottom line. That is not exactly a robust endorsement of procurement's impact on the overall enterprise. How do you show someone the money when you don't even know what the money looks like?

At this stage, one might reasonably suspect that I would write about the long and angst-ridden road that has been uneasily traveled together by those in procurement and finance. After all, isn't this a book about procurement? But when Kelly and I put pen to paper to write this chapter, we decided that it shouldn't only focus on finance and purchasing. Our reasoning was simply this—the disconnect between finance and purchasing is likely symptomatic of the disconnect between all departments within a whole organization.

In a January 18, 2011 *Information Management* article "Why Marketing and IT Don't Get Along," David M. Raab[3] shared the results of a chief marketing officer (CMO) Council study that found not only misalignment between the two departments, but *isolation and mutual distrust in both camps.* As he went on to explain, "The broad findings are no surprise—CMOs and chief information officers (CIOs) know they need to work together but don't do it very well. But it's worth digging into the details to understand the dynamics of this dysfunctional relationship, in the hope of helping them to improve it."[4]

In a more recent article "Finance and Marketing: Can't We All Just Get Along?" Matt Davis concluded that the departments speak "two completely different languages."[5] The resulting challenge sounds much like the problems procurement has in demonstrating and documenting savings, "in most organizations, there's often a disconnect between the marketing expenses the CMO reports and the bottom line the CFO tracks. To get those numbers to match up, members of both the marketing and finance teams spend a lot of hours reconciling and number-crunching."[6]

Not even HR always gets along with finance. They cross swords more frequently than one would suspect. This notion was a little surprising to me, as I have always considered HR to be the organization's great peacemakers. They are the ones who will invite everyone to lock arms around a fire and lead a rousing rendition of Kumbaya.

In 2011, Samuel Dergler wrote a guest article for the Canadian HR Reporter asking his own *Why can't* question, as in "Why can't finance and HR just get along?" It would seem that the difference in their areas of respective focus (people and money) gets in the way. According to his experience, "The biggest point of this interdepartmental friction comes from the intersection of their interests—HR deals with people, whose costs are usually the largest expenditure in a company, while finance is mandated with managing costs."[7]

Even those who occupy the loftiest heights in the corporate hierarchy seem to be at odds with one another on a frequent basis. Ron Ashkenas provided proof of this last fact in his April 2nd, 2015 *Forbes* article "What to Do When Senior Managers Don't Get Along." "It's virtually impossible to like everyone you meet. It's even more unlikely that you will get along with everyone at work. People have different personalities, biases, values, ambitions, and interests, all of which affect the chemistry of their relationships."[8] After all, even senior managers are just people. Clearly harmony is an elusive quest.

Like a bad episode of Jerry Springer or Geraldo Rivera—and yes, they are all bad—it seems that everyone at one time or another has thrown the occasional chair or, had to be restrained by a Steve Wilkos type. By the way, don't ask me how I even know their names, because I don't actually watch the shows, just the commercials for the shows. But that is another story.

Procurement needs to come to the realization that there is indeed life beyond the confines of historical feuds and the defense of functional imperatives. For those of us who are able to do this—to step outside of the die that was cast for us so many years ago—we will finally make the transition to the brave new world of enterprise accountability. We will finally make the transition from being purchasing people to procurement professionals. There is, of course, a world of difference between the two.

In purchasing, antiquated terms such as cost avoidance, lowest price, and vendor rationalization will be replaced by procurement's strategic spend, best value, and relationship development. Contracts with their onerous conditions will no longer become the lever through which we will achieve desired outcomes. Instead, charters and partnering agreements will ascend to a position of prominence. While not replacing contracts outright, these new frameworks or models will not only govern how we acquire goods and services, but how we will collaboratively and cooperatively co-manage outcomes with key stakeholders internally as well as externally.

We are not alone in this transformation toward harmonious cooperation. A few years ago, a survey of CIOs by *CIO Magazine* found that the majority believed that their role had to evolve. Specifically, it found that they had to leave the comfort of their own world and to better engage the people in other departments. In fact, they felt so strongly about the need to redefine their traditional role that there were suggestions that their CIO designation be changed to reflect a more inclusive intent.

In the end, the world is changing rapidly. Global enterprise is no longer confined to mega corporations with tens of thousands of employees working in disassociated divisions. Today, we are as likely to form partnerships with smaller, more innovative organizations of ten people on the other side of the world as we are with the behemoth around the corner. This means that relationships and relationship building are no longer based on feel-good sentiment, but an essential component of a successful and highly productive organization.

Whether we are ready or not, the petty differences and myopic internal feuds of the past have no place going forward. The professionals who understand this reality and are able to foster communication based on the best interests of the whole enterprise will rise to the top regardless of whether they come from procurement, finance, marketing, HR, or for that matter, Timbuktu.

Surrendering the Cold War Mind-set

Even though the Cold War created a heightened degree of fear and tension, there was also a certainty—perhaps even an uneasy comfort—in knowing that there was a clear-cut enemy. That enemy had a known identity, location, and mode of operation. The question at the time was if and when that enemy might strike. The majority of the preparation at the time was focused on building up defenses and training people of all ages how to respond in case of an attack. Fortunately, the feared attack never came.

Historically, it has been clear that finance—for as long as anyone can remember—has been procurement's nemesis. Just like in the 1950s and 1960s, procurement responded to the *threat* with defensive planning and safety drills. In the Cold War, allies and enemies were contained by geographical boundaries. The formal ambassador/foreign policy framework was successful because whether a country was a friend or a foe, they had the same basic structure of contacts and authority. The same was true of procurement and finance. Both had relatively similar organizational structures and understood where they fell in the overall corporate hierarchy.

At the end of the Cold War, the global landscape became increasingly confusing through the splintering of the threat from one large defined adversary to many smaller yet equally lethal adversaries. The same can be said about the finance-procurement relationship. With the structures and objectives of all major functions in flux, procurement is dealing with uncertainty on a number of fronts. And while there is little deliberate sabotage going on, there are ample opportunities for overlap and competition for authority.

It is no wonder, then, that many procurement professionals, especially those who have been at their jobs for longer than ten years, might be inclined to ruefully and with a touch of nostalgia, reflect on bygone days when they could place all of their problems at the feet of a single enemy. In some cases, professionals still habitually bemoan finance even when they have long since been surpassed by some other concern as procurement's biggest problem.

Today everyone is scrambling, including finance and IT professionals, to redefine themselves and their roles within their organization and the greater market itself. Relevance and job security are no longer tied to the familiar roles with which many are most comfortable. Country lines are being redrawn, and foreign policy is being conducted at a lower, more fragmented level.

Against this backdrop of progressive and tumultuous transformation, procurement professionals need to readjust their thinking to a new reality. In this new reality or era, the *defined* roles of the past are merging into a holistic blend of business acumen that knows no real boundaries beyond producing results. It would seem that everyone is a *double agent* as professionals are moving in and out of functions with more regularity than in years past. Someone in procurement is as likely to have a background in finance or IT as anything else, and that experience changes their perspective and prevents them from accepting the Cold War view that would otherwise dictate both allegiances and enmity.

As indicated, the changes that procurement faces today are not unique to us. Every other corporate function is going through a similar shift. IT, for instance, is dealing with the extinction of enterprise applications and mainframe technology while the use of mobile technology and security requirements are on the rise. This change is similar to when the personal computer appeared on the scene to replace mainframes. All at once, an area of responsibility that used to be just a portion of their territory has become a core and critical competency. If this were a standardized test, we might pose this analogy: Security is to IT as [?] is to procurement. This idea provides us with an opportunity to learn from the experiences of colleagues in other functions. We must ask ourselves: What is it that procurement is doing today that will be the majority of our focus tomorrow?

Finding the answer to that question requires us to look at the corporate landscape differently, very much the way you have to allow your eyes to go out of focus to see an optical illusion. It is highly likely that we will not like all of the changes that need to take place, but the potential from achieving a clear line of sight in the organization is so significant that is it worth whatever adjustments have to be made.

As this is a chapter on finance, or more specifically the relationship between finance and procurement, the remainder of this chapter will focus on understanding the dynamics of how these two important elements of a holistic enterprise can and should interact. However, we would be remiss, as demonstrated by the aforementioned IT reference, if we did not mention that the very same principles of engagement and mutual discernment involves all stakeholders both within and external to the enterprise. In other words, you can replace finance with IT or procurement with suppliers, and the same approach would still be applicable. And taking a big picture view, this is really a communication and collaboration chapter in which the principles of engagement are applicable to everyone whether in IT, finance, procurement, etc.

And Now for Something Completely—Finance

Rather than focusing on finance as a dominant or competing function we should focus on what they are trying to accomplish and how we can advance it. We should take this same approach with any stakeholder group, whether they are inside or outside of the organization. Any areas of shared impact or interest should be the highest priority for both. For instance, we should be working to understand how procurement can affect liquidity: ours' and our suppliers'. Movement of cash is the real continuity in the supply chain—our management of risk, suppliers, goods, and services is all about maintaining liquidity. As Chuck Prince, former Chairman and Chief Executive of Citigroup, infamously said to *The Financial Times* during the credit crisis of 2007, "When the music stops in terms of liquidity, things will get complicated. But as long as the music is playing, you've got to get up and dance."[9] Granted, he was talking about leveraged buyouts, but he had a point that transcends that specific context. Every link in the chain needs to set up their payables and receivables such that they have the liquidity to operate and invest for the future. And while the going is good, everybody has to stay in the game.

It is fair for us to look at the world in a certain way because we are procurement. There is just as much value in having a unique perspective as there is the risk of limiting blind spots. We just have to make sure we don't narrow our view to the detriment of big picture performance. Having too narrow of a scope—both of our actions and of the consequences (intended and otherwise)—creates risk and negative outcomes that we may not be able to recover from without significant loss.

The real questions this raises going forward are simply these—what does the big picture actually look like and how do we recognize it when we see it? It is one thing to accept that we can't stay confined within the walls of our home silo, but what are we supposed to do instead? Before we answer this question, consider what the big picture isn't. Another way of approaching a better big picture view is to focus on what in the current landscape prevents us from seeing it.

Case Study: Candy and Supply Base Synchronization

How important is effective internal collaboration? Just ask a candy company in the midwestern U.S. As the manufacturer of a number of leading brands, this organization grew dramatically in a very short period of time through a series of acquisitions. Unfortunately, an extemporal supply base was a byproduct of the transactions, leaving the acquiring company with a highly suspicious, deeply segmented group of suppliers.

The biggest challenge as expressed by a senior procurement manager for the parent organization was convincing the suppliers of each acquired company that becoming part of the larger pool would expose them to opportunities for increased sales. The suppliers didn't buy the *increased opportunity* mantra and as a result, the transition process was challenging to say the least.

What is worth noting is that the degree of collaboration between the different purchasing organizations was also not clearly established from the beginning of the consolidation process. This only served to fuel rather than douse the internal fires of division resulting in both a practical and operational lack of cohesiveness and coordination. The end result was a *territorial* struggle that manifested itself in a divided supply base. This is hardly the ideal environment for a successful consolidation.

The candy company case study demonstrates how we can obfuscate our own view of the big picture. The previously independent procurement teams were more focused on maintaining their individual spend territory than they were on advancing the best interests of the consolidated enterprise. Can it be any surprise that the suppliers did not embrace the idea that this change presented them with an opportunity? Clearly procurement made a feeble attempt to sell something that they did not buy themselves. The other disconnect it highlights is that problems arise even when everyone shares a similar viewpoint. The procurement organizations being consolidated by the parent candy manufacturer all had similar points of view, at least functionally speaking, and yet they were still unable to align and work together for the greater good.

For procurement professionals to see the big picture, even when working with other procurement professionals, we must stop thinking in terms of *us* versus *them*. In fact, this is *especially* true within our own ranks. When multiple procurement teams try to integrate, there is a natural but unproductive jostling for dominance: our process is more mature than yours—we have a more integrated contract management process and our suppliers view our account as more important than they do yours. The situation very quickly devolves into a schoolyard brawl that cannot hope to lead to a successfully integrated supply base. Such a brawl is most likely to occur in a leadership vacuum. A strong chief purchasing officer (CPO) is able to establish order through frank and open discussions with all parties. Lack of willingness to participate fully results in swift and clear negative consequences while contributions to the greater good go unrecognized. Keeping the focus of the group on the collective goal rather than fragmented and selfish interests is the best way to reach the target.

We have to immerse ourselves, whether by invitation or self-directed intervention, into the overall business and its objectives. Only then will we be in the position to leverage our expertise to have the greatest and widest impact beyond the limited scope that has previously defined and confined our contributions.

For example, and with a merger or acquisition such as the one referenced in our previously mentioned case study, procurement has to adopt and demonstrate a proactive solution-oriented mind-set long before a merger or acquisition occurs. Just like with collaboration, which we discussed at length in the last chapter, procurement must think and see collaboratively in order to act collectively. If we continue to think and see defensively, our actions—particularly those that involve other functions—will be constrained, artificial, and unconvincing. They will also be seen as an attempt to establish a *quid pro quo* dynamic: I will do this for you, but only if you do that for me in return. This reveals the fact that the *right* approach is not being taken for its own sake, and that procurement may not even believe in it. Ultimately, it will undermine the success of the effort and it will do little to improve the positioning and regard for procurement in the enterprise.

In her March 25th, 2015 article "The Employee's Guide for Surviving a Merger & Acquisition," executive coach and branding expert Roz Usheroff answered the question, *how do I survive a merger or acquisition?*, with the following advice: "Be outgoing in meeting and engaging with your coworkers and senior management. It's all about your ability to build and sustain rapport. Undertake assigned tasks with both energy, passion and enthusiasm. Remember that similar to relationships, there are going to be good days and challenging ones as well, so think in terms of running a marathon as opposed to a sprint."[10]

The political or influence capital that you might have to spend to survive a merger, acquisition, or consolidation requires time to build up, and it has to be authentic. As we saw with the procurement professionals at the candy company who failed to convince suppliers of the opportunity at hand because of their own lack of belief, you have to act upon the right priorities and interests—not just affect them outwardly—in order to be successful.

CROSS-FUNCTIONAL INTERACTION AND INCREASED POTENTIAL

One of the reasons so much time and space has been devoted to finance in particular is that they are seen as the driving force behind procurement's quantitative performance metrics. Just as procurement has a certain perspective on the work we do and the results we generate, each other function in the enterprise will have a different take. Our work means something different to finance, IT, HR, operations, etc. The connection between the groups we collaborate with and how highly our contribution is valued by them provides procurement with a reason to actively pursue increased interaction rather than just tolerating it. The more multifaceted we are seen as being in our capabilities and results, the more dimensions will be represented in our performance expectations.

This emphasis on cross-functional collaboration is something that leading procurement organizations have long understood. As described in *Procurement 20/20*, "Their [leading companies'] procurement organizations regularly extend their efforts beyond cost reduction and supply chain performance, measuring a combination of price, quality, and supply chain performance and striving for other strategic goals—for example, access to intellectual property. None of this happens without a cross-functional, collaborative approach."[11] By seeking out a multifaceted understanding of the organization's goals and how we can contribute to them, procurement allows big-picture nuances to direct our work and improve it. That, in turn, leads to increased performance from procurement—not to mention new opportunities for involvement— thereby continuously increasing our impact and influence over time.

There are several examples in this book of traditional notions or hang-ups that we have encouraged procurement to look beyond. Just as we suggest in this chapter that we need to get over our hang-up on finance in order to improve our relations with all internal teams, we previously suggested that the fastest path to influence is letting go of the need for a seat at the executive table. Both recommendations include big picture approaches and neither is intended to suggest that we should turn our backs on making progress in those areas. We should not stop trying to improve procurement's relationship with finance any more than we should turn down a C-level position for procurement. The idea is to get out of our own way and to prevent speedbumps from turning into total roadblocks. Any opportunity to make progress on either front requires us to invest daily in order to win big. We just can't allow a myopic obsession with either to stymie our overall development.

Of course we would be remiss if we did not once again reference our Cold War analogy and the comfort that even an uneasy and, at times, acrimonious relationship represents. Let's face it, in many instances, change, or the ability to change, is not determined by opportunity or intelligence; it is determined or embarked upon as an act of will. This means that there must be a willingness and conscientious effort to shed the shackles of complacent familiarity. The question is one of critical mass. At what point does the pressure (or desire) to change become so great that it can no longer be ignored?

This is a critical point that requires some discussion before we can even begin to contemplate what a seat at the executive table really means, let alone being invited to sit down at one. Tantamount to what the ring meant to Gollum in the Lord of the Rings, we will, of course, talk about this infamous seat at *the table* shortly. But first things first.

A Formula for Change

Back in the early 1960s, David Gleicher developed his formula for change, now known as Gleicher's Formula. He identified three variables that when multiplied, must be larger than the resistance to change. So what are the factors that go into the formula? (See Figure 6.1.) They are: (1) A dissatisfaction with how things are now, (2) The ability to envision another reality, and (3) The first steps that need to be taken toward that new vision. "Since the formula involves the multiplication

Gleicher's Formula for Change

Dissatisfaction with how things are now	X	The ability to envision another reality	X	The first steps that need to be taken towards that new vision

Figure 6.1 Gleicher's Formula for Change

of the three variables, if any variable is completely missing or is too low, the end result will also be low. This implies that falling short on any one of these variables will make it difficult to get past the resistance."[12] In other words, dissatisfaction, vision, and the path forward have to be equally strong in order to motivate change. If the formula were based on addition, a high value in one of the variables would be enough, but that is not the case.

In the 1980s, Kathie Dannemiller refined Gleicher's Formula and applied it on an organizational level. Roland Sullivan, a career change management agent, summarized her view of the post-change state, "organization members see themselves for the first time and the company differently, they have new mind-sets both individually and collectively. This breakthrough in mind-set gives the organization the ability to shift their behaviors to align with the future they aspire for instead of repeating unproductive patterns of the past."[13]

Even though Dannemiller applied these factors at the organizational level, Sullivan makes it clear that they must ultimately happen on an individual level, with enough people to create the proverbial tipping point that results in change. Also of interest is the break between the old and new mind-set, especially if the up-and-coming generations have already, in their own way, natively embraced the change that the rest of us need to experience.

If one is to accept the above formula for change, then determining the current level of dissatisfaction with how things are today within the collective ranks of our profession is an important place to start. Properly channeled levels of dissatisfaction—even if they are high—can be a powerful tool. Anyone in a change leadership role must be sure the players are prepared to fight rather than take flight in the face of change. As we have already mentioned, the vision and plan may be in place from a leadership perspective, but if the energy of the group cannot be channeled, the change will not occur.

We are not talking about the same old Rodney Dangerfield lamentations that we *get no respect,* or the little sibling-style grumblings that occur in the same confines of procurement conference rooms. We need to espouse a confident belief that the trajectory of our profession has mirrored procurement's increasing strategic importance to the enterprise as a whole. If we do not believe this is the case, we need to identify what we are individually and collectively prepared to do about it.

There is a likelihood that the majority of old procurement pros would not be willing to undertake the personal risk and discomfort required.

This is perhaps why—and it bears repeating again—Handfield suggests that there is a definite and definitive divide between yesterday's purchasing people, and the up-and-coming Generation Next procurement pros.

The latter group is not manacled to a familiar past in which purchasing was largely viewed as an adjunct function of finance, whose only real contribution was more administrative than strategic. In reality, this younger generation has no more knowledge of the old pecking order or hierarchy, than they do cassette tapes and hula hoops. This means that theirs is a new, more global vision, in which a seat at the table is not pursued with hopeful anticipation, but is expected. But is this expectation well founded?

Given that the Generation Next professionals from other functions are going through similar evolutions, one would have to say yes. Therefore the steps that they have taken toward procurement are not those that are taken toward a vague and distant vision, but are an expected matter-of-fact reality. Change, or the need to change, is not an issue because they are in and of themselves representative of the change the old pros have to reenvision and then pursue. They are automatically wired to not only see themselves and what they do in a new and exciting light, but through their exposure to social media and networking, are predisposed toward a much broader collaboration model.

KELLY'S PERSPECTIVE: *Change Management as Easy as ABC*

I have heard a number of speakers address the subject of change over time. Since change is an ever present factor in so many aspects of our lives, it is also a popular presentation or speech topic and usually draws an eager crowd. Some of my favorite thoughts on change management have come from Dr. Aubrey Daniels, sometimes referred to as the *father of performance management*. He often discusses the ABC Model for change management, shown in Figure 6.2, the parts of which are

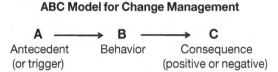

ABC Model for Change Management

A ⟶ B ⟶ C
Antecedent   Behavior   Consequence
(or trigger)   (positive or negative)

Figure 6.2 The ABC model for change management

the antecedent, the behavior, and the consequence. In order to cause change, you have to address the antecedent (or trigger) for the behavior as well as the consequence.

One thing I have learned is that a consequence can be either positive or negative. Although in most cases, it is implied that a consequence is negative, this is not necessarily the case. In fact, positive consequences are far more effective and lasting. As William B. Lee and Michael Katzorke wrote in *Leading Effective Supply Chain Transformations,* "'Be careful that victories do not carry the seeds of future defeats.' With positive reinforcement, people give their best because they *want to do so*. Nobody has to watch them, except to applaud. Negative reinforcement is only effective as long as people are watched adequately to sustain the behavior."[14]

This more individual level of change management helps us better understand how to execute the third step of Gleicher's Formula. People may be dissatisfied, and one or more of them may have a vision for how to make it better, but if you can't spur the group or action, no improvement will ever be realized. Rewarding examples of collaborative thinking and action are likely to result in more of the same as well as a more positive work culture. Keeping the focus on the positive reinforcement and off of the new behavior may even incent those who are averse to change to get on board.

Just as organizational change has to be executed on an individual level, individual successes should be recognized and celebrated on an organizational level. Rather than pointing out the differences between the person or persons who effectively made the change take place, early wins that allow the entire group to take ownership are a first step toward redefining how the team sees themselves and how they act in the future.

Helping spread effective change requires a review of all three elements, just like sowing the seeds of change did in the first place:

- Antecedent: How did the team know this was an opportunity to accomplish something better? What are the signs that would help us recognize a similar opportunity in the future?
- Behavior: What steps did the team take beyond the usual processes that took the opportunity from concept to reality? Are there additional training or resources worth investing in to prepare the rest of the team to act similarly?
- Consequence: What are all of the different positive results that came from the improved series of events? How did procurement

win? How about the other functions involved and the enterprise as a whole?

So Where Does This Leave Yesterday's Procurement Professional?

There is a growing consensus—extending well beyond Handfield's chasm—that the day of the dinosaurs is rapidly coming to an end. Whether or not someone belongs in the dinosaur category has little to do with their length of time in the profession or age, and more to do with their mind-set. In other words—and this brings us back to Gleicher's Formula—in particular a dissatisfaction with how things are now, anyone and everyone can become part of the new vision by choice. This also has very little to do with being in procurement. We could just as easily have opened this chapter with the question, "Do we really need another book about procurement?" Every function in an organization needs to be constantly reexamining the status quo and making plans for an evolving future.

Think of this in the context of being forewarned is being forearmed. The new vision is here. The change has already happened. What are you prepared to do? This decision, and this decision alone, will determine what your future will look like. Being part of change does not require that each individual fully understand the new vision and what is required to make it happen. However, as we learned from the multiplication in Gleicher's Formula, someone has to. All three factors—dissatisfaction, vision, and plan—must be present in equal measure for the organization to make a change happen. This is the great power of increased internal cross-functional collaboration. Procurement may be dissatisfied, finance may have a vision, and operations may have a plan. As long as the three groups find a way to work together, they will have all of the pieces required to make change a reality.

People Who Need People

The need to work well with all other functions (okay, people)—for real—is an absolute requirement for anything ambitious we may have in mind. No one should expect to be asked to join a cross-functional C-level leadership team if they don't work well with other people at the individual contributor level. *Procurement Leaders'* Paul Teague has made the observation that it is—and should be—difficult for anyone to earn a seat at the head table. "That table everyone wants to sit at is really pretty small. There really aren't a lot of chairs. You only get a seat if you can do something while you're there—like add value to discussions on the company's future."[15]

As with any promotion, the common wisdom is that you have to prove you can carry out a job before you will get it—and all of its associated perks. If procurement wants to make the case that we deserve to have sway at the highest level of the company, we need to demonstrate that it is in the organization's best interests to put us there—again, long in advance of getting the opportunity to sit in the seat. Strong relationships with all of the major players (again people—do you see a theme here?) will propel us to the top with as much certainty as poor ones will hold us back.

We've already discussed collaboration, although mostly from the perspective of building relationships with our external supply partners. All of the same incentives and requirements exist with internal colleagues: being a partner of choice, gaining greater traction when it comes time to implement change, and creating greater value through the investments of both parties. All of these require good communication—not a strength that procurement has often been credited with in the past.

ONE BIG HAPPY TALENT POOL

Most of our focus in this chapter has been on what the people already on the job in procurement need to do in order to work cross-functionally to achieve enterprise-wide objectives. We have stressed the need for a broad mind-set that supports complete alignment in thought, word, and deed. If this is the kind of capability we want and need on the team, it is highly likely that we are going to be competing for top talent with all of the other functions in the organization.

In May 2015, ThomasNet and the Institute for Supply Management hosted a panel-style discussion forum with some of the 2014 30 Under 30 Supply Chain Rising Star award recipients; they recorded it and made it available afterward as a podcast. The forum started with each of the participating recipients and program mentors introducing themselves and then moved on to a press-conference style question and answer session with representatives from the procurement media sites.

Bob Trebilcock, *Supply Chain Management Review's* Editorial Director, asked how these rising stars ended up in supply chain. Two of the award recipients, both of which happened to come to procurement from finance, debunked the idea that all Millennials—or Generation Next procurement professionals—purposefully select it as a career from the outset. At least in the case of these two young professionals, they fell into the field just like many of us already in the field did. Most of the rising stars we heard from in the podcast—although not all—ended up in procurement by some indirect path. In some cases they chose to enter the field and had to push to get here. In other cases they were recruited for their skills. But even when they were selected for experience they already had, knowledge of procurement had less to do with the decision than mind-set and outlook.

Amy Schwantner, manager of strategic sourcing at CBS Corporation, interviewed for a job in procurement without knowing what strategic sourcing was. And she's certainly not alone in that. As it turned out, it wasn't even a problem. As Schwantner explained, "I could not be in finance any more. ... I started Googling anything with analyst in the title and came across CBS Corporation. I had my phone interview and the woman asked if I knew what strategic sourcing is and I say 'no.' I was embarrassed, mortified, but that wasn't the intent."[16] In her case, the hiring team preferred to have someone with the right mind-set and skills than with experience or prior working knowledge of procurement processes and techniques. As she explained in the forum, the HR rep gave her this advice for her interview: "Just don't go in there with your finance hat on."

What makes these professionals different than those of years past is how qualified they are when they come to procurement. We've already written at length about the dead weight and misfits our field has been plagued with in the past. The fact of the matter is, these young professionals were rising stars long before anyone made it official with an award—the trick was getting them into procurement and supply chain.

If the notion that bright kindergarteners are going to start telling grown-ups they want to be in procurement or supply chain when they grow up is a false one; this may be yet another area where those of us already in the field need to step up and take control. When we profile the kinds of professionals we want for open seats, having a collaborative mind-set should absolutely be on the list of desired qualifications.

The problem with taking a more open approach is that, at least at an entry level, all functions are going to be looking for very similar qualities in their candidates. Which new hires should be assigned to each function? If these young but promising achievers are willing to be professionally opportunistic, we have to make sure procurement looks like the best opportunity for them—in the long and short term.

TWO EYES AND ONE MOUTH FOR A REASON

In the first century A.D., the stoic philosopher Epictetus made the enduring observation that "we have two ears and one mouth so that we can listen twice as much as we speak." The only addition we might make to this wise observatory statement is that we also have two eyes and two feet. If procurement is going to form and maintain productive relationships with other functions in the organization, we absolutely have to listen more than we speak, but we should also observe and take a walk in others' shoes before we make recommendations or pass judgment.

In other words, we must find a balance between emotional intelligence and social intelligence. A realistic self-awareness combined with empathetic insight into those with whom we come in contact, is a powerful force in terms of influence.

Sure, there are a lot of changes happening in procurement right now, but there are a lot of other shifts taking place elsewhere at the same time. If we focus too much on what is happening within our own boundaries, we risk missing the larger context and putting in place a new structure or set of governing priorities that is out of step with the rest of the enterprise.

Believe it or not, being able to effectively empathize with other functions may be the shortest path for us to take on our quest to build influence. In an excerpt of the book *The Zen Leader* by Ginny Whitelaw, which was run in Fast Company, she talks about the role that empathy plays in leadership. "'Become the other person and go from there.' It's the best piece of coaching advice I ever received, coming from Tanouye Roshi, and it applies equally to influence, negotiation, conflict, sales, teaching, and communication of all kinds."[17] She doesn't explicitly list procurement or finance, but they are both there in implied form.

We cannot afford to make the mistake of thinking that to listen, observe, and empathize puts us in a weakened position. This is another piece of the corporate mind-set that is evolving out. Knowledge is power, as Sir Francis Bacon told us in the sixteenth century. And the knowledge we acquire by better understanding our colleagues is no exception. In this case, we may be even better advised by Ralph Waldo Emerson: "Skill to do comes of doing; knowledge comes by eyes always open, and working hands; and there is no knowledge that is not power."[18]

When looked at in this way, it quickly becomes clear that by better understanding all of our stakeholders, we build a clearer view of the total picture. We don't have to agree with them, just understand their mind-set so we can interact more productively. This expanded and diversified view of the current situation and possible responses allows us to make enriched judgments and decisions and improve our performance in turn.

CONCLUSION

This is perhaps where the Generation Next procurement professionals have a leg up on those who have been around for a number of years. Their experiences and the roads that led them to procurement involve both timing and choice, and are far more diversified than in years past. In other words, the younger set have generally seen more and experienced more, thereby creating a broader horizon of vision and understanding of the world beyond their profession. To these young men and women, the definition of any role is a natural extension of what they have learned and what they bring to the position rather than a generalized collective identity.

Theirs is a world of wearable technology where the mobile supply chain is rapidly becoming the only supply chain. In fact, in his post titled "Building for the way the world should work and the Indian P2P economy," Nilesh Gopali indicated that most "SME suppliers do not know how to use a PC or a notebook computer."[19] Gopali's statement is based on the findings of a study which indicated that the majority of business people under the age of 35 have never actually used a *traditional PC device* to connect to the world.

Of particular interest is the fact that there is no mention of, or differentiation between, people from various professions. We are all one in this brave new hyper-connected world, and therefore it is assumed—at least in principle—that we are also better positioned to achieve a more seamless state of capability and experience.

In this context, the incentive for each profession or group to act in their own best interest is significantly reduced. This reduction in turn leads to a greater mutual or shared understanding of the global enterprise as a whole by *all* parties.

Bridging the gap between procurement and other organizational functions is as much a mindful progression as it is a circumstantial one. Everyone is equally connected with one another and therefore information and the flow of information is not limited or restricted to specific pockets of individuals. Everyone can see everything if they choose. The technological means has, in essence, created the opportunity. What procurement professionals decide to do with this opportunity will determine their place and their position in the new hierarchy of the emerging business world order.

REFERENCES

1. Christina Schuh, Michael F. Strohmer, Stephen Easton, Armin Scharlach, and Peter Scharbert, *The CPO: Transforming Procurement in the Real World*, (New York: Apress, 2012), 23.
2. Vijay Govindarajan, "The First Two Steps Toward Breaking Down Silos in Your Organization," *Harvard Business Review*, August 9, 2011, https://hbr.org/2011/08/the-first-two-steps-toward-breaking -down-silos/.
3. David M. Raab, "Why Marketing and IT Don't Get Along," *Information Management*, January 18, 2011, http://www.information -management.com/issues/21_1/why-marketing-and-it-dont-get -along-10019516-1.html.
4. Ibid.
5. Matt Davis, "Finance and Marketing: Can't We All Just Get Along?" *Allocadia*, November 6, 2014, http://www.allocadia.com/mpm/ finance-marketing-cant-just-get-along/.
6. Ibid.
7. Samuel Dergler, "Why can't finance and HR just get along?" *Canadian HR Reporter*, November 21, 2011, http://dergelcfo.com/wp -content/uploads/2011/11/why-cant-finance-and-hr-just-get-along -samuel-dergel.pdf.
8. Ron Ashkenas, "What To Do When Senior Managers Don't Get Along." *Forbes*, April 2, 2015, http://www.forbes.com/sites/ ronashkenas/2015/04/02/what-to-do-when-senior-managers-dont -get-along/.
9. Michiyo Nakamoto and David Wighton," Citigroup chief stays bullish on buy-outs," *Financial Times*, July 9, 2007, http://www .ft.com/cms/s/0/80e2987a-2e50-11dc-821c-0000779fd2ac.html# axzz3eTeNh1RY.
10. Roz Usheroff, "The Employee's Guide for Surviving a Merger & Acquisition," *The Remarkable Leader*, March 25, 2015, https:// remarkableleader.wordpress.com/2015/03/25/the-employees -guide-for-surviving-a-merger-acquisition-revisited/.

11. Peter Spiller, Nicolas Reinecke, Drew Ungerman, Henrique Teixeira, *Procurement 20/20: Supply Entrepreneurship in a Changing World*, (Hoboken: Wiley, 2014), 21.
12. Sidharth Thakur, "Gleicher's Formula: A Scientific Approach to Change," *Bright Hub Project Management*, July 29, 2011, http://www.brighthubpm.com/change-management/122241-gleichers-formula-a-scientific-approach-to-change/.
13. Roland Sullivan, "Collectively Creating a Paradigm Shift," *Roland Sullivan's Blog*, Accessed July 8, https://rolandsullivan.wordpress.com/2014/08/25/the-change-management-or-organization-development-formula-that-i-have-used-extensively-for-years/.
14. William B. Lee and Michael Katzorke, "Leading Effective Supply Chain Transformations: A Guide to Sustainable World-class Capability and Results," (Fort Lauderdale: J. Ross, 2010), 174.
15. Paul Teague, "Want a Seat at the Table? Prove You Deserve it." *Procurement Leaders*, Accessed July 3, 2015, http://www.procurementleaders.com/blog/my-blog--paul-teague/want-a-seat-at-the-table-prove-you-deserve-it-332554.
16. "The "30 Under 30" #SupplyChainStars Speak Out," narrated by ThomasNet, *Sound Cloud*, June 2015, https://soundcloud.com/thomasnet/the-30-under-30-supplychainstars-speak-out.
17. Ginny Whitelaw, "Empathy Is the Most Powerful Leadership Tool," *Fast Company*, Accessed on July 7, 2015, http://www.fastcompany.com/1835574/empathy-most-powerful-leadership-tool.
18. Ralph Waldo Emerson, *The Conduct Life of Society and Solitude*, 1892, 303.
19. Nilesh Gopali, "Building for the way the world should work and the Indian P2P economy," *LinkedIn*, June 8, 2015, https://www.linkedin.com/pulse/building-way-world-should-work-indian-p2p-economy-nilesh-gopali?trk=prof-post.

Web Added Value™

This book has free material available for download from the
Web Added Value™ resource center at *www.jrosspub.com*

7

Can Procurement Technology Benefit from the Uber Effect?

"Uber is a $3.5 billion lesson in building for how the world *should* work instead of optimizing for how the world *does* work." Aaron Levie Tweet, August 23, 2013.[1]

Over the past year, the above Aaron Levie tweet about Uber (with his original emphasis) has appeared on our radar screen on two separate occasions. In the first instance, it was referenced in a post on the Nipendo blog by Erin Livneh,[2] and then again more recently by the Country Head for India from cloudBuy, Nilesh Gopali.[3] Both referred to the tweet in the context of how technology—or the idea of technology—in the procurement world, must dramatically change in terms of expectations and deliverables.

A change is definitely needed given that the vast majority of technology-based eProcurement implementations have consistently failed to deliver the expected results—at least before the Gartner-defined *postmodern enterprise resource planning (ERP) era*. But was the technology or some inherent flaw in a program's coding to blame? Or was the intent good while the technology itself fell short?

Technology for its own sake is irrelevant. Its constraints cannot be allowed to take precedence over how the real world operates. When a process or procedure needs to be adjusted because *that's not how the system works*, the team's priorities have fallen out of balance. It is therefore not the programming or implementation strategy of a particular application that leads to its failure, but its mistaken placement as the focal point of a business transformation effort.

Think about this last point for just a moment.

In Chapter 9, we will discuss the way in which the media covers the procurement industry, including the pitfalls surrounding the features, functions, and benefits analysis of technology provided by the majority of information sources. There are countless problems with this *technology first* approach to evaluating technology, both in the context of informing decision makers and in empowering the market to determine and reward the *right* or *best* solution. This has become particularly true since the advent of the software-as-a-service (SaaS) delivery model. Companies and their solution providers stay far more closely connected post-implementation today than they did in the times of implementations behind the firewall. This increases the importance of the people on both sides of the arrangement as well as their ability to work together in a prolonged fashion.

Although normal attrition is to be expected at any and all companies, the sudden or unexpected departure of a C-level executive at a solution provider underlines one of the challenges relating to this last point. Since leadership sets the tone as well as the priorities of the organization, their departures and arrivals have more of an impact on the company's direction, and therefore changes in their ranks serve as important signposts for anyone evaluating the company.

The following case example is based on a real-life story. As you read it, think about how the people behind the technology are more important in terms of your potential for achieving a successful outcome than the features of the solution itself. And by *outcome*, we are referring to the ability to effectively leverage technology to improve the procurement process so that you will be able to achieve your organization's objectives.

WARNING SIGNS

Baseball is a great game. In fact, it is America's pastime. Keeping this in mind, we would like to consider the story of one technology company and the dynamics of their executive team within the context of a batter coming up to the plate. As you will see, it is impossible to separate the offering from the overall leadership and stability of the company when evaluating them as a supply partner.

For those unfamiliar with the game of baseball, the batter gets an opportunity to hit the ball until they have three strikes against them. If they fail to make contact and get on base safely, they are out. The idea of a limitation on strikes, whether three or otherwise, is often applied in business and legal contexts as well as baseball. In 2002, Jerry Helzner, a long-time stock columnist for Barron's and former equity research professional, wrote an article titled "Look for 'Red Flags' on Stocks," which provides us with a clear calling on this at bat for the company in question. Of the four red flags he detailed in his post, the company in our story met the first three. And since every buyer-supplier relationship, including the ones procurement manages with their eProcurement solution providers, is truly an investment, we would be wise to heed Helzner's warnings.

Strike 1

"It's an especially bad sign when a company's chief financial officer (CFO) leaves suddenly. No one knows more about a company's financial condition than the CFO."[4]

Similar to when a chief executive officer (CEO) starts selling his or her shares, it is rarely a good sign when a CFO leaves a company on short notice and with little explanation. In what was characterized as an *abrupt departure*, a publicly held company announced that their CFO was leaving the position he had held for approximately five years. There was no reason given for the move, no information offered up about the now former CFO's plans moving forward, and no elaboration on the timing.

Strike 2

"It's true that insiders sell stock for a variety of reasons [...] but multiple insider sales of a single company's stock is one of the clearest warnings that things aren't going right. If the insiders are selling a stock, you should be getting out too."[5]

The CFO's appointed successor had previously been the head of the finance team at the company and stepped into the CFO role with expectations for a smooth transition. In what appeared to be one of his first moves as the top finance person at the company, he sold a number of shares for a total value of more than $35,000. Putting aside the questionable timing of facilitating such a transaction less than a week after assuming the CFO reigns, the sale of the shares by itself may not have been an issue. However, when considered alongside the additional revelation that the company's CEO had been selling his shares through what appeared to be a 10b5-1 plan, that should give current shareholders along with existing and prospective clients something to think about.

Strike 3

"All big companies get sued from time to time—it's part of the price of being big and having deep pockets. But when you see a number of similar lawsuits being filed against a company, it's a good time to exit that stock."[6]

When the news that the company was being sued for breach of contract by a U.S.-based nonprofit corporation came out, an important question was raised: was this a sign of a more pervasive problem? In the years before the CFO transition, the company had lost a number of high-profile clients across multiple sectors. Even with the implementations that were already in place, concerns were raised regarding the usability of their solution. When it was reported that another client had paid seven figures worth of licensing fees, but had never really used the company's application, questions regarding implementation difficulties were magnified.

It did not help that the company's CEO denied responsibility for the above problems, choosing instead to point the finger of blame at the clients themselves or explain away the negative results as a sales execution problem.

Despite an understandable desire on the part of the CEO to position the situation in as positive a light as possible, client lawsuits and failed initiatives provided unavoidable evidence that there might be a number of serious problems with the company's offering and operations.

If You Wouldn't Invest, Why Would You Buy?

While you will not likely read about the aforementioned developments in the features, functions, and benefits analysis of companies and their solutions that are so common in our industry, the information is nonetheless relevant to solution implementation decisions. The people behind the technology are the ones who ultimately determine a provider's ability to meet end-user requirements. At the very least, the executive team is responsible for keeping their company in business so they can continue to meet their contractual obligations to clients and employees. It is also the leadership who determines when, and even if, shareholders will ever realize the hoped for return on their investment. If executives and shareholders are more focused on covering themselves or deflecting blame than executing on a vision of technological excellence, there is little chance of anyone realizing value.

Given what becomes apparent when we look beyond the traditional coverage of a solution and examine the company behind the offering, would you invest in a company like the once referenced earlier? The decision to invest is not just limited to shareholders. It is also relevant for anyone who is considering becoming a client or an employee to ask themselves that question. If you wouldn't invest in a company, doesn't it stand to reason that you shouldn't buy anything foundational from it either? Although implementations are easier than they used to be, there is still an investment of time and effort required, not to mention a learning curve and change management effort both to and from. No one in procurement wants to tell their leadership team or stakeholders that they will be changing providers *again* because the selected one went out of business. Everything that contributes to the stability of an offering should be taken into account during the selection process and beyond, including both financial and management stability.

Given that, and although it makes complete sense to want a 360 degree view of every supplier, many times the coverage of solution providers only covers the 180 degrees of the analyst's view that addresses functionality directly. Even if the media and other concerned parties don't take notice of these developments and what they represent, executives at competing solution providers certainly do. The sudden departure of the aforementioned company's CFO generated an interesting reaction on social media. In particular, it received Twitter responses from senior executives at a competing company. The following exchange involving the competing company's vice president of strategy and market development and an industry blogger demonstrates how market interest has now extended beyond the confines of traditional industry coverage:

@blogger: What does the departure of the company CFO really mean to you?

@CompeteExec: @blogger interesting question

@blogger: Thanks ... I think it is in the often overlooked details where the true insights are found.

@CompeteExec: @blogger couldn't agree more ... you have to read between the lines

So why are we sharing this information with you in a chapter on technology? It is because a company's technology means very little if the people and management structures behind it are in a state of disruptive change. If a company and the technology it offers are in disarray, there is no chance that it will lead users to the benefits they so dearly need and have selected that company to help them achieve. This is especially true if the technology is (misguidedly) being relied upon as a catalyst for transformation rather than as a supporting factor.

In other words, you have to look at the team first, and *then* the technology. When we talk about technology we are really talking about people: the people behind the vision of a solution provider or vendor and the people within your own organization. For all of our talk of collaborative relationships and strategic partnerships, many procurement organizations have very low expectations for the interactions they will have with their own solution providers. Although there is nothing transactional about the nature of such a contract, decision makers often make the mistake of oversimplifying what is needed for success. When you consider the risks, opportunities, and needs in this broader context, there can be no question that technology is not about features, functions, and benefits: it is about people.

For example, and referring back to the question posed at the outset of this section, which of these would be more useful to you in terms of insight:

1. An assessment of the company's current technology, or
2. The true current and longer-term financial and managerial state of the company, particularly if it includes the unexpected departure of the CEO or CFO, senior executives selling shares, and/or active or pending client lawsuits.

It is our position that a myopic focus on *technology first* is the antithesis of truly leveraging automation to achieve desired procurement outcomes. The high rate of eProcurement initiative failures of the past offers sad proof of this assertion.

Before you continue reading the remainder of this chapter, we invite you to create a new mind-set for yourself relating to technology and procurement. In taking this approach, it is our hope that you, too, will view eProcurement solutions from the standpoint of how the world *should* work, as opposed to addressing how it *does* work.

KELLY'S PERSPECTIVE: *A Two-sided Look at the Role of People in Technology*

I've been very lucky to fill a number of roles within the procurement field—I was a practitioner; I was a consultant at a solution provider; and of course, now I combine the perspectives of both sides as a blogger. I had the opportunity (yes, I consider it an opportunity) to experience tough implementations as a practitioner and as a consultant with the same solution.

I was on the eSourcing evaluation and implementation team at a grocery retailer when we selected Emptoris (pre-cloud and before they were acquired by IBM). They were moving to a new version of their software just as we were scheduled to implement. We decided to roll out the new version rather than starting with the current version and upgrading at a later date. To make a long story short, there were some issues with the new release. When you combine that with the fact that we were implementing full eSourcing for the first time, what you end up with is a bit of a mess.

I can still remember, as clear as day, sitting in the Emptoris executive conference room with my project manager and most of the executive team at Emptoris to figure out what we were going to do. For the sake of simplicity, let's just say there was tension in the air. However, because everyone ultimately wanted the roll-out to be a success, each person in the room—starting with our project manager—offered up what he or she was going to do to improve the situation without deflection. Both sides owned their part of the problem and we moved forward. Although the challenge may have started with the technology, the people were the solution. If there had been a different combination of people in that room, I can easily see us having an outcome other than the successful one we reached.

After I joined Emptoris as a consultant, I had the opportunity to work on a number of projects—including implementations. I'm going to let you in on a little secret here: all implementations are tough for someone. There is always a change or adjustment that has to be made, and people don't typically embrace changes that they didn't decide to make on their own. This is true of every kind of technology ever invented. On at least one occasion, I found myself back in that same executive conference room, with the same tension in the air, only this time I was sitting on the Emptoris side of the table. I never forgot the lessons I had learned the first time I sat there. When problem statements were directed at *it*, meaning the technology, the solution was always to be found in *us* and *we*. I learned that ownership and cooperation were always to be prioritized over avoiding or assigning blame.

The focus on people versus technology needs to be cross-functional in order to be pervasive. It should be just as clear in the sales team as the executive and customer service teams. Some sales people preferred to close deals based on the technical details of the solution. Others often asked a member of the consulting or implementation teams to accompany them on sales calls—even when the final contract did not include a consulting statement of work. But those clever (wily) salespeople understood that just as people are always the solution, people are also a great way to close a deal. The ones who understood that, and the prospective customers who insisted upon meeting the team, recognized the importance of people in a technology decision long before the cloud forced everyone to think of the ongoing relationship between provider and user that way.

THE UBER EFFECT

As a result of these observations, procurement's new framework should be based on an assessment of the people at all stages of the collective technology relationship. This means that we will look at the innovators, the end users, and the end clients for input, vision, and direction.

When we talk about the innovators, we are really speaking about the technology architects: the individuals whose vision for a better way of procuring goods and services have led (and are leading) to the transformation of our industry. They push us to adopt new models and experiment with new capabilities in response to the business challenges they have observed. Who are these innovators and what characteristics must they and their companies possess in order to earn a high degree of confidence?

Before we can truly answer that question, we have to move beyond the *no one ever got fired for choosing IBM* mind-set that has dominated our profession for such a long time. It is important to point out that it is not just the procurement profession that has followed this edict. Equally risk-averse positions and perspectives exist within the finance and information technology (IT) worlds as well. This is yet another reason why Handfield's reference to the fact that "integration across the business is not the responsibility of a few but rather a challenge that must be embraced company-wide"[7] rings true in so many areas of focus.

Since procurement cannot control the behaviors or thought processes of other professionals in the enterprise, we must be willing to take a leading role—starting with changing our own way of thinking. If we do, then that long elusive seat at the executive table might actually become a reality, along with the even more meaningful and lasting achievement of true influence.

Before we delve into the Uber Effect, allow us to make one last point. The old adage about the relationship between the decision to select IBM and the risk to one's professional upside supports our position that client confidence is tied more to corporate or brand identity than the product actually being purchased. In this context, the brand or the company identity, both of which are inextricably linked to its people, actually transcend its technology. While this idea is not really new, what *is* new is applying it to the process for selecting technology partners in a way that allows us to realize a new kind of result. We must force ourselves to realize that no matter how good a brand is, each solution or offering must stand on its own merits and be subject to scrutiny. Any selection that we automatically conclude is good (without challenge) simply because it was generally accepted to be good in the past, will certainly lead us down the wrong path. Any contract we sign without evaluating both the company and their individual solutions is based on an unsound foundation.

Today, the potential for innovation and likelihood of success are not linked to the old standards of company size or length of time in business. For many—especially for the up-and-coming Generation Next—being an old, established company is more likely to be viewed as a potential weakness than a strength. Part of the reason for this thinking is that older, established firms are also viewed as being unduly entrenched. Even if they are not complacent, these behemoths are simply not as agile or responsive in the face of change as newer, younger, less-invested firms. Let's face it, *towers of gold* and *feet of clay* stability aren't exactly reflective of a fast moving, mobile world in which the majority of young professionals have never used a desktop or notebook. Many are more familiar with their mobile devices and bristle at the idea of being anchored to a desktop system. Their expectations about the technology they employ—both personally and professionally—is more closely linked to *procurement in 140 characters or less*, than to an unwieldy enterprise solution, no matter how *proven* the providing company is.

Some prognosticators have gone so far as to suggest that the mobile supply chain is likely to become the only supply chain in the not too distant future. "The computing power and internet access speed that's now in the palm of our hand, means we can deliver pioneering supply chain software solutions—via mobile computing—that are both cost-effective and feature-rich," Matthew Slinn, CEO and founder of SCM and EDI vendor Perceptant, told Enterprise Apps Today.[8] When one thinks of our profession within the framework of the providers of the past and looks at our track record for harnessing the potential of mobile devices and applications to date, none of the holdover solution dinosaurs come across as poster brands for this brave new hyper-connected world. This is where the Uber Effect comes into play.

Uber was founded in California in 2009 by Travis Kalanick and Garrett Camp. In June 2010, they released the Uber Mobile app which allows users to submit a trip request. Each request is then routed to a network of crowd-sourced drivers who can commit to pick up the passengers. The young company has raised tens of millions of dollars and is available in 58 countries and 300 cities worldwide. Uber is expected to earn $10 billion in revenue by the end of 2015.[9]

Looking beyond the growth and reach of the Uber application, it is easy to miss that the idea for Uber came about as the result of a human need, not innovative new technology seeking a profitable application. As Andrew Anthony wrote in *The Guardian Observer*, "Legend has it that he [Kalanick] discovered what he wanted to sell on a wintry night in Paris in 2008, when he and his Uber cofounder Garrett Camp couldn't find a cab."[10] Uber's story is an inspiring example of innovation but why is it relevant to a chapter on technology in a book about procurement?

The success, or at least the disruptive innovation, of the Uber story speaks directly to the need for our profession to stop using the same old methods for assessing technological capabilities. In too many cases we overemphasize the value we get from what we know, as opposed to embracing what is possible and what we may not yet fully understand. Looking to the same experts to provide the same advice within the same framework in order to generate different results is the very embodiment of the Einstein definition of insanity: "doing the same thing over and over again and expecting different results."[11]

If we expect technology to help us to achieve our objectives, we have to start looking as closely at the company and the people behind the company as we do the product it offers. This is not to say that we should ignore the product offering, or fail to test it to determine its viability for our organization. At the end of the day we still need to end up with a working solution that delivers against our objectives.

We need to redefine dependability and performance indicators by confirming whether or not the people behind the solution have their act together in terms of creative vision and commitment. Ironically, this is no more and no less than we do in every strategic sourcing initiative we run. We would never think of just collecting pricing and specifications from suppliers—we ask about financial stability, we inquire about pending litigation, and we collect all kinds of peripheral material on strategic vision and future potential. We also validate the information we receive from suppliers using third-party information sources. Why don't we do the same when allocating our own spend?

Returning to the example of the company referenced earlier in this chapter (see *Warning Signs?*): they may have a good solution—they obviously offer value because they have achieved a certain level of success in a field where others have not. That being said, if we ignore the aforementioned signs of a company that may be in trouble, or in which the leadership appears to be responding defensively to events and circumstances that are beyond the public view, we do so at our own risk. Because the company's technology—anybody's technology—cannot overcome poor execution in the medium to long term, no matter how good it may be. This is why procurement professionals need to look beyond the technology to see the real company picture and assess the potential for a viable partnership.

JON'S PERSPECTIVE: *Once You've Seen It All, There's No Going Back*

One of the great things about having been around since the days of mainframes, punch cards, and 8-inch floppies is that I have *seen it all* technology-wise.

While the years have not dampened my enthusiasm for technological advancement, they have given me a broader perspective than most people have. The reason is quite simple. I have adapted and actually utilized each new breakthrough product—in spite of the fact that the buttons have gotten much smaller as has the print on the small screens. Sharing a familiarity reminiscent of an old married couple, technology and I have been through a lot—the good days and the bad.

So what is the one piece of advice that I can give to you, whether you remember the good old days of CP/M or are of the brave new Uber generation? Well here it is—technology is irrelevant! Not what you expected to hear, is it? Especially in a chapter that is focused on technology. However, it is nonetheless true. From the early days of Visicalc spreadsheets, to the current *we got an app for that* mobile landscape, one thing has become irrefutably clear: technology will never overcome poor processes resulting from a lack of collaboration and cooperation. Technology, as it turns out, is not a magic bullet. It cannot transform a bad or questionable business practice into a good one—this requires people.

The greatest breakthroughs will not occur within the circuitry of the latest and greatest gadget or platform, but instead through the way in which we work—both individually and collectively. The real break-throughs as of late, and going forward, are more relational than tech-nological. When I say relational, what I am really talking about is the ability for organizations to communicate internally (and externally), in a transparent fashion that stimulates their desire to focus on a shared outcome or mutual benefit. In essence, technological prowess and suc-cess begins with people.

This is because technology, especially when it is misaligned with the targeted environment, renders itself irrelevant and ineffective. Misalign-ment occurs when there is a lack of open communication between stake-holders. In instances such as these, all technology ultimately achieves is to hasten the arrival of inevitable failure.

I have often referred to the growing realization that process, and not technology, is the main force behind successfully achieving results from efficiency and spend rationalization. Process understanding and refine-ment, when combined with the ability to adapt to how the real world operates on the front lines, allows credible targets to be established and ultimately met.

The Commonwealth of Virginia is one of the few enduring examples of the veracity of this latter point based on the success of their eVA (Virginia's eProcurement portal) initiative. When Bob Sievert, Director of the eProcurement Bureau for the Commonwealth of Virginia, con-tacted me via e-mail in the fall of 2007 to schedule a conference call, he indicated that Virginia had been *living with SaaS for eProcurement on a broad and deep scale*. When he emphasized that *few customers have taken the plunge* as far as they had, especially given the *complexities* of govern-ment procurement practices, I knew that there was a story to write.

As we all know, there are definite challenges in trying to address the diverse, and some would say competing, elements within a decentral-ized purchasing environment. This is especially true for public sector initiatives which, for the most part, are center-led monolithic under-takings that are largely driven by legislative control mechanisms versus independent departmental needs.

Virginia recognized this difference, and in doing so was able to understand that government is not just a *single business*, but is actually comprised of many different *lines of business*. Unfortunately, the majority of e-procurement initiatives are championed by senior-level managers who, while recognizing the potential of a technology-centric program, lack a firm understanding of operational challenges. As a result, they usually underestimate the impact of a proposed strategy at the department level.

Looking beyond the organizational chart, Virginia saw that government is comprised of higher education, K-12 education, corrections, public safety, transportation, health, social services, construction, etc. They really understood the *special needs, special rules, and special challenges* associated with the procurement practice of each entity—both individually and collectively. As a result, they prevented eVA from becoming just another software project. They were able to shift the emphasis from an exercise in cost justification, to one of process understanding and refinement. In the end, eVA's effectiveness had (and has) little to do with the technology and more to do with the methodology the Virginia brain trust employed. It is when technology (originally called software) is seen as the primary vehicle to drive results that it becomes ineffectual and mostly irrelevant.

The Virginia example helps us to realize two important things. The first is that there are still too few organizations that have reached the point of understanding the diverse requirements within their own organizational hierarchy. This is a communications or relational issue as opposed to one that is rooted in technology. The second is the emergence of cloud-based SaaS, eProcurement solutions and the impact they are having on the market. With the newer, more nimble technologies, both strengths and weaknesses in a process can be quickly recognized.

The problem is that while we can recognize issues faster, if we have not established a relational framework to ensure an open and effective dialogue, we will not be in a position to take the needed action. Knowing that an issue or benefit exists is not the same as being able to effectively leverage the insight to everyone's betterment, which brings us back full circle to my original point about technology being irrelevant.

PROACTIVE LEADERSHIP, NOT ABDICATION

Phil Fersht wrote the following in his February 22, 2014 *Horses for Sources* post titled "Are some 'independent' analysts the worst offenders of pay-to-play?": "There is only one opinion, at the end of the day, you can rely 100% on—your own. You'll hear all sorts of puff and bluster, observe all sorts of fancy grids and scatterplot charts, and you'll be able to pick up a lot of useful datapoints, especially with the plethora of free information available today. But the only opinion that ultimately matters is what you see with your own eyes—and hear from other customers who've experienced the products and services."[12]

Fersht is insightful and on the money. Fortunately, he is not alone in his belief that the client is ultimately the one who must take ownership for the success or failure of an implemented procurement solution.

During a Blog Talk Radio interview in October 2013, Joe Payne and Bill Dorn from Source One Management Services offered their insight on the end user or client mind-set with regard to analyst advice and the role it plays in decision making. As Dorn said in the interview, "The people in many cases are more at fault for not really challenging what they find in that report or reading that report and saying, 'okay this customer was evaluated in the lower left-hand quadrant, but the three things that they were dinged on are all things that are not important to my business so they might have been a good provider for my business.' So from that side there is a disconnect where people have an over-reliance on those reports."[13] In other words, the end user or client must bear some responsibility for the historic failings that continue to plague the industry. After all, beyond the challenges of having limited resources, Payne and Dorn suggested that clients either do not know the right questions to ask or are just not willing to pose the questions they have. Instead they appear to choose to blindly follow the lead of analysts and bloggers whose interests may be influenced by the very companies about whom they are supposed to be providing objective and meaningful coverage.

What is even more telling about the previous comment is that it came from the vendor perspective—Source One is a procurement service provider that offers outsourcing, market research, and strategic sourcing services that may be used by procurement organizations or in their stead. Fersht, Payne, and Dorn have come to an important realization that must be acknowledged and addressed by the rest of the profession if procurement ever hopes to be taken seriously. Procurement has a tendency to abdicate their due diligence responsibilities when it comes to technology, either by choice, laziness, or a true lack of knowledge. Expectations have reached the point where pointing to analyst reports should not suffice as the defense for a poorly selected technology.

For whatever reason, there is an inexplicable willingness to *follow the leader*—any leader—be it an analyst or a blogger, without personally going through the necessary cycles to qualify a technology-based procurement solution. Part of the problem is generational, meaning that in the past, procurement's requirements for automation were most often an afterthought in a major ERP implementation.

In the past, these efforts were driven by finance, IT, or an uneasy alliance between the two. Purchasing was rarely (if ever) consulted until after a decision regarding the selection of a solution was made. At that point, they were *advised* that any functionality required would have to be submitted to the implementation team and would be addressed on a prioritized basis. In plain English, this meant that procurement's needs were usually not considered until after all of the *real* requirements of the company had been satisfied.

Of course ERP implementations were not like today's SaaS-based cloud solutions, which can be implemented in a matter of weeks or even days at a fraction of the cost and complexity. Back then, implementing an ERP solution usually spanned several years and cost millions, if not tens of millions, of dollars. It did not help that these implementations were so complex that even vendors such as Hewlett-Packard (HP) had trouble implementing ERP solutions for their own business.

Regarding HP, a 2008 CATA Alliance white paper titled "SAP Procurement for Public Sector" cites HP as an example of a company trying to sell its services to deliver something it could not successfully execute in-house. As they stated at the time, HP's failed SAP rollout was noteworthy, "And not just because of the apparent size and resources of the companies in question. Although the HP case study should be somewhat disconcerting given that organization's level of sophistication and supposed expertise as an SAP integrator."[14]

As RedMonk analyst James Governor put it, "What better case study in proving your R/3 and Netweaver capability than a good old dog food eating session–show everyone how to merge two SAP systems and they will come to you the next time they make a merger or acquisition and want to do the same thing."[15] The problem is, while HP was trying to demonstrate that they could rival IBM's application management capabilities, they were falling short in their own efforts in such a way that the CEO was forced to acknowledge it publicly. Governor concluded by saying, "Who would go to HP now for a large-scale SAP integration? The CEO just publicly said HP can't effectively manage such a project."

If purported (and self-declared) implementation experts such as HP could not do the job, you can certainly understand purchasing's reluctance to step out on a limb to take the lead in recommending a solution based on its perception of what was required to automate the process, especially when their opinions were not deemed worthy of consideration during the selection process.

Fortunately, times have changed considerably. Today, ERP complexity has been replaced by cloud-based solutions with streamlined supplier on-boarding capabilities and an intuitive end-to-end P2P process designed to meet the expectations of mobile-enabled, seasoned Internet shoppers. Mainframes and vast networks of desktop computers have been replaced by mobile devices offering more power, greater speed, and even greater convenience. The days of the overarching ERP initiative have been relegated to the scrap heap of unfulfilled expectations and unrealized savings.

Despite this revolutionary transformation in technology, many procurement professionals still have a *run for cover* survivalist response when the subject of automating the procurement process is raised. After all, it is better to say nothing and simply follow orders than risk making a mistake in which the potential payoff does not justify owning the associated uncertainty. As the professionals who are often brought in to select and implement solutions used by other parts of the enterprise, procurement finds ourselves in much the same place as HP did—not wanting to admit that we were unable to do for ourselves what we professed to be able to do for others.

The persisting reality of this thinking was demonstrated in a series of discussions about procurement technology with a vice president of procurement from a major U.S.-based energy company. During one of these discussions, the vice president was asked about his thoughts regarding the potential for implementing a new cloud-based eProcurement system that would likely save the company considerable sums of money.

While the vice president acknowledged that the new system looked good, and that he was certain it would deliver on its promises, he also indicated his intent to promote it internally from behind the scenes. In other words, he would not openly or officially endorse the new technology, but would do all he could to encourage its adoption from a position of safe anonymity.

The obvious follow-up question to his remarks was to find out whether he thought that his staying in the shadows was the best way to accomplish the goal of having this system adopted by the company. His answer still reverberates in the memory of those who heard him reply: "No, I do not believe that this is the best way to go about it." He then went on to explain that his reason for taking a discrete route was that he planned to retire in a few years and if the system had failed to deliver on its promise by then, it would negatively impact his legacy. Even if the system performed as anticipated and met or exceeded all expectations, he would not be around long enough to enjoy the benefits of being its champion. In short, there was no upside for him if he were to take on the additional risk of advocating for the solution, but there *was* the potential for downside.

This was not a buyer or a middle manager, but the vice president of procurement for a large, publicly traded corporation; in other words, someone in a *leadership* position with a great deal of influence. If he was unwilling to take a risk from the lofty heights of the executive suite to lead his department and his company in what he believed was the right direction, how could anyone expect someone on the front lines to step up to the plate? His decision to put personal risk before corporate potential serves as further evidence of the fact that regardless of how good the technology is, the people involved matter more. Although we do not know this for certain, it seems reasonable to assume that this same vice president also made *safe* choices in other areas—such as hiring, strategic planning, or conflict resolution.

There are plenty of other people in leadership positions who exhibit this same mind-set. However, the above example is the best one we know that captures the limiting effect of not taking personal responsibility for vetting and enabling a successful implementation. In reality, playing it safe with new technology is akin to working against it from the outset. As we discussed in our chapter on collaboration, there are all kinds of communication—verbal, written, and *body language*. By working to advance the implementation cautiously, the vice president communicated his lack of confidence in the outcome. It would have been different if this was, in fact, the most politically expedient way to collect the necessary approvals, but he made the decision to take this approach in order to protect himself. His hesitation likely cost the company more than the risk of any failure might have.

The trouble is that while technology has changed significantly, old habits and conditioning have stayed deeply entrenched in the procurement psyche. Perhaps this is why Handfield talked about a definite and definitive chasm between the purchasing people of the past and today's Generation Next procurement professionals. It is also the reason why Kate Vitasek emphasized the point that advances in the profession relative to increased credibility would not occur until *all of the dinosaurs have died off*—i.e., left the profession. While the leaders of the past associate new technology implementations with risk based on what they have experienced, young professionals assume or take for granted that the newest thing is actually *the best* just for the sake of being the latest. They would likely need a reason to hold back rather than a reason to proceed forward.

When the safety, but stagnation, of the past has finally ceded way to the bold future, then and only then will procurement as a profession step up and take the reins of technological promise to the next level.

THE CLOUD AS THE GREAT COMMODITIZER

If technology and the evaluation of technology are more about people than solutions, how are companies supposed to make decisions about which solution is right for them? Part of what should be weighed is cultural fit; how well do your organization and the provider's organizations mesh? Solutions still have to be evaluated, but this too has changed over time. The advent of the cloud and SaaS delivery models has made it much easier to not only implement solutions, but also to change from one solution to another. Selecting a technology partner no longer has to be a relationship for life. As technology continues to change, so too do the mechanisms to transition between platforms.

As technological approaches of capabilities mature, they go through a number of standard phases. Each phase has an effect on the revenue potential associated with that technology. Some phases justify a premium with a select number of customers while others increase revenue through scalability due to a rapid increase in the number of users. Chris Anderson, former Editor in Chief at *Wired* magazine, has a theory on technological maturation that he calls his *grand unified theory of predicting the future*. As described by the TEDxClassroom Project, "This theory is based on the belief that every single technology product at least goes through one of four stages throughout its life span."[16] The four stages of technology are shown in Figure 7.1.

- The first stage of technological growth is critical price—this is where an idea catches on and becomes affordable for the average company (or an individual, in the case of B2C technology) through scalability.
- The second stage represents the achievement of critical mass, as the number of users skyrockets in response to the affordability of the solution and therefore, the improved return on investment.
- In the third stage, a technology replaces or encompasses other existing technologies. In the case of procurement technology, you

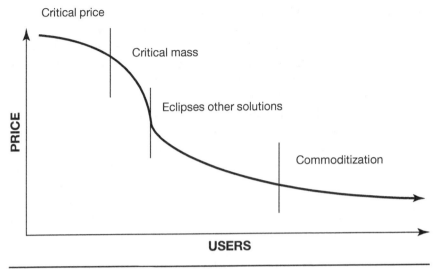

Figure 7.1 The four stages of technology

might say the third stage is when we start to rely upon an eSourcing solution's collaboration functionality rather than using e-mail or Excel to collaborate and exchange details with suppliers. It is interesting to note that this transition has less to do with affordability or scalability than usability. As the cost comes down and more users are able to adopt it, their collective feedback improves the capabilities of the solution and allows it to eclipse other in-use solutions.

- In the fourth and final stage, the technology becomes a commodity, where all solutions are effectively the same and the technology itself plays a much smaller part in why you choose to work with a provider than their capabilities in other areas such as proprietary data enrichment, knowledgeable staff, cultural fit, integration capabilities, or experience with an important category of spend.

In a video produced in response to Procurious' Big Ideas 2015 open call, Market Dojo addressed procurement technology commoditization.[17] In their big idea response video, they explain that most procurement solution providers are in either stage two, where the number of users is increasing but the solution is not yet infringing upon alternatives, or stage three, where the number of users is relatively stable, but the use of the solution is expanding into complementary areas.

From a practitioner or user's standpoint, Market Dojo is right in that most procurement technology is in the second or third stage of maturation. When you look at the market in isolation, however, and just consider the solutions themselves, we have already seen a significant amount of commoditization. It is no longer regarded as misguided or high risk to work with one of the smaller providers in the procurement space. The cloud has made proven backbone and security options available to companies regardless of how large they are.

Gigaom writer Katie Ferenbacher wrote about the leveling force of new hosting and delivery models in 2013: "One point of pressure is that the costs of the underlying technologies have dropped dramatically—much of these technologies are now commodities that lean startups (or really anyone) can buy with a bit of funding and a solid business plan."[18] While this relieves one pressure for solution providers—the need to differentiate on their underlying technology—it creates another in that they have to find a new way to differentiate.

They can set themselves apart with better visual design, a skilled in-house team of consultants, or the accessory-type functionality or connectivity they choose to roll in. Whatever path they choose, they differentiate in an area that saves them from commoditization. When you segment the capabilities of an end-to-end procurement solution, it becomes possible to consider how commoditized each area of functionality is. For instance, basic RFx functionality has been a commodity for a long time, while optimization still provides an opportunity for a solution to distinguish itself. This does not mean that optimization is immune to commoditization. It provides us with a view to the connection between longevity, adoption, and maturity. Optimization is not as easy to adopt and therefore is not as mature from a technology evolution perspective, or at least, not yet.

This variance in maturity and competitive advantage becomes challenging for procurement in the selection of a procurement solution, requiring yet another mind-set shift. We are so accustomed to focusing on technical features and functionality—hence our reliance on industry analysts up to this point—when trying to match a solution to our needs. When the decision will be made more on subjective capabilities than specifications, many of us may stumble or at least feel uncomfortable with the new process. But since the decision needs to be made, procurement needs to make sure we don't drop the process and allow it to fail, or to fall into the laps of the IT folks lurking nearby.

CHICKENS ARE INVOLVED, PIGS ARE COMMITTED

Some reading this book may remember Phil Donahue. He was the quintessential daytime talk show host before Oprah. For our Generation Next readers: he was the Zach Galifianakis (Between Two Ferns) of the late 1960s through the mid-1990s. During one of his segments, he was interviewing a guest about achieving success and what was required to accomplish all that he had, up to that point in time. The guest responded by referencing the business fable about the chicken and the pig. As the story goes, in the making of a hearty fresh breakfast, the chickens are involved, but the pigs are committed. When you are sitting down the next time to have breakfast, look at your plate and think about this for a moment.

If you look at your plate, you will see that the pig provides the ham. In accomplishing this task, the pig is required to sacrifice everything to be part of the breakfast meal—there is no going back for the pig. The chicken sacrifices very little, especially in comparison to the pig. The chicken is therefore involved and important, but is not nearly as committed as the pig. We use this analogy because it represents the range of engagement levels stakeholders bring to the procurement relationship relative to automation.

For example, suppliers can make or break an eProcurement initiative. But are they pigs or chickens? A story from a vice president at a major U.S.-based consumer packaged goods (CPG) company may provide us with an answer. After going through the time and expense required to implement an eSourcing solution, not a single supplier responded to the first RFx run by the company. The whole project was eventually scrapped for lack of return on investment. The company put too much reliance on the technology to create the change they wished to see in their supplier interactions. Rather than jumping in *whole hog* and *bringing home the bacon*, they were *chicken*, and their lack of commitment prevented an effort with significant potential from generating any results. (Our heartfelt apologies for the puns.)

Even in those instances when suppliers do utilize a buying company's technology, the quality and price of the end product that is offered to the consumer is equally affected by the quality of the relationship between the buyer and their suppliers. One of the industries where this has been consistently tracked, measured, and analyzed is in auto manufacturing. The Annual Automotive Original Equipment Manufacturer (OEM)-Supplier Relations Study tracks automakers' working relations with their suppliers. It is closely watched by the leadership teams at those manufacturers because, "an OEM's supplier relations rating can be directly correlated to its profitability and competitiveness—including which OEM customer is first to see a supplier's newest technology and gets their best pricing. ... Over the years, the study has shown convincingly that automakers with Good-Very Good working relations realize considerable benefits."[19] Those companies without good supplier relationships, or whose relationships lag behind their competitors, lose out on market-leading pricing, supplier support, and early opportunities to be involved in innovation.

As a result of findings such as these, there has been a steadily increasing focus on ways to leverage technology to address the supplier concerns that lead to those poor relationships, such as slow invoice payment. A far cry from when procurement was only asked about their technology requirements as a secondary afterthought, supplier requirements and interests are represented front and center in the selection process—or at least they should be. In today's business world, technology—and to be more specific eProcurement solutions—must be able to meet stakeholder needs that originate both inside and outside of the buying organization.

However, and unlike in years past when the electronic data interchange (EDI) limited such real-time interaction to a few hundred companies, today's technology provides a *love all, serve all* capability that has removed the traditional barriers of engagement associated with enterprise solutions. What this ultimately means is that there are no longer limitations in terms of being able to connect and collaborate in real time, at least based upon the technology. The companies and people on both sides of the technology need to be prepared to take advantage of its capabilities. The big question, therefore, is no longer how we can communicate with our suppliers as well as other key stakeholders, but if we will do what is required to communicate with them to the full extent made possible by today's technology. We must be willing to give the effort our full commitment, even if it means investing everything.

There is a world of difference between the old and new ways of technological integration in that the latter is based on not only an ability to collaborate, but a desire and willingness to collaborate. The investment of time and effort may be significant. As we saw with the CPG CPO's eSourcing failure, the technology does not bring about a solution. It exists as a platform where people can serve as the real change agents. This is, after all, more than an exchange of information and data. It is an exchange based on mutual benefit and shared effort, things that technology will never replace.

Like so many of the other crossroads described in this book, we must move away from the adversarial mind-set that has dominated the buyer-supplier relationships of the past. Far from the early ERP implementations where finance and IT might throw purchasing a bone near the end of the process, supplier requirements for the technology need to be as represented in the decision-making process as anyone else's. It is the communication and collaboration that take place in technology between buyer and supplier that ultimately create value. It is the quality of those exchanges that determines whether the technology will be associated with success, not its functionality.

This means that seemingly unrelated topics, such as how well we negotiate with suppliers, become critical success factors in evaluating technology performance. If the relationship being automated via technology is faulty or unhealthy, the results will be subpar as well. In a 2010 *Commitment Matters* blog post, International Association for Contract and Commerical Management CEO Tim Cummins pulled findings from "A Conspiracy of Optimism," a paper by the International Center for Complex Project Management to illustrate the connections between mind-set, behavior, relationships, and performance. "For example, in its recent paper 'A Conspiracy of Optimism', the International Center for Complex Project Management identified the 'conspiracy' that leads executives on both sides of the table to 'lie' to their trading partners and to create a combined version of 'the truth' that leads to mutual delusion over what they can achieve, by when, and for how much. Indeed, how truthful are any of us when we are seeking to impress someone with whom we want a deal or a relationship?"[20]

So what does this have to do with technology? Everything! Based on our premise that people—not technology—are the true basis for results, a relationship or contract based on lies is like a strategy based on faulty technology and without a clear and present leader. It cannot hope to stand the test of time.

CONCLUSION

There is an old saying that goes *garbage in—garbage out!* and it perfectly sums up the disconnect between being able to communicate through technological advances and actually communicating. This is the reason why we chose to focus on the people side of the potential offered by technology. It is also the reason why the principle behind the Uber Effect, or emphasizing the need to design processes and solutions for how the world should work as opposed to optimizing for how the world does work, is so important.

The changes that procurement needs to make in order to achieve our full potential require increased complexity of vision, approach, and understanding. This is why even a chapter about technology is not really about technology. It is about the organizational health of the parties involved—whether they are solution providers, suppliers, or procurement professionals. The technology is just a conduit for interactions that must stem from properly minded people.

Far too many people consider technology through the optimization lens and then wonder why procurement as a profession has not progressed as much as it should have in terms of its recognized strategic importance to an enterprise's bottom line. It is only when we realize that the changes in mind-set are the determining factor for advancement as opposed to technological breakthroughs, that we will achieve a true symmetry between technology and our profession.

REFERENCES

1. Aaron Levie, Twitter post, August 23, 2013, 1:16 a.m., https://twitter.com/levie.
2. Eran Livneh, "What is the Internet of Things and what does it mean to the P2P world," *Nipendo*, April 22, 2014, http://www.nipendo.com/blog/what-is-the-internet-of-things-and-what-does-it-mean-to-the-p2p-world/.
3. Nilesh Gopali, "Building for the way the world should work and the Indian P2P economy," *CloudBuy*, June 11, 2015, https://cloudbuyblog.wordpress.com/2015/06/11/building-for-the-way-the-world-should-work-and-the-indian-p2p-economy/.
4. Jerry Helzner, "Look for 'Red Flags' on Stocks," *Optometric Management*, 1 July, 2002, http://www.optometricmanagement.com/articleviewer.aspx?articleID=70498.
5. Ibid.
6. Ibid.
7. Gerard Chick and Robert Handfield, *The Procurement Value Proposition: The Rise of Supply Management*, (Kogan Page: Philadelphia, 2015), xii.

8. Herman Mehling, "Business Intelligence and Mobile Devices Will Change Supply Chain Management," *Enterprise Apps Today*, June 29, 2011, http://www.enterpriseappstoday.com/supply-chain-man agement/mobile-business-intelligence-supply-chain-management .html.

9. Alyson Shontell, "Uber Is Generating A Staggering Amount Of Revenue," *Business Insider*, November 15, 2014, http://www .businessinsider.com/uber-revenue-projection-in-2015-2014-11.

10. Andrew Anthony, "Travis Kalanick: Uber-capitalist who wants to have the world in the back of his cabs," *The Guardian Observer*, December 20, 2014, http://www.theguardian.com/theobserver/ 2014/dec/21/travis-kalanick-uber-cab-app-observer-profile.

11. "Quotation #26032 taken from Michael Moncur's (Cynical) Quo- tations," *Quotations Page*, Accessed July 16, 2015, http://www .quotationspage.com/quote/26032.html.

12. Phil Fersht, "Are some 'independent' analysts the worst offenders of pay-to-play?" *Horses for Sources*, February 22, 2014, http://www .horsesforsources.com/independents-worst-offenders_022214?utm _source=dlvr.it&utm_medium=twitter&utm_campaign=Feed%3A +HorsesForSources+%28Horses+for+Sources%29.

13. "The End of Procurement Industry Analysts & Bloggers?" narrated by Jon Hansen, PI Window on Business, *Blog Talk Radio*, October 8, 2013, http://www.blogtalkradio.com/jon-hansen/2013/10/08/ the-end-of-procurement-industry-analysts-blogger.

14. "SAP Procurement for Public Sector," *CATA Alliance 2008*, Accessed July 1, 2015, http://www.slideshare.net/piblogger/sap-a-propensity -for-failure.

15. James Governor, "Adaptive Differencing? HP and Partner Synchronization," *Redmonk*, August 17, 2004, http://redmonk.com/ jgovernor/2004/08/17/adaptive-differencing-hp-and-partner -synchronization/.

16. Andrew R. "Chris Anderson: Tech's Long Tail," *The TEDxClassroom Project*, April 11, 2010, https://tedxproject.wordpress.com/2010/ 04/11/chris-anderson-techs-long-tail/.

17. Market Dojo, "Market Dojo's Big Idea for Procurious Big Ideas Summit 2015," *YouTube* video, 1:13, May 1, 2015, https://www .youtube.com/watch?v=p5FOaj-DDcg.

18. Katie Ferenbacher, "As the underlying tech becomes a commodity, design emerges as the answer," *Gigaom*, October 17, 2013, https://

gigaom.com/2013/10/17/as-the-underlying-tech-becomes-a
-commodity-design-emerges-as-the-answer/.

19. "2014 Annual Automotive OEM-Supplier Relations Study Shows
Toyota and Honda on top; Nissan displacing Ford in the middle;
Chrysler and GM falling behind," *PR Newswire*, May 12, 2014, http://
www.prnewswire.com/news-releases/2014-annual-automotive
-oem-supplier-relations-study-shows-toyota-and-honda-on-top
-nissan-displacing-ford-in-the-middle-chrysler-and-gm-falling
-behind-258885661.html.

20. Tim Cummins, "The Power Of Negotiation," *Commitment Matters*,
September 1, 2010, http://commitmentmatters.com/2010/09/01/
the-power-of-negotiation/.

This book has free material available for download from the
Web Added Value™ resource center at *www.jrosspub.com*

8

Are the Differences Between the Public and Private Sectors Real or Perceived?

Each side of the divide has strengths and weaknesses, but in every case the public sector is providing something the private sector cannot: A backup that's there if and when you need it; a benchmark for private providers; and a backstop to make sure costs don't spin out of control. "When Government Competes Against the Private Sector, Everybody Wins," Eric Schnurer[1]

Many years ago, during a seminar for one of the purchasing associations, the following question was posed to the audience: when it comes to procurement, what is the difference between the public sector and the private sector? Within seconds a Fortune 500 vice president's hand shot up and without missing a beat, she said, "When we screw up in the private sector, we are not likely to find ourselves on the front page of the local newspaper." Everyone nodded. And while it is hard to argue with that kind of self-assured logic, everyone who has spent time in the private sector knows we are all just one paycheck from the unemployment line. Pick your poison, as it were.

Anyone that follows their local or national news is likely to have come across more than one story that provides *obvious proof* of outrageous waste and disregard for taxpayer money by the public sector. Stories of million-dollar toilet seats and research into the effects of Swedish massage on rabbits skew our perspective and minimize our trust in government agencies. Unfortunately for public sector procurement, all of this negative press has done serious damage to their reputation within the professional community as well.

PUBLIC SECTOR BAD, PRIVATE SECTOR GOOD?

It would be easy to conclude that public sector procurement is awash in a sea of incompetence, where its professionals are hapless participants in a cumbersome system ill-equipped to deliver the desired outcomes and unconcerned by its own failings. In fact, since most people only have contact with public sector procurement in exposés of willful or unwitting wrongdoing, the assumption is planted early on that public sector procurement is a total joke.

In 2010, DTZ, a global provider of property services, conducted research into perceptions of public sector procurement on the part of developers, contractors, and service providers. The results, shown in Figure 8.1, illustrate a clearly negative skew against the public sector. All of the respondents are presumably members of the private sector themselves, and had frequent contact with the government in the course of doing their business. One important point about the research is that it follows a concerted effort on the part of the UK government to incorporate more private sector approaches and individuals. As explained in the research, "In recent years a series of government appointees have called for more professional and commercial procurement people and processes in order to achieve better value for money for the public purse."[2] However, "Recent advances in public sector procurement processes may be doing more harm than good."[3]

Conversely, the private sector has traditionally been seen (at least by outsiders) as being the epitome of excellence, and this benefit of the doubt extends to private sector procurement. Staffed by deep benches, private sector procurement professionals are believed to be on the leading edge of operational efficiency. Just as many people assume that public sector procurement is flawed, they assume that private sector procurement is highly qualified and strategic.

Of course, you know the old saying about what happens when you assume; you make an *ass* out of *u* and *me*. When we first put pen to paper (or keypad to screen) to write about the differences between public

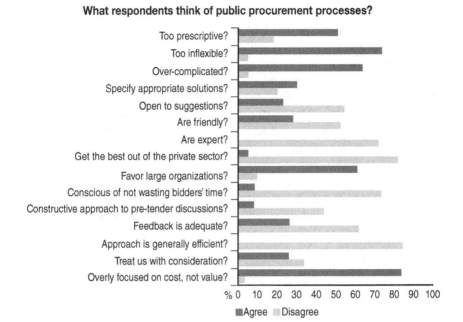

Figure 8.1   What respondents think of public procurement processes (*Source*: DTZ.com)

sector procurement and private sector procurement, our own ideas were based on many of the same assumptions that trip up others. The preconception is hard to avoid, since there is no shortage of research and case studies that support the common perception that public sector procurement is less proficient than its private sector counterpart. A logical extension of the notion that the private sector is skilled and the public sector is flawed is the belief that public sector practice should be transformed to emulate the private sector way of doing things.

For example, in 1995, Dr. Ronald D. Utt, the Herbert and Joyce Morgan Senior Research Fellow of the Thomas A. Rowe Institute for Economic Policy Studies at the Heritage Foundation in Washington D.C., wrote a post titled, "Privatize the General Services Administration Through an Employee Buyout." In it, he explained not only why the General Services Administration (GSA) was ripe for privatization, but also the many benefits that would result from the transition. Dr. Utt noted that "Its many services are available from the private sector, whose more successful firms offer a blueprint for how a privatized GSA could survive and thrive in a competitive environment."[4] He did not base his recommendations solely on the belief that the private sector *way* was preferable to the public sector's historic approach. Dr. Utt went on to write that "besides saving a considerable sum for the taxpayer, privatization of the GSA could become a model for many of the other privatizations lawmakers and Administration officials say they intend to pursue."[5] In other words, it is not just procurement that would be better handled through private sector methodology, but a wide range of public sector functions.

A prime example of the challenges that remain even after privatization is the U.S. Postal Service. The USPS is a quasi-private (or semi-independent) agency. While it is a part of the government, and its employees are in the civil service, it does not rely upon taxpayer subsidies. In some ways they have to deal with the worst of both worlds. While they do not receive funding from the government, they also can't refuse to perform services that hurt the bottom line, such as delivering mail to Alaska or Hawaii. They can't even make major decision about their own operating model, such as ending Saturday delivery, without approval from Congress.

If Dr. Utt's proposal was to have a chance of success, the privatization of the GSA would need to be complete, not quasi or semi. In the end, Dr. Utt's recommendations were not acted upon at all. Twelve years later, the GSA had seen little improvement in many of the challenging areas pointed out in Dr. Utt's original article. A 2007 *Procurement Insights* post, based on the recommendations, made the point that bureaucracy and inefficiency are responses to the negative coverage of public sector procurement as much as they are the causes of it. "Many within the public sector ranks point to the 'media's exploitation of past anecdotes of alleged incompetent buying,' such as the U.S. Department of Defense paying $436 for a hammer, that it is often behind the seemingly pervasive bureaucratic fear of ending up on the front page of the local newspaper. Some even perceive this to be one of the key drivers of public sector procurement policy."[6] If this is the case, private sector professionals and processes would likely suffer from the same apparent inefficiencies once they found themselves under equally intense scrutiny.

In 1991, Christopher Hood, a British expert on executive government, regulation, and public-sector reform, published the now wellknown paper "A Public Management for All Seasons?" in which he discussed the New Public Management method, or NPM. As he stated near the end of the paper, "NPM can be understood as primarily an expression of sigma-type values. Its claims have lain mainly in the direction of cutting costs and doing more for less as a result of better-quality management and different structural design."[7]

The NPM *philosophy* has been viewed as the vehicle for "redefining managerial and governance practices in the public sector," so that said practices would be more "in line with objectives typical of market economies."[8] Proponents of the belief that the private sector had somehow figured it all out also contend that the NPM ideology in which efficiency, accountability, decentralization, and marketization are the main components or drivers, is the answer to public sector procurement inefficiency.[9]

In an October 2014 International Association for Contract and Commercial Management article titled, "If you want to make a private sector approach work for public procurement—start small," a detailed step-by-step process outlined an alternate approach to both the Dr. Utt employee buyout plan and a wholesale adoption of the NPM model. This most recent article looked at the public-private debate from the standpoint of leveraging just a few of the successful elements from a private practice, as opposed to the wholesale changes related to privatization and NPM adoption. It noted two huge differences between public and private procurement that have largely been overlooked:

1. "Governments need to do more than just make savings. They need to leverage their purchasing power to drive regional economic benefit and innovation. They also have an overriding need to ensure the request for proposal (RFP) process is deemed fair.
2. "The private sector's main objective is simply to use the best methods possible to get the desired outcome.

"These differences must be recognized and a true symmetry of purpose or intent established before a private sector approach can be viable in the public sector."[10]

Given all of these approaches to migrating some or all of the private sector's methods to the public sector, you would think the material superiority of the one over the other had been conclusively proven. That, however, remains a question for study and debate.

THE COPPERFIELD EFFECT

There are two moving pieces in the relative superiority question that we have to consider. One is the apparent mediocrity of the public sector, and the other is the apparent proficiency of the private sector. In a way, while we seem to be bombarded with examples of how awful the public sector is, we should expect to see more examples of how advanced the private sector is. We falsely assume that news of good and bad performances reach us equally regardless of sector.

In Simon Horton's book *Negotiation Mastery: Tools for the 21st Century Negotiator,* he tells the story of *evil dolphins* and survivorship bias. The basic idea is that because all of the stories we hear about dolphins are good—such as when they save swimmers or lead lost boaters to shore a la *Flipper*—we deduce that dolphins are always nice. We use the information available to us to make what seems like a logical judgment call. The problem with this is that we don't know that we have all of the information or even a representative sampling. As Horton states in the book, "We do not know any stories of evil dolphins forcing swimmers away from the shore because we simply would not hear of them, the victim would not be able to tell us. This is known as the Survivorship Bias. We make our judgments purely on the evidence of the winners or survivors, ignoring those that were not so successful."[11] For the most part, we only hear the stories of public sector failure, so we assume they are bad. We don't really hear any stories about private sector procurement, so we assume they are not having those same problems.

We have spent the better part of this book examining the challenges procurement faces, and in most cases when we talk about procurement, we are speaking of the private sector. The fact of the matter is, if private sector procurement were as proficient as we appear to be when contrasted with the public sector, we would not have needed to write this book. Similar to the amazing work of illusionist David Copperfield, reports of private sector superiority are more of an illusion than a reality. In fact they are not reports at all, but rather a lack of coverage of private sector failures—a *no news is good news* philosophy. In reality, the stories are there, you just have to know where to look. For every public sector embarrassment, it is possible to find one or more anecdotes from the private sector that are equally shameful or scandalous.

A Case in Point: The Fleecing of the DoD

Back in the 2007 *Procurement Insights* post "CNN drops the ball with $1 million DoD washer purchase story,"[12] reference was made to the historic tendency on the part of the press to sensationalize stories about purchasing inefficiencies at the U.S. Department of Defense (DoD). In this case, the example was how the U.S. paid $1 million to ship two $0.19 cent washers.

A flawed system designed to rush supplies to troops in Iraq and Afghanistan let a small-parts supplier improperly collect huge shipping fees for two washers. The supplier, South Carolina-based C&D Distributors, charged 38 cents for two washers and then it charged and collected almost $1 million to ship them. It is only natural that a story of such egregious waste should make the news. Yet, in the coverage on August 16 and 17, 2007, on CNN, the reporting included only a thinly veiled acknowledgment that public sector procurement was *at it again.*

In CNN's first mention of the story, there is no suggestion of wrongdoing by the supplier; there is no mention of fraud, just discoordination on the part of the government. "The Pentagon says it accidentally paid a small parts supplier almost $1 million to ship two 19-cent washers. It blames a flawed system designed to rush supplies to troops in Iraq and Afghanistan. It says loopholes letting the mistake happen have been closed and the money has been returned."[13] Silly Pentagon, everyone knows it doesn't cost a million dollars to ship less than a dollar's worth of merchandise! You could probably ship two washers to the moon for less than a million dollars.

On their second day of covering the story, CNN introduced the fraud element. "Defense contractor C & D Distributors pleaded guilty to bilking the Pentagon out of $20 million over nearly 10 years. Now, the Defense Department blamed a flawed system designed to rush supplies to troops to Iraq. And that system allowed the smart parts supplier to charge millions in shipping costs."[14] Adding in that missing detail certainly increases the fairness of their coverage. Now we can see it wasn't just the silly Pentagon and their broken system, there was also a nefarious supplier involved. But they weren't done with their coverage. CNN couldn't resist tacking on a final reminder of who was really to blame, "And they were paid."[15] In other words, the system was broken, and the supplier was bad—but the DoD missed the opportunity to catch the fraud internally before the funds were dispatched for the fraudulent invoices. All this is true enough, but since we only hear similar tales of fraud in the private sector when criminal charges are filed, the impression given is that only the public sector could mess their procurement processes up so badly.

The main issue with CNN's coverage was that they failed to mention C & D's wrongdoing was part of a fraud investigation that went back to September 2006 and that the perpetrators were prosecuted. As Reuters news service more thoroughly reported on August 17, "Loopholes in the automated purchasing system have been fixed and the ill-gotten gains are being returned to the U.S. Treasury, said Army Lt. Col Brian Maka, a Pentagon spokesman."[16] The blame is more properly associated not only with a deceptive supplier, but also with the system the DoD had in place for managing their orders and payments—a system which, no doubt, was designed by the public sector.

The story naturally made the DoD and their purchasing department look very foolish and fed into preexisting stereotypes of illogical and unsubstantiated costs. Journalistic practices that can only be referred to as the equivalent of a *drive-by ambush* in which all the facts are not presented and only serve to rile rather than remedy the situation. Such reporting is sensationalist and irresponsible in that it perpetuates the urban legend mind-set regarding public sector inefficiency and incompetence.

Don't get us wrong, we are not attempting to justify the obvious holes in the DoD's procurement practice that led to this unfortunate series of transactions. However, given that the DoD spent $265 billion involving millions of contracts in 2006, one would hope that collectively, these facts would put the whole matter into perspective.

The $20 million that was fleeced by this unscrupulous, private sector supplier represents an infinitesimal fraction of the DoD's total expenditure for the year. It is safe to assume that similar levels of pilferage occurs at all levels of private corporations on a daily basis without us knowing about them. A June 2004 article by Jane Herring Stanford titled, "Curing the Ethical Malaise in Corporate America" demonstrates that wastefulness and misuse of resources—even under the watchful eyes of shareholders and the Securities and Exchange Commission—extend well beyond the levels reportedly taking place at the DoD. As she wrote, "reports that something was seriously awry in the business world only hinted at the shocking revelations to come—the true cause of a growing number of corporate downfalls. Financial difficulties can strike even the best was the common train of thought at the time; that is, until the media explosion began."[17] It was only a matter of time before similar stories of waste began to come out about the private sector.

FoxMeyer Drugs: Those Who Live in Glass Houses...

The irony of the CNN/DoD story is that private sector procurement failures of similar or greater magnitude seem to elude the public's radar. At the very least, they are confined to those who are brave enough to buck the trend in terms of industry coverage. Even when private sector problems are covered, they are relevant to a far smaller percentage of the population than the DoD, which is funded by all taxpayers and therefore of broader interest.

The FoxMeyer Drugs bankruptcy story serves as the ultimate example of how private sector organizations can get it just as wrong, and at a cost that is substantially higher than the reported $20 million DoD shipping fiasco. Following an unsuccessful SAP R/3 implementation in the mid-to-late 1990s, the FoxMeyer Drugs' bankruptcy trustees filed a $500 million lawsuit against SAP and another $500 million lawsuit against co-implementer Anderson Consulting. In both suits, they claimed that the companies' software and installation efforts had contributed to the drug company's demise.

An article on Bright Hub Project Management about implementation horror stories spotlighted the disparity between the new SAP system and the legacy one already in place. "By 1994, the SAP system was processing only 10,000 orders a night, compared with 420,000 orders under the old mainframe. FoxMeyer also alleged that both Andersen and SAP used the automation project as a training tool for junior employees, rather than assigning their best workers to it."[18]

In the end, SAP reached a settlement agreement with FoxMeyer, but the damage had been done. FoxMeyer went from being the fourth largest distributor of pharmaceuticals in the U.S., worth $5 billion in 1993 to being purchased by competitor McKesson for $80 million in 1996. The decision to acquire and implement a complex enterprise resource planning solution led to the financial collapse of a large chain. They were either unprepared for what was required or did not do their homework in the first place, resulting in them being fleeced just like the DoD was—only inside their own walls.

All Good Things Must Come to an End

Let's assume that the Fortune 500 vice president we mentioned at the start of this chapter was right when she characterized the primary difference between public and private sector procurement as an ability to avoid having your mistakes appear on the front page of the newspaper. When private sector errors or embarrassments are kept behind closed doors, it allows corporations to protect their brand and reputation from harm and negative perceptions. No one deliberately airs their dirty laundry—public or private—unless a whistle is blown or someone is fired, arrested, sued, or exposed by the media.

A significant change to this is coming as the result of the trend in recent years to contract out—or more accurately *outsource*—an increasing percentage of internal operations to suppliers. As the supply chain or supply network expands, so does the exposure to the risk of bad press.

In 2015, the UK-based consultancy Proxima Group commissioned a study of how consumers, American consumers specifically, feel about companies that find themselves on the wrong end of a supplier scandal. According to an initial data release Proxima shared at the time, "74% of respondents stated they would be unlikely to buy products or services from a company involved in controversial supplier practices. Furthermore, nearly 66% would stop giving such a company their business even if that company was the most convenient and cheapest option."[19] Those consumers who are willing to punish corporations who end up on the front page—even for the actions of their suppliers that they took no active role in themselves—are the same taxpayers that have little tolerance for nonsense in public sector procurement. By leveraging the cost advantages of working with third-party providers, private sector procurement is parting the curtains that have for so long protected them from the scrutiny the public sector has never been able to avoid.

While the short-term news cycle moves stories in and out of the general consciousness with greater speed than accuracy, there is a longer-term impact that may be hard to track and quantify. Bad news may or may not travel fast, but it sure does travel. Decisions, opinions, and word of mouth are clearly more affected by negative news than by positive news. We must ask ourselves whether there is a correspondingly positive reaction by consumers when companies are lauded for good supplier practices. Would an overwhelming majority of consumers go to extra lengths to support a company with exceptional supplier relations? Would they pay more to do so, or spread the word to family and friends? The answer to all of these questions is probably no. As a result, the private sector may be about to learn what the public sector has known for a long time: bad news will punish you more than good news will reward you. If there is a collaborative relationship between supplier and customer, the likelihood of financial reward or positive publicity is much greater.

Different but Equal

We could continue to regale you with salacious tales of spectacular failure in the public and private sectors, but what value (beyond entertainment value) does that really offer? The two groups are, at their core, different but equal. We have similar types of goals and processes, and both the public and private sector are susceptible to missteps when proper governance is not in place. As we form an opinion about either sector, especially one that may affect how we interact, we must be sure the information contributing to that opinion is representative.

It may seem as though there are less controls in place in the public sector, but there are also different considerations driving their efforts, not to mention the fact that their spend is often much larger than that being managed by private sector procurement. Public sector procurement plays by a different set of rules. They are also asked to shoulder the blame for systemic problems that have more to do with government in general than public sector procurement specifically. In fact, this is one of the less obvious but no less important points raised in the article by Dr. Utt that we referred to earlier in this chapter. He recommended a buyout of the GSA by its current employees. His belief was that it was the bureaucracy of the government and the inefficient structure of the relationship between the GSA and the public sector entities it was designed to serve, and not the incompetence of the GSA employees themselves that was at the root of the problem.

In fact, when we get down to it, public sector procurement is not even one thing. Since we have made the argument that the public and private sectors are different, effectively limiting the types of comparisons we can draw, we should also point out that it is not always possible to make meaningful comparisons between different public sector procurement entities. If we define the public sector as being everything under the control of the government, there are a wide range of organizational types, structures, and sizes included. Local, state, and federal governments may loosely resemble each other in structure, but one does not roll up into the other, and the higher level entities do not usually have mandate authority over the localized ones. This does not even begin to address the agency model that focuses on a specific operational area such as education, defense, communications, or transportation. We should keep in mind that while buying a V-22 Osprey and hiring a contractor to pave Main Street are both examples of public procurement, they are not the same thing.

RELATIONSHIP WITH CHANGE

Once we accept the fact that public sector procurement is not the private sector's *goofy cousin*, we can examine their challenges in isolation and without judgment. The public sector is facing many of the same forces that are making themselves felt in the private sector: generational shifts, rapidly expanding access to data, and increased emphasis on diversity and sustainability. And while the public sector is subject to the same internal and external forces that are leading to change in the private sector, what may be different is how they respond to them.

External Forces: Cyclical versus Linear Change

While at first glance it might look like the public sector is guilty of just doing things the way they have always done them, they have actually been dealing with smaller, more cyclical changes on a regular basis over a longer span of time as visualized in Figure 8.2. Through their connection to election cycles and changes in administrative priorities, the public sector is forced to absorb changes—sometimes minor and sometimes quite significant—on a regular, ongoing basis. Even when these changes are small, they are an accepted part of the public procurement landscape. In this context, it is the regularity of the change and not the significance of it, that is relevant.

In order to survive what would otherwise have the same impact as turbulence on a jetliner, the public sector has had to learn to absorb, adapt, and move on. Corresponding changes in the private sector, such as the appointment of a new CEO/CFO and being involved in M&A

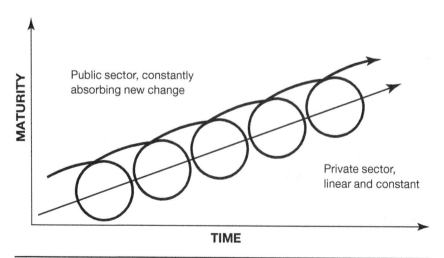

Figure 8.2   Public versus private sector change and maturity increase over time

activity, are less frequent and are usually accompanied by major adjustments in resources and expectations. The uniqueness of those changes determines the way private sector procurement handles them. Responding to more frequent changes with the care and consideration that are typically given to an acquisition would be like treating every supplier as a strategic partner; it would require unsustainable levels of energy and manpower.

Even when you look at common regulatory changes, which affect private sector procurement much like administrative changes affect the public sector, they are usually relegated to certain industries and a subset of spend categories. When a new person or staff of people who have direction-setting authority over a public sector procurement organization are ushered into office, especially at the federal level, the changes are not only immediate and ongoing, but they are potentially regularly spaced every four, six, or eight years. A team's relationship with change would have to adjust as a result.

Internal Change: Millennials and the Public Sector

"Well, when I said 'I just hope I haven't let you down,' that said it all. I had. I let down my friends. I let down the country. I let down our system of government, the dreams of all those young people that ought to get into government but will think it's all too corrupt and the rest."[20]

From where we stand, the preceding excerpt from the famous Frost/Nixon interview in 1973 is a ringing reminder of how the perceptions of the past—whether based in fact or fiction (or a combination of both)—have far reaching consequences. This is especially true in terms of Generation Next procurement professionals, which of course includes Millennials. Many of the changes being seen today in the workforce in general, and in procurement more specifically, are due to the increasing numbers of young workers entering the workforce and the characteristics and momentum they bring with them. There is no reason to think that they will not affect the public sector the same way they are affecting the private sector.

According to an IBM Institute for Business Value (IBV) study titled "The Real Story Behind Millennials in the Workplace," one of the key myths dispelled was centered around career goals—specifically that Millennials' career goals and expectations are different from those of older generations.

As the IBV said of the study's findings, "We discovered that Millennials want many of the same things their older colleagues do. While there are some distinctions among the generations, Millennials' attitudes are not poles apart from other employees."[21] In other words, and similar to their older coworkers, Millennials want to:

1. Make a positive impact on their organization,
2. Help solve social and/or environmental challenges, and
3. Work with a diverse group of people.

These goals are admirable and necessary and would seem to be natural drivers for Millennials to enter the public sector. Unfortunately, all three can be easily undermined by a perception of futility, corruption, and a lack of professionalism in the public sector. This is why the CNN DoD washer story we shared is so damaging. It contributes to and perpetuates the myth that the public sector is somehow reminiscent of a *Who's on first?* comedy routine.

Even though those who have been in public sector procurement for many years have, to a certain extent, become numb to such misperceptions, it is unlikely that newer generations will want to pick up and carry the energy sapping baggage this represents. It would make far more sense for them to seek employment in the private sector. Of course, they may be in for a surprise once they realize things are not necessarily better in the private sector.

We have already discussed the fact that public sector procurement is not *one thing*. Millennials seem to understand that, looking at individual agencies as having profiles different than that of the government in general. "A Reason-Rupe survey of 2,000 Americans between the ages of 18 and 29 [Millennials] finds 66 percent of Millennials believe government is inefficient and wasteful—a substantial increase since 2009, when just 42 percent of Millennials said government was inefficient and wasteful."[22] When you depart from the notion of government as a whole and break it down into agencies and departments, their perception of it changes. In 2013, Universum surveyed over 65,000 college students, asking them about their goals, what employers can do to attract them, and who they consider as *ideal employers*. The public sector featured surprisingly well in the results. "The good news for government is that federal agencies were among the most preferred employers for students across main fields of study: the FBI, National Institutes of Health, NASA, Department of State, and Peace Corps all ranked among the top ten, alongside companies like Google, Walt Disney Company, Apple, and Microsoft."[23] If the public sector can rate alongside Google and Apple, then maybe Millennials really will ride in on a wave and bring change to public sector procurement just as they are starting to do in the private sector.

Of course, in order to make that happen, Millennials actually have to land jobs in the public sector, and that is proving tough to accomplish. The public sector workforce is aging as a whole and may find it hard to catch up on the recruitment front if they don't actively start working to attract young talent. "According to the Census Bureau, the median age of government employees is 45.3 compared to the median age of 42.3 in the U.S. workforce as a whole. Sixty percent of federal employees are over the age of 45, compared to 31 percent in the private sector."[24] Twice as many employees are over age 45 in the federal government than in industry. Dinosaur thinking is not always tied to age, but when it is, the long tail of legacy thinking will extend further into the future for the public sector than the private sector.

Many of the changes that we think we need to actively bring about in procurement will happen on their own if just given the chance. How those changes affect any organization has a lot to do with their preexisting relationship with change: how much of it there has been, and how regularly, over time. Do they embrace it or fear it? Once change has been effected, the challenge remains to alter public perceptions so that they align with the new, improved reality. Private sector procurement has certainly seen this lag, and especially if the public sector continues to get negative press, it is likely that they will continue to struggle with this as well.

CAN OIL MIX WITH WATER?

We've considered how public sector and private sector procurement organizations are the same and how they are different, but what about when the two sectors have to work together? When the private sector meets the public sector (or vice versa), it is often like oil meeting water—they just don't seem to mix. And while the two can be put into the same container, they remain separate and distinct. This doesn't mean that a public-private sector partnership can't work. It can—provided that the public sector takes the lead in terms of a project's or initiative's direction, just like a client would do in the private sector. As an aside, this is yet another reason why *sad sack* or *goofy cousin* perceptions have to be dispelled. If a private sector supplier does not respect their public sector client in mind-set as well as actions, the project cannot hope to have a successful outcome. That respect is only gained by meaningful interaction between the two parties with each benefiting from the activity.

In our chapter on collaboration, we discussed the fact that not all procurement needs to be based on strategic relationships. However, in the cases when it does, there has to be mind-set alignment between the organizations engaging in the collaboration. Experts such as Andy Akrouche and Kate Vitasek, champions of relational, collaborative supply methods, both advocate an approach in which parties are empowered to openly communicate and work toward a common goal or outcome. They view relationships, as opposed to contracts, as the foundation for success. In a *shared risk shared outcome* model, there is no room for passing of the *responsibility buck*. All stakeholders, whether in the public or private sector, have to be in the effort together and completely.

This last point is critical because it creates a common ground of mutual understanding and respect for the strengths and weaknesses of both parties. This allows for a truer understanding of the task and related challenges, particularly when the inevitable changes in circumstances and goals require adaptation as opposed to enforcement. When the oil and water paradigm is in place, the public and private sectors can't collaborate—almost by definition. But they don't have to be oil and water. *Oil and water* is more a matter of circumstances than being, and the public and private sectors have more control over it than they realize. While oil might not be able to mix with water, the aforementioned changes in both mind-set and approach ultimately render the question moot. Since both sectors now regularly experience pressure or heat from stakeholders and the general public, they must learn to perform well in those conditions—separately and together.

Privatization: The Ultimate Example of Strategic Outsourcing

One of the major trends in public sector procurement is privatization. Many of the jobs and services that have been fulfilled by public sector employees in the past are now being completed by companies in the private sector. In the private sector, sometimes we call this outsourcing. Other times we don't label it at all, missing the trend in increased spend flowing out of the organization to suppliers. Either way, it is the same trend in pursuit of the same objectives: efficiency, specialization, and cost reduction.

When the public sector spends considerable money with the private sector in an outsourced-type relationship, the benefits, while realized, are often seen more in the private than the public sector. This is especially when money is invested in new product development. At the end of the effort, the public sector entity hopefully gets their bridge, or communication capability, or spacecraft. The private sector, while they have to make an investment of funds and employee bandwidth to meet the challenge, develops proprietary, market-leading expertise that they can use to win other contracts and differentiate themselves from the competition.

KELLY'S PERSPECTIVE: *To the Moon, Procurement! To the Moon!*

I've been fascinated with the idea of SpaceX ever since the company's mission was first made public. Founded in 2002 by Elon Musk of PayPal and Tesla fame, the ultimate end goal is to establish a colony on Mars. (No, really, that's the goal.) In 2006, NASA awarded SpaceX a *Commercial Orbital Transportation Services Contract* to design and demonstrate a launch system to resupply cargo to the International Space Station. I challenge anyone in the private sector—no matter how strategic or mature—to produce a template for a Commercial Orbital Transportation Services contract. That requires what you might characterize as *extremely* specialized category expertise.

Now if anyone were going to find themselves in an *oil and water* situation with the government, you would think it would be Elon Musk. Often described as an *eccentric billionaire*, Musk is known for his unorthodox opinions and willingness to go against the grain in pursuit of his radical ideas. When asked about his relationship with NASA, he seemed to instinctively understand the core point we have been making in this chapter about the difficult position public procurement often finds themselves in. "NASA's in the position it's in not through any desire of its own. The public is often asking NASA to have a perfect track record and a perfect safety record, yielding excessive caution and institutional gridlock."[25] Yet, despite the enormous obstacles to be overcome and the failures SpaceX and NASA have faced together, the joint effort would have to be characterized as a success.

Ironically, and in the spirit of the coverage disparities we described earlier in this chapter, SpaceX's failures have literally been *called* successes. On June 28, 2015, a SpaceX Falcon 9 rocket exploded 19 seconds and 20 feet into its planned flight. As a Forbes article titled, "How SpaceX's launch failure is also a measure of success," explained the scenario, "while the failure marks a high-profile stumble for the commercial spaceflight industry's poster child, it's also indicative of a company, and an industry that is operating at the very edge of what's possible."[26] In an interesting twist, particularly relevant to readers of this book, the test was being run to validate whether SpaceX's efforts to reduce launch costs (ahem, procurement…) had been effective.

Something tells me that if the failure had been NASA's alone, Forbes would not have been explaining away their failure for them. The assumption that if anyone can do it, Elon Musk can, added to the fact that this really was their first launch failure in 19 attempts, made their failure more palatable. If nothing else, the benefit of the doubt is a worthwhile return from a well-structured, collaborative public-private effort.

JON'S PERSPECTIVE: *An Apple Is Still an Apple!*

In the months that Kelly and I have actively collaborated on the writing of this book, our interaction can best be described as being harmonious along the lines of an evening at the Cleaver house. For those of you who might be too young to remember the Cleavers, look up the show "Leave It to Beaver," and check out the interaction between Ward and June Cleaver. You will get the drift fairly quickly.

Politically outdated stereotypes notwithstanding, my point is simply this—we rarely, if ever, disagreed on anything of any real consequence. This isn't to suggest that we are mere carbon copies of one another. Even though we shared the same values and viewpoints, we did so from a perspective that was uniquely our own, as distinctive as a fingerprint.

The utopian collaborative ideal came to a crashing end when we hit Chapter 8—this chapter, on the differences between public and private sector procurement. As it turns out, and for a period of time, what Waterloo was to Napoleon, Chapter 8 was to us.

It wasn't so much that we were in disagreement in terms of the underlying principles associated with distinguishing between the two. It had more to do with how we arrived at the pages you are now reading. This is perhaps one of the main reasons why, unlike the other chapters, Chapter 8 had to be written, rewritten, and rewritten again … and again … and yet again.

Then it dawned on me!

Our collaborative effort at working toward a mutually desired outcome was, and is, the perfect analogy of the differences between the public and private sectors.

It is not a matter of wanting completely different things or having substantially different ideas. What it all came down to was simply our perceptions of the same thing. In other words, an apple is an apple, no matter the angle from which it is being viewed. This is the greater or larger truth. However, the apple may still appear to be different depending on the unique angle from which it is being viewed by the individual. One side could be shaded and therefore appear dull, while the other side that is exposed to the light may appear to be bright, even luminous. Both would, of course, be correct in their point of view.

Problems arise when one tries to assert his or her view as being the only one, losing site of the fact that both are looking at the very same apple. So what is the moral of the apple story?

At the end of the day, and like the apple, procurement is procurement. Whether in the public or private sector, the angle of view ultimately doesn't matter as long as you keep your eye on the big picture. [Additional note from Kelly: Just like June Cleaver, I always work with my pearls on.]

CONCLUSION

We have identified a number of *dinosaurs* in this book that have outlived their practical lives and now only stand to prevent procurement from achieving its full potential. Of all of these, the notion that the public sector is bad and the private sector is good is the *T. Rex*. Not only are the two groups more similar than we realize, the instances where differences do emerge are critical because they meet a need or requirement that the private sector is not faced with. If anything, the public sector needs to reach the point where it can assert itself in partnerships with the private sector, demanding, deserving, and receiving respect all at once.

There are a number of preconceived, regularly fed notions about public sector procurement, and those of us in the private sector need to remember that as taxpayers we see public sector procurement's efforts much as the rest of the company sees us in the private sector. We would do well to show them the respect we so often clamor for ourselves.

REFERENCES

1. Eric Schnurer, "When Government Competes Against the Private Sector, Everybody Wins," *The Atlantic*, March 11, 2015, http://

www.theatlantic.com/politics/archive/2015/03/when-government
-competes-against-the-private-sector-everybody-wins/387460/.

2. "Recent advances in public sector procurement processes may be doing more harm than good," *DTZ*, December 3, 2010, http://www .dtz.com/UK/Recent+advances+in+public+sector+procurement +processes+may+be+doing+more+harm+than+good.

3. Ibid.

4. Dr. Ronald Utt, Ph.D., "Privatize the General Services Administration Through an Employee Buyout," *The Heritage Foundation*, May 26, 1995, http://www.heritage.org/research/reports/1995/05/ bg1036nbsp-privatize-the-general-services.

5. ———, "Privatize the General Services Administration."

6. Jon Hansen, "Can present day PWGSC woes be traced back to a 1995 article on the General Services Administration in the U.S.?" *Procurement Insights*, October 26, 2007, https://procureinsights .wordpress.com/2007/10/26/can-present-day-pwgsc-woes-be-traced -back-to-a-1995-article-on-the-general-services-administration-in -the-us/.

7. Christopher Hood, "A Public Management for All Seasons?" *Royal Institute of Public Administration*, Volme 69, Spring 1991, (3-19), 15, http://www.ipf.se/static/files/12/hood_the_paper.pdf.

8. David Osborne and Ted Gaebler, *Reinventing Government: How the entrepreneurial spirit is transforming the public sector*, (Massachusetts, Addison-Wesley: 1992).

9. J.E. Lane, "Public Sector Reform: Rationale, Trends, and Problems," (London, Sage: 1997).

10. Jon Hansen, "If you want to make a 'private sector' approach work for public procurement—start small," *Contracting Excellence*, October 1, 2014, https://www.iaccm.com/news/contractingexcellence/ ?newsletterid=37.

11. Simon Horton, Negotiation Mastery: Tools for the 21st Century Negotiator," (London: MX Publishing, 2012), 24.

12. Jon Hansen, CNN drops the ball with $1 million DoD washer purchase story, *Procurement Insights*, August 20, 2007, https://procureinsights.wordpress.com/2007/08/20/ cnn-drops-the-ball-with-1-million-dod-washer-purchase-story/.

13. "Peru Quake Search and Rescue; California Overdue for 'The Big One'; Wall Street's Wild Ride," *The Situation Room*, CNN, August 16, 2007, http://www.cnn.com/TRANSCRIPTS/0708/16/ sitroom.03.html.

14. "America's Credit Crunch Intensifies; China and Russia Hold War Games," Lou Dobbs Tonight, CNN, August 17, 2007, http://www .cnn.com/TRANSCRIPTS/0708/17/ldt.01.html.

15. "America's Credit Crunch Intensifies," CNN.

16. Jim Wolf, "U.S. paid $1 million to ship two 19-cent washers," Reuters, August 17, 2007, http://www.reuters.com/article/2007/08/17/ us-iraq-fraud-washers-idUSN1638072120070817.

17. Jane Herring Stanford, "Curing the ethical malaise in corporate America: organizational structure as the antidote," SAM Advanced Management Journal, Volume 69, Issue 3, Summer 2004, http:// www.freepatentsonline.com/article/SAM-Advanced-Management -Journal/122415525.html.

18. N. Nayab, "A Review of Three Project Management Horror Stories and the Lessons We Can Learn From Them," *Bright Hub Project Management*, March 15, 2012, http://www.brighthubpm.com/ monitoring-projects/15893-lessons-we-can-learn-from-three -project-management-horror-stories/.

19. "New study suggests American consumers intend to punish companies involved in supplier-driven scandals," *Proxima Group*, May 14, 2015, http://insight.proximagroup.com/new-study-suggests -american-consumers-intend-to-punish-companies-involved-in -supplier-driven-scandals.

20. Carole D. Bos, J.D., "Richard Nixon—Apologizes for Watergate," *Awesome Stories*, Oct 27, 2014, https://www.awesomestories.com/ asset/view/Richard-Nixon-Apologizes-for-Watergate0.

21. Myths, exaggerations and uncomfortable truths, The real story behind Millennials in the workplace" *IBM Institute for Business Value*, Accessed July 21, 2015, http://www-935.ibm.com/services/us/gbs/ thoughtleadership/millennialworkplace/.

22. "Millennials Think Government Is Inefficient, Abuses Its Power, and Supports Cronyism," *Reason Rupe Poll*, July 10, 2014, http:// reason.com/poll/2014/07/10/reason-rupe-2014-millennial-survey# .dbjucc:a5ca.

23. Bob Lavigna and John Flato, "Millennials Are Attracted to Public Service, But Government Needs to Deliver," ERE Recruiting Intelligence, January 22, 2014, http://www.eremedia.com/ere/ millennials-are-attracted-to-public-service-but-government -needs-to-deliver/.

24. Ibid.

25. John Carter McKnight, "MarsNow 1.9 Profile: Elon Musk, Life to Mars Foundation," September 25, 2001, Space Ref, http://www .spaceref.com/news/viewsr.html?pid=3698.
26. Clay Dillow, "How SpaceX's launch failure is also a measure of success," Forbes, July 1, 2015, http://fortune.com/2015/07/01/ spacex-launch-failure/.

 Web
Added
Value™

This book has free material available for download from the
Web Added Value™ resource center at *www.jrosspub.com*

9

The Media and Procurement: Are We Really Covered?

"All you have to do is write one true sentence. Write the truest sentence that you know. So finally I would write one true sentence, and then go on from there. It was easy then because there was always one true sentence that I knew or had seen or had heard someone say." A Moveable Feast, Ernest Hemingway[1]

Even though *Procurement Insights* has always had a strong industry presence through a solid base of core followers, a story that broke in late 2014—and evolved into a major controversy in early 2015—has seen the number of reads for the blog triple. The #CodeGate coverage, which began with a single straightforward post in December 2014, gained traction and continued to develop, sometimes with new news breaking every day for weeks. That being said, the traffic to the site was not confined to the newest post, but saw visitors to the site looking at multiple posts per visit.

The story absolutely merited the traffic it attracted, but part of the associated growth was undoubtedly due to the fact that no other site or media source covered the events related to Periscope Holdings' purchase of the National Institute of Governmental Purchasing (NIGP) and their classification code and the potential conflict of interests this created. Perhaps more important than even reporting the facts, no other source attempted to help readers and professionals in the industry piece together what implications the story might have for them. While the rest of the industry's loss was definitely *Procurement Insights'* gain, when we look at the situation purely in consideration of the best interests of the procurement industry, such silence is extremely troubling.

There are many things the authors of this book have in common, from writing styles to a certain way of viewing our profession and the business world in general. However, it is the willingness to tell it—or in the case of this book and our blogs, write it—*like it is* and regardless of the consequences, that seems to separate us from the pack. Generally speaking, our willingness to be honest and take risks has put us at odds with some in our industry while bringing us closer to others—creating a loyal readership base who have come to trust us based on our no-holds-barred objectivity.

This distinction is not just about our near-obsessive commitment to research and the desire to get the story right, as opposed to being right ourselves—and there is a significant difference between the two. Neither *Procurement Insights* nor *Buyers Meeting Point* is covering the procurement industry solely from an inside-out perspective. We cover it from the outside-in as well. Specifically, and unlike the vast majority of industry analysts and journalists, we are not solely dependent on the procurement world for our financial stability or success.

This means that while we are heavily invested in the industry, we do not have to make a choice between our earnings potential and being honest about our perspectives and insights. The objectivity associated with our outside-in vantage point, coupled with our inside-out experience as procurement professionals, supports the balance necessary to maintain journalistic integrity. We serve our readers first and foremost. This is not to suggest that the others who cover the industry lack integrity. They do not. However, they do lack visibility and at times exhibit questionable priorities about which stories justify the greatest investment in coverage, as you will discover through our discussion later in this chapter of the differences in coverage of the Persicope-BidSync merger. It is within the context of all that is written here, that we ask you to view or read this chapter.

SO WHAT EXACTLY HAPPENED AT NIGP AND WHY IS IT IMPORTANT?

The NIGP code had its genesis in 1983 when the director of general services in Texas led a group that included representation from Texas,

Oklahoma, Florida, and Illinois, along with some other states, cities, and counties. In 2001, NIGP, who held the copyright for the data file, appointed Periscope Holdings as the custodian for the code. Their responsibilities included "licensing, overseeing code change requests, publication of version releases, communication with end users, phone support, training, integrity of the codeset, and commodity coding services for the conversion of contract and inventory files."[2] The code as well as the *crosswalk* that allows agencies to align the NIGP code with other common classification systems are available to solution providers and user agencies for an annual license.

In late 2014, Periscope Holdings merged with BidSync through a *control* recapitalization spearheaded by Boston-based Parthenon Capital Partners. Unlike more generalist eSourcing or eProcurement solution providers, BidSync specializes in serving the public sector. According to their Bloomberg Business profile, their combined suite of solutions "are designed and built to meet the procurement demands of public agencies by ensuring spend management through automating, consolidating, and centralizing procurement information and processes. ... It serves government-specific verticals, such as state entities and departments, counties, cities, parishes, school districts, and universities."[3] Stated plainly, the custodian of the NIGP code bought eSourcing functionality from a company that already had a specialization in public sector procurement. This acquisition brought Periscope into direct competition with other providers looking to serve the public sector—the same companies paying to license the NIGP code from them.

It didn't take long for this overlap of roles to cause friction. Not even a year after Periscope's acquisition of BidSync, the combined company lost a bid issued by the state of Missouri. In response, Periscope wrote a protest letter to the state of Missouri—which it should be noted was co-signed by NIGP's CEO, making accusations against Perfect Commerce, the winning company. Periscope and NIGP stated that, "Within their offer Perfect Commerce made false claims regarding contractual rights with the NIGP Code...,"[4] because Perfect Commerce failed to disclose that the NIGP code was the property of NIGP. As was pointed out in the Procurement Insights coverage at the time, "What is to prevent Periscope from employing similar tactics going forward to challenge all contract awards? In other words, NIGP's support of Periscope by threatening—in writing mind you—to pull the winning vendor's licensing rights to the code, is tantamount to giving Periscope the only gun in the field."[5]

The initial posts on *Procurement Insights* led to further information being provided by confidential sources—at least one of which was outed by the NIGP themselves. What started as a simple post turned into a full investigative series, delving into the politics and financial status of professional associations in procurement. It included a *side excursion* into the process NIGP used when they made the decision to replace their in-house consultants with a third-party service provider. The process, which they described as a competitive RFI (request for information), included an unusual array of participants and settled on—brace yourself—Periscope Holdings as the award recipient. This put two very big NIGP eggs in the Periscope basket.

The reason why this matters and why it belongs in our chapter on procurement media coverage, is because through a number of seemingly independent steps, NIGP was putting a privately held company that competes directly with other service providers in the public sector in charge of what should have remained an independent entity—the code. Even if we concede the possibility that there might be a legitimate reason for any of the moves between NIGP and Periscope, isn't it the responsibility of the media to ask why, and consider the implications? And yet no one—absolutely no one—other than *Procurement Insights* pursued the story or did the research necessary to shine a light on what was taking place and how it might affect the industry. As Jon wrote on *Procurement Insights* at the time, "While I am hard pressed to understand the reasons why industry blogger and analyst coverage of the Periscope acquisition of BidSync has been limited to the usual commentary, with no real follow-up beyond the initial announcement, one thing of which I am certain is this ... being the lone voice has its benefits."[6]

EVERYONE IS ENTITLED TO AN OPINION

We are certain that some of our colleagues on the procurement media side of the coverage fence—and we use the word fence for a reason—will scorn us for being harsh or arrogant, holier-than-thou know-it-alls by expressing concern that procurement does not have a sufficiently independent commentary sector. Some might dismiss us as just plain dumb or naive, while others will scream foul, claiming that we are panning them without merit just to sell a few books. That is fair enough. Everyone is, after all, entitled to their opinion.

Without apologizing for our standpoint, we are sorry if you are one of those who feel this way. If we did not write what we believe, or allow the truth of a particular story to lead us wherever it takes us with no thought of influencing (or benefiting from) its outcome, then we would be less than honest with ourselves. More importantly, we would be less than honest with you. In the end, this would be a far more difficult thing to face than the criticism of a few.

This isn't about being crusaders for truth, because we are not in the position to judge anyone. Nor are we particularly interested in chasing windmills on behalf of interested third parties who would like to use our platforms for their own purposes. This is a critical point because a willingness to *tell it like it is*, is not the same as being a *tell-all*. There are details that come across our desks that we choose not to publish, because they serve no one—not the people and organization they pertain to, nor the reading audience. In order to be newsworthy, information must not just be interesting, it must hold actual value to procurement practitioners.

Procurement is an industry experiencing tumultuous changes without any meaningful coverage on the part of most analyst firms and bloggers. That sounds harsh, yet it is the truth—a truth born by proximity and relationship oligarchies in which those covering the procurement world have a too-close-for-comfort relationship with their subjects.

To be perfectly clear, this does not demonstrate an intentional or deliberate intent on anyone's part to deceive. It is more a reflection of the way things used to be done. We are talking about a time when there were few bloggers, and the ones that did exist had close ties to the vendors being discussed through an analyst firm to client relationship, or past employment. Under such a scenario, it is virtually impossible to remain truly objective, but at the time, no one expected it. Everyone knew about most of those connections and understood the role it might play in coverage. Over time, however, these connections and trails have a way of fading into obscurity.

As individuals who are part of the procurement world and therefore can view the industry from the inside-out, we understand this part of the business more deeply than you know. As investigative journalists looking at the industry from the outside-in, the task, while still challenging for the aforementioned reasons, is one that has to be undertaken—and not just by us. If the procurement world is to ever progress beyond what it has been, to become all it could be, then the way the industry is covered by its media must also change.

DON'T FENCE ME IN

For some time, there has been a growing recognition that traditional analyst firms' and industry pundits' credibility in the market is waning.

Specifically, and being caught between serving cross-purposed agendas, firms such as Gartner continue to fail[7] in terms of delivering sound and unbiased insight into industry trends and vendor capabilities. "Forrester, Gartner, IDC, and others insist their output is squeaky clean, yet they also rake in millions providing services to the very same companies they monitor... Which leads to a question that continues to dog the research firms: how much influence do technology vendors have over their work?"[8] Generally speaking, this should not be a surprise to anyone who thinks through the economics of large analyst firms. Relying primarily on paying vendor clients to provide the critical case references that contribute to an analyst's or blogger's assessment of capabilities is tantamount to the fox guarding the hen house.

This is not a procurement-specific issue. Most analyst firms are reliant upon the markets they cover for research sponsorship. As David Rossiter, Director of Analyst Relations and Insight at Sunesis, wrote for the Institute for Industry Analyst Relations, "Any analyst firm which values its long-term reputation in the market has to ensure that its research is independent (and also seen to be independent)."[9] These firms, whether large or small, must guard against bias as well as the appearance of bias. And while sponsors typically make their identity known in the proud distribution of research as a marketing asset, some bias is easier to discern than others.

The end user client must bear some responsibility for the historic failings that continue to plague the industry. After all, beyond the challenges of having limited resources, it has been suggested that clients either do not know the right questions to ask or are just not willing to pose the questions they actually have. Instead, they appear to blindly follow the lead of analysts and bloggers whose interests are (to a certain extent) influenced by the very companies about whom they are supposed to be providing objective and meaningful coverage. Following the lead of respected organizations is fine; blindly doing so is not.

Individuals bear some responsibility in separating independent from *independent* coverage of the industry. In 2014, Horses for Sources chief executive officer (CEO) Phil Fersht wrote a blog post that called out analysts, bloggers, etc., that portray themselves as objective sources of information yet are dependent upon the companies they cover for income. He wrote, "Suddenly, in today's media-insane environment, everyone is an expert and can put out their own version of the world in many different forms and soundbites, across many different information channels. It must be getting really, really hard for some people to keep track of what is real versus propaganda."[10] While the majority of his post is dedicated to criticizing pretend objectivity, Fersht also points out that none of this would be able to happen if readers held their sources of information to account. Being a critical thinker and reader requires careful consideration of any position of interest held by the writer or creating organization.

Client abdication issues notwithstanding, this does not absolve the analysts and the vendors they cover from shouldering the lion's share of the responsibility for failed initiatives such as the detailed example we described in Chapter 7. When multiple clients experience implementation problems with the same solution, those covering the industry are faced with a he-said/she-said situation. The leadership at the solution providers may point to mitigating factors—either in the market or in their clients' organizations—as the cause of the failure. Their (sometimes former) clients are so focused on stopping scheduled payments and seizing implementation work that they are not concerned with telling their side of the story. In some cases, perhaps because of lack of coverage, solution providers are even able to continue making presentations about their knowledge and expertise or accepting industry awards without having to answer sufficient questions about all of their clients. Stories such as these may go effectively uncovered by the procurement commentary sector even though they represent major developments and have a significant impact on stock price and brand reputation. The fact of the matter is that major failed implementations should not be considered discretionary when it comes to news coverage.

This raises some interesting (and perhaps troubling) questions. Can traditional analyst firms and industry pundits such as bloggers be relied upon for sound advice or are their days really numbered? What side of the bias fence are they actually on in terms of their coverage? Would it be possible for them to survive financially without the sponsorship dollars that bring the accuracy and objectivity of their coverage into question? If not, is it better to work in an industry covered by biased institutions or to have no coverage at all? After all, there has to be some source of income for these firms and organizations, but it cannot be earned at the cost of their ability to fulfill their purported role.

In the past, pundits and bloggers were considered to be industry insiders, the gatekeepers of knowledge and understanding. But things have changed in a way that has altered their influence and perhaps even their ongoing viability. The persistently high rate of initiative failures costing end-user clients hundreds of millions of dollars over the years is without a doubt the impetus behind said change.

However, it is the emergence of the Generation Next professionals who can, through a panoply of devices and sources, gain access to information on their own, that has raised the bar in terms of industry coverage. The news cycle is faster today, but more importantly, it is less-filtered and more direct. Everything is expected to be absolutely current. The pundits of the past, used to serving the important role of news filter, find themselves distanced from their potential audience. In order to hold value to the up-and-coming generation of procurement thinkers, they cannot just report the news, they must provide additional insights that are valuable, unbiased, and of interest to readers.

There are also some (albeit not many) examples of providers questioning the conclusions that are supported by procurement media coverage. In a uniquely clear observation, Chirag Shah, Executive Director of Xchanging Procurement, made the following comment about the fact that so much focus has been placed on talent as procurement's major challenge while research sponsored by his company concluded that capacity constraints are the real issue: "If you were to go by media headlines and conference topics over the past few years, you might well think that talent shortage was the only problem plaguing the procurement function. Whilst our study confirms it's still an operational challenge, there is a much bigger issue found in the form of 'team time pressures'."[11]

This is an interesting, frank observation about the role that organizations in the commentary sector have on procurement's understanding of their own field. Although it was certainly not the main point of their research, it demonstrates a clear view and a critical thought process. Statements such as Shah's are enough to make anyone in the function question which of the generally accepted ideas are false and which trends are going unmonitored.

Once again, we want to emphasize that we are not suggesting a malicious intent to deceive. These are, generally speaking, decent and honest individuals who had the misfortune of bad timing relative to the origins of the procurement world's media. Some industry pundits now find themselves confined by the very close proximity relationships that initially benefited them professionally and financially. They have become fenced in by their own familiarity with the vendors and people they are supposed to be covering. The challenge that follows is how to *unring* the bell of well-intentioned, but misguided advice that ultimately did more harm than it did good.

JON'S PERSPECTIVE: *A Case (or Story) in Point*

Vice President and Gartner Fellow Andy Kyte was recently quoted in an article about the changing nature of the relationship between stakeholders and technology solutions. At the peak of the enterprise resource planning (ERP) movement, CEOs and other executive leaders prioritized reliability and the potential for integration when selecting a solution provider.

At the time, those requirements—particularly in combination—served as a way to narrow the field of options. While the need for reliability and integration still exists, a solution's ability to provide them is no longer a differentiator—it is instead an entry requirement. Technology has progressed to the point that all solutions that are considered competitive are able to satisfy this requirement. As Kyte explained in the article, "their requirements have switched to the twin concerns of lowering information technology (IT) costs and seeking increased flexibility. A system that is not sufficiently flexible to meet changing business demands is an anchor, not a sail, holding the business back, not driving it forward."[12]

The first problem with this assertion is that what Gartner now refers to as *highly customized ERPs*, never delivered on the promise of being reliable, integrated solutions. The second is that having championed these ERP systems, thereby creating the heyday about which they could then write, how can we trust Gartner's take on anything going forward? This is especially true with what they are now calling *postmodern ERPs*.

In a 2008 *Procurement Insights* post "Optimization Modeling and the Modern Supply Chain,"[13] and again in the 2009 entry "Riding the Crest of a New Wave: How the Original SaaS Companies Have Gained the Upper Hand,"[14] I made reference to the findings of a 2000 Software & Information Industry Association (SIIA) whitepaper titled "Strategic Backgrounder: Software as a Service." The SIIA eBusiness Division authored the paper, about which I wrote the following:

"In its opening paragraph, this seminal effort to explain the evolution from traditional licensing models in which 'packaged desktop and enterprise applications will soon be swept away by the tide of Web-based, outsourced products and services,' accurately establishes the core principles or elements of the SaaS or on-demand model. Specifically, that the new model will 'remove the responsibility for installation, maintenance, and upgrades (and the associated heavy costs) from over-burdened MIS staff.'

"Even though the SIIA report at the time of its publication stressed that 'due to technical and business issues, such drastic predictions,' had not yet happened, it nonetheless sent up the first flare indicating that a change was definitely on the horizon."[15]

At the end of the day, everyone, and I mean everyone—including Gartner, knew that this *postmodern ERP* era was going to happen. However, rather than empowering the end-user market to more rapidly embrace what is now considered to be the only way to fly—technologically speaking—Gartner seemed to have chosen instead to serve the best interests of its paying customers. I am talking about the ERP companies, whose solutions have consistently failed to deliver the expected results more than 80% of the time over the years.

This is a harsh reminder of what are both the reality and the curse of the technology world. Specifically, that when it came to a choice between serving the best interests of the end user/customer or the financial interests of those who for far too long had driven the market, the former always got the proverbial short-end of the stick. Once again, and given this history, why would anyone trust Gartner or for that matter any of the other similar-type analyst firms and industry pundits going forward?

From my perspective, any insights they offer are likely to be driven by an effort to rebrand their past mistakes as the natural progression of an industry that should have been where it is today, five years ago.

Don't Lump Us in with Gartner!

Opinions such as the one Jon expressed above, channeling frustration at Gartner's coverage choices relative to the knowledge they had of changes coming to the ERP market, are more likely to be thought than spoken. And yet, this is not an absolute. There are occasions when either individual or collective positions are revealed.

In 2015, Pierre Mitchell, Spend Matters Chief Research Officer and Managing Director, commented on a *Procurement Insights* blog post that called into question the lack of public coverage of the relationship between the NIGP code and Periscope Holdings. Whether his comments represented his own individual opinion or the beliefs held by Spend Matters as a whole, they were telling. "Please reach out to us if we're missing stuff like you've uncovered… before you roll us over and lump us in w/ Gartner! We did do a deep dive analysis in our premium subscription, but it was mostly from a technology buyers perspective regarding a SWOT type of analysis..."[16]

The above commentary says a great deal in that it provides evidence of a long-standing blog such as Spend Matters distancing itself (or at least trying to distance itself) from a long-standing analyst firm like Gartner. And yet, when Mitchell responded to Jon's claims of missing coverage, he referenced subscriber (translation: paid) access to a *deep dive analysis.* By his own admission the coverage only focused on a *technology buyer's* perspective.

Moving forward, as procurement technology (and in fact most enterprise technology) becomes increasingly commoditized, technology-focused coverage probably won't mean as much as it used to. If solution providers have to differentiate on something other than their technology, and if coverage is primarily intended to serve procurement decision makers, shouldn't coverage be predominantly focused on evaluations of the *other?*

There are clearly questions that exist in the market about the ties between the administration of the NIGP code used by many public sector agencies and licensed by a number of eSourcing providers, and an eSourcing provider that competes in the eSourcing space. As Mitchell commented later in the same comment stream, "Non-profits, especially those geared towards acquisition professionals and transparent procurement, shouldn't point their members to 'standards' owned by them and licensed in a monopolistic setting by a commercial entity with close ties to that non-profit. If it looks bad, and smells bad, and sounds bad, and feels bad, it's probably bad!"[17] Periscope Holdings sued the State of Missouri, alleging improper selection of Perfect Commerce as their bid winners. Shortly thereafter, Perfect Commerce was threatened with the loss of their license to use the NIGP code in direct connection with the Missouri bid. That meets all of Mitchell's criteria; it looks bad, smells bad, and feels bad. That being the case, why didn't anyone other than *Procurement Insights* cover it?

There are multiple ways to respond to Mitchell's characterization of Spend Matters' coverage of the story. Not the least of which is the ongoing viability of a pay-to-access content business model. But going back to Fersht and his post about the accountability that must be assigned to consumers of procurement media sites, no one can be all things to all people. This creates the need for readers to have multiple go-to sources—one focused on technology, another on news, another on regulation, and perhaps one tracking executive-level shifts and trends within the industry. Procurement professionals should be expected to do some amount of digging on their own, even after reading something like a professionally done SWOT (strengths, weaknesses, opportunities, threats) analysis. "There is only one opinion, at the end of the day, you can rely 100% on—your own," Fersht wrote. "… the only opinion that ultimately matters is what you see with your own eyes—and hear from other customers who've experienced the products and services."[18]

Should Pierre Mitchell or Spend Matters be *lumped in* with Gartner? Well, it depends. Gartner is an analyst firm; they serve a specific role. The knowledge that they hold, however, does not qualify them to serve as a source of general industry news or opinion-based commentary. That is why there are news sites and blogs. Each comes with a different purpose, structure, audience, and burden for quality. The challenge lies in determining which to be and setting appropriate expectations with the target audience. As Bruce Horovitz, long-time marketing reporter for *USA Today* wrote in his final article for the paper about the core problem facing anyone trying to market a brand today, "It's that you still haven't decided what you want to be. You can't do everything well. But you can do a few things well … In headhunter lingo, find your niche."[19]

KELLY'S PERSPECTIVE: *Diversity of Voice and Diversity of Perspective*

I found myself in the procurement commentary sector after years of working as a procurement practitioner and a consultant, which means that I was (and in some cases still am) a consumer of the products and services of the organizations that now serve as what you might call Buyers Meeting Point's competition. I don't usually like to use the word competition, because it suggests a sort of conflict, which is not really the case. Maybe something like co-opetition would be better? For the most part, the people associated with the media sites in procurement get along fairly well.

I've had great exchanges with the teams at many of the sites that Buyers Meeting Point shares procurement professionals' scarce reading time with. Limiting these relationships to direct competitor status would have held me back more than it could ever have propelled me forward. One of the best pieces of advice Jon Hansen ever gave me was early in my days at Buyers Meeting Point. He told me that there can be no direct competition when you base your value proposition on the uniqueness of your own perspective, capabilities, and voice. I have never looked at other blogs and media sites the same way since. I have, however, encountered a cold shoulder or blind eye here and there.

The benefit to there being quite a few established, reputable sources of news and commentary in procurement is that we are all free to specialize in something a little different. Because they have been around the longest, I believe many people in procurement see Spend Matters as the de facto source of information in our industry. Such regard is both a blessing and a curse. While everyone wants to be in a leadership position, there is a reason why migrating birds rotate the front spot as they fly. There is wear and tear and more than a few unfair expectations that go along with a top seat.

Spend Matters' coverage of the Periscope Holdings-Bid Sync merger through a SWOT analysis is a perfectly acceptable approach. It does not, however, present the entire picture. The conflict of interests associated with Periscope owning the standard public sector taxonomy while it competes against eSourcing companies that license that taxonomy from them require a bigger picture perspective. The disconnect here is that I would venture Spend Matters never claimed their SWOT assessment represented the entire picture. If practitioners assumed the story ended there because Spend Matters' coverage ended there, that isn't Spend Matters fault. *Enquiring minds want to know*, as the tabloid saying goes. If procurement needs anything to jettison itself into the next phase of existence, it is more "enquiring" minds.

In the book I wrote with Jeanette Jones, *Supply Market Intelligence for Procurement Professionals*, we discussed the importance of triangulation when doing research. This ensures that a strategy or action plan is not drafted based on an isolated data point. A pragmatic researcher understands that every source of information, especially when analysis and interpretation are involved, is a slight variation on the truth. Not, as we have said previously in the chapter, that anyone is deliberately misleading their audience, but each editorial discretion, no matter how small, leads to a different presentation of the facts. Even in the writing of this book we had to make such choices. In one section (I will not reveal which one) Jon had used the word *pedestrian* meaning *lacking in vitality, imagination, distinction, etc.; commonplace; prosaic or dull.*[20] I envisioned having to enter witness protection after the book was published and talked him down to another term. In the end, we were working with shades of grey, but while both terms would have been equally truthful, the one we decided on in the end was an editorial choice that will shape the impression we give our readers.

By looking at how multiple people or sources represent the same information, a researcher can get as close as possible to validated truth. Granted, reading is not researching, but maybe that is part of the problem. Researching is an active way of processing information, while reading is more passive. This is especially true in today's high-speed world of skimming 140-character summaries and catchy titles leading to articles that may or may not be read. It is not reasonable to expect that by reading one story on an event or revelation that one is properly informed. Reading one story simply prepares us to better understand the next version we read.

If procurement professionals want to be seen as multidimensional sources of value creation, we must learn to treat our own industry as such. On important topics, plan to read a number of types of coverage and ultimately to rely on our own opinions, not the advice or recommendations of others.

THE EMERGENCE OF A NEW MEDIA MODEL

Every industry needs its thought leaders, pundits, and bloggers. Ideally, each person or organization would select one role and stick to it. The challenge for anyone who aspires to fill one of these roles is how to do so in such a way that they can make a living without compromising their perspective and content decisions. It would seem that there are two basic revenue streams associated with media content: the readers and the companies that would like to reach them. Readers can be made to pay for access to content, or companies can pay for advertising—which we commonly class-up by referring to it as *sponsorship*—designed to shape readers' thoughts and opinions.

Assuming the greater risk to objectivity comes through advertising or sponsorship dollars, paying for access to content seems like the preferable approach. But that does not mean it will work. Can a blog, or for that matter any media platform, survive and thrive by asking its readers to foot the bill? When we consider this question, we need to take a step back and look at what is happening outside of the procurement world.

In a *PI Window on Business* blog post discussing the subject of social media monetization, a reference was made to a September 2009 interview with media expert and author Shel Israel. In that interview, Israel stated his belief that the monetization of any social media venue would never be tied to a content access model, but to other things such as sponsorship dollars. Even then, he did not give it too much thought. Referencing his own blog, he indicated that if a sponsor is happy, they will continue to sponsor his blog, if not, then they won't, and someone else will. It is as simple as that.

While most do not share Israel's seemingly cavalier attitude regarding the revenue model question (because it is nice to eat), to many, monetizing social media has become a question of survival. This challenge of how to balance the need to grow readership with the desire to secure revenue affects all media organizations, large and small, generalist and specialist. Even publications such as *The New York Times* are not exempt from the challenge. In January 2011, they announced their intent to start charging for online access to their content. "*The New York Times* is expected to begin charging readers next month for unlimited access to its website, but the introduction of multiple subscription packages will not affect the majority of the site's readers, the *Wall Street Journal* reports."[21]

For traditional print media, making the move to the virtual realms of the Internet, as well as creating a new revenue model, has proven daunting. *The New York Times* decision to begin charging (an albeit small percentage of its electronic readership) an access fee was viewed as innovative and revolutionary. For those following the story closely, however, it was seen more as desperation than innovation.

According to a 2009 prediction by veteran media industry expert J. William Grimes, daily newspapers in the United States would cease to exist within five years. A 2009 post titled "Death of Print Newspapers in 5 Years (J. William Grimes)" considered the Grimes comment and its implications for print media.[22]

Citing statistics which showed that print newspapers' share of the $37 billion spent on advertising was 15%—down from 25% a decade earlier—Grimes pointed out that only 5% of our collective time is spent reading newspapers. This, he concluded, *is not a sustainable model*. As a result of these declines, Grimes pointed out, both the *Washington Post's* and *The New York Times'* traditional print businesses were losing money at a surprisingly rapid rate.

At the time of this book's publication, we find ourselves six years into Grimes' five-year prediction. And while newspapers have not disappeared from the media landscape completely, they are—according to a Carpe Diem blog graphic that reflects revenue through 2014 (see Figure 9.1)—continuing on a steady decline toward an inevitable end.[23]

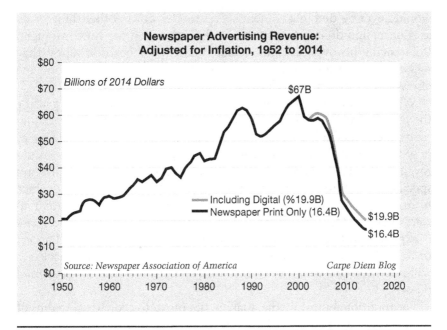

Figure 9.1 Newspaper advertising revenue: adjusted for inflation, 1950 to 2014

The inevitability of the predicted outcome is based on the fact that the revenue decline is not limited to the newspapers' print editions. The steep mirroring dive of advertising revenue for the online versions of the newspapers, after an ever so brief upsurge between 2000 and 2002, indicates that going digital and charging a fee to access content will not boost readership or advertising dollar return. It is very hard to compete with *free*—and even harder when the target audience *expects* a product or service to be free, as they do with news today.

This brings us back to the viability of monetizing procurement industry content through the offering of premium access programs. If people are reluctant to pay to access the content of *The New York Times*, why would the procurement world's media outlets be any different? This leaves us with the option of drawing revenue from sponsorships and made-to-order deliverables. Clearly the challenge of making money and remaining uncompromised will continue in the future.

If a Tree Falls in the Woods, and No One Reports on It, Did It Happen?

The nature of the content being offered and how its value is quantified or proven would seem to be a critical factor in answering this question. Once again, let's look at Pierre Mitchell's comment in the *Procurement Insights* post regarding the link between the Periscope-BidSync merger and the emergence of the #CodeGate scandal.

While Mitchell talked about doing a *deep dive analysis* for the blog's premium subscribers, the focus was on a SWOT analysis of the combined technical offering resulting from the merger. In terms of covering the #CodeGate story, he explained it more as a limitation of time and resources than omission. "We didn't omit this because of lack of courage, but more because lack of time to stay on top of every issue in every industry with every provider!"[24] In other words, Spend Matters made a conscious choice to remain focused on the Periscope-BidSync deal from a traditional technology assessment standpoint because they did not have the headcount to cover every story from every angle.

Given the serious implications of #CodeGate in terms of the public sector procurement world and everything we have discovered since *Procurement Insights* began to unravel the details behind the scandal, one would have to question what this means for the value proposition of their *PRO* paid access. Because Spend Matters' coverage of the Periscope-BidSync merger was at best, partial, and at worst, perfunctory; a lack of deeper coverage could have undermined the value of the blog's premium service offering in the eyes of their subscribers.

Think about this last point for just a moment. PRO subscribers are paying a premium to access *insider information* on Spend Matters. In return for your investment you receive a SWOT analysis of the combined offering that is supposedly going to help you to decide if the features, functions, and benefits of the merged technology align with accomplishing your procurement automation objectives. Let's say the story ends here and the majority of readers, who, because they are pressed for time, never read alternate coverage of the story on another blog. From the decision-making standpoint of those professionals, it would be as if the conflict did not exist.

There would be no #CodeGate. No revelation that Periscope, through what Mitchell himself referred to as being a monopolistic setting, had teamed up with the NIGP to threaten to pull the NIGP Code license of a competitor who just happened to have beat them out for a major government contract.

There would be no assessment as to how this could affect public sector procurement going forward. For example, would the merged organization force government entities to deal with a single vendor, because said vendor had control over the much needed NIGP taxonomy? What about other eProcurement vendors? Would they back away from bidding against Periscope on new contracts if there was a risk that they would lose their license to the NIGP Code, and with it the ability to support their existing clients?

None of this would have ever come to light. And even if it did, under a pay-to-access content model, would it have gained the exposure that was necessary to effect needed change in the industry? Which information is worth more to you? An overview of a vendor's technology, the access to which you are required to pay a premium fee, or *free* access to content that uncovered a conflict of interest relationship, that if left unchecked would have a significant and lasting impact on public sector procurement?

The answer to this question is in the application of the news. Which information is more valuable from the standpoint of selecting a vendor? The features, functions, and benefits or the questionable terms under which said vendor operates? Which would be more important for you to know, and how much would you be willing to pay?

From our perspective, the way in which a company does business—including its corporate values—far outweighs the functionality of the technology it offers. This is especially true given the fact that the eProcurement solution world is becoming an increasingly commoditized market, in which the risks associated with the complexity of enterprise implementations of the past are no longer an issue.

While some may disagree with the above assessment, the fact is that today's SaaS, cloud-based models can be implemented in a matter of weeks versus years and for relative pennies as opposed to tens of millions of dollars. These new-age solutions—especially for technology savvy Generation Next professionals, no longer require the *deep dive* analysis that was necessary during the ERP era. As a result, why would anyone pay to access this information?

It is this questionable value of traditional industry coverage, coupled with the resistance on the part of readers to pay to access content that would seem to concur with Israel's perspective.

CONCLUSION

The changes taking place in procurement today create plenty of fodder for analysts, bloggers, and journalists to churn on. But given the strategic development of our field, and the shifts being seen in our technology solutions, there is little black and white fact that can be reported without opinion and analysis. Media entities must remember that companies and individuals make decisions based on their reporting, and they must regard that trust highly enough to walk the straight and narrow—even if it means losing a few friends or sponsors along the way. But the burden is not theirs alone. Readers and decision makers also have a role to play. They must employ critical thought whenever possible; double and triple-check claims and sources; and be prepared to form their own opinion before taking or recommending action.

REFERENCES

1. Ernest M. Hemingway, *The Poetry Foundation*, Accessed July 6, 2015, http://www.poetryfoundation.org/bio/ernest-m-hemingway.
2. "The NIGP Code," *Wikipedia*, Accessed July 6, 2015, https://en.wikipedia.org/wiki/NIGP_Code.
3. "Overview of RFP Depot, LLC," *Bloomberg Business*, Accessed July 6, 2015, http://www.bloomberg.com/research/stocks/private/snapshot.asp?privcapId=223025293.
4. Jon Hansen, "Missouri Award Protest: The Gettysburg of Public Sector eProcurement," *Procurement Insights*, March 31, 2015, https://procureinsights.wordpress.com/2015/03/31/missouri-award-protest-the-gettysburg-of-public-sector-eprocurement-by-jon-hansen/.
5. Ibid.
6. Jon Hansen, "The Silence of the Blogs (and Industry Analysts)," *Procurement Insights*, April 17th, 2015, https://procureinsights.wordpress.com/2015/04/17/the-silence-of-the-blogs-and-industry-analysts-by-jon-hansen/.
7. Jon Hansen, "Madison Avenue ooops … make that Gartner, names Oracle as a leader in supply chain planning," *Procurement Insights*, January 7, 2011, https://procureinsights.wordpress.com/2011/01/07/madison-avenue-ooops-make-that-gartner-names-oracle-as-a-leader-in-supply-chain-planning/.
8. "Credibility of Analysts," *Information Week*, February 3, 2006, http://www.informationweek.com/credibility-of-analysts/d/d-id/1040282?page_number=1.
9. David Rossiter, "Ethics and Independence Among Industry Analysts," *Institute of Industry Analyst Relations*, March 7, 2008, http://analystrelations.org/2008/03/07/ethics-and-independence-among-industry-analysts/.

10. Phil Fersht, "Are some 'independent' analysts the worst offenders of pay-to-play?" *Horses for Sources*, February 22, 2014, http://www .horsesforsources.com/independents-worstoffenders_022214?utm _source=dlvr.it&utm_medium=twitter&utm_campaign=Feed%3A+ HorsesForSources+%28Horses+for+Sources%29.

11. "Global Research Reveals Procurement's Internal Comms Crisis," *Xchanging Procurement*, May 19, 2015, http://www.xchanging.com/ news/global-research-reveals-procurement-internal-comms-crisis.

12. "Gartner Says By 2016, the Impact of Cloud and Emergence of Postmodern ERP Will Relegate Highly Customized ERP Systems to 'Legacy' Status," *Gartner*, January 29th, 2014, http://www.gartner .com/newsroom/id/2658415?utm_content=buffer7c72b&utm _medium=social&utm_source=linkedin.com&utm_campaign= buffer.

13. Jon Hansen, "Optimization Modeling and the Modern Supply Chain (A PI Q and A)," *Procurement Insights*, March 18, 2008, https:// procureinsights.wordpress.com/2008/03/18/optimization-modeling -and-the-modern-supply-chain-a-pi-q-and-a/.

14. ———, "Riding the Crest of a New Wave: How the Original SaaS Companies Have Gained the Upper Hand," Procurement Insights, March 20, 2009 https://procureinsights.wordpress.com/2009/03/20/ riding-the-crest-of-a-new-wave-how-the-original-saas-companies -have-gained-the-upper-hand-a-procurement-insights-knowledge -leadership-publication/.

15. Ibid.

16. Pierre Mitchell, April 21, 2015, comment on Jon Hansen, "The Silence Of The Blogs (And Industry Analysts), *Procurement Insights*, April 17, 2015, https://procureinsights.wordpress.com/2015/04/ 17/the-silence-of-the-blogs-and-industry-analysts-by-jon-hansen/.

17. Jon Hansen, "The Silence of the Blogs (and Industry Analysts)," *Procurement Insights*, April 17th, 2015, https://procureinsights .wordpress.com/2015/04/17/the-silence-of-the-blogs-and-industry -analysts-by-jon-hansen/.

18. Phil Fersht, "Are some 'independent' analysts the worst offenders of pay-to-play?" *Horses for Sources*, February 22, 2014, http://www .horsesforsources.com/independents-worst-offenders_022214?utm _source=dlvr.it&utm_medium=twitter&utm_campaign=Feed%3A +HorsesForSources+%28Horses+for+Sources%29.

19. Bruce Horovitz, "Shoe is On the Other Foot: Selling 'Me,'" *USA Today*, May 27, 2015, http://www.usatoday.com/story/money/2015/ 05/15/marketing-workforce-job-hunting-bruce-horovitz/27365613/.

20. "Pedestrian," Dictionary.com, Accessed July 21, 2015, http:// dictionary.reference.com/browse/pedestrian.
21. "New York Times preps online paywall," *CBC News*, January 24, 2011, http://www.cbc.ca/news/new-york-times-preps-online -paywall-1.981042.
22. Jon Hansen, "Death of Print Newspapers in 5 Years (J. William Grimes)," *PI Window on Business*, August 30, 2009, https:// piwindowonbusiness.wordpress.com/2009/08/30/death-of-print -newspapers-in-5-years-j-william-grimes/.
23. Mark J. Perry, "Free-fall: Adjusted for Inflation, Print Newspaper Advertising Will be Lower This Year Than in 1950," *Carpe Diem*, September 6, 2012, http://mjperry.blogspot.hk/2012/09/freefall -adjusted-for-inflation-print.html.
24. Pierre Mitchell, April 21, 2015, comment on Jon Hansen, "The Silence Of The Blogs (And Industry Analysts), *Procurement Insights*, April 17, 2015, https://procureinsights.wordpress.com/2015/04/ 17/the-silence-of-the-blogs-and-industry-analysts-by-jon-hansen/.

Web
Added
Value™

This book has free material available for download from the
Web Added Value™ resource center at *www.jrosspub.com*

10

Where Does Procurement Go from Here?

"It's quickly dawning on us instead that our education was at best a thin foundation that needs to be continually refreshed in order for us to stay competitive." The Power of Pull, John Hagel III, John Seely Brown, and Lang Davison[1]

American author and social philosopher Eric Hoffer once said, "In times of change, learners inherit the earth … while the learned find themselves beautifully equipped to deal with a world that no longer exists."[2] In this simple yet powerful statement, Hoffer sums up the procurement professional's greatest challenge, as well as his or her greatest opportunity. The only question left to be answered is this: what does making the transition from being learned to learning entail, and are we up to the task?

In this final chapter of our book, we examine what it means to change the way we see our profession, including our understanding of its role within the modern competitive enterprise. From moving beyond the adversarial aspects of past supplier engagement practices, to becoming relational and collaborative in our interactions with external as well as internal partners, we hope you will find this chapter to be an essential survival and transformational guide for your career as a procurement professional. Change is on the near horizon. We can no longer deny or avoid it any more than we can precisely predict what it will look like. We can, however, adapt and become relevant beyond what we ever thought possible. First we have to decide what it means to become relevant and what relevance looks like in this brave new world.

THE TAKEAWAYS

In this book we have posed and discussed—we would not dream of saying answered—nine questions that we see as being of critical importance to the procurement profession and to the careers of those currently within it. The fact that there is no clear answer to any of these questions not only opens up the floor for debate, but also demonstrates that the place and role of procurement is nuanced. If nothing else, this fact alone should demonstrate that we are not tactical. If we were, there would be little to discuss, and since we must be strategic in order to be relevant, we have met the first requirement on our journey to influence.

Who is Procurement?

We are a fabulously (and increasingly) diverse group of professionals who want to be all we can be for our own sakes and for the sake of the company. Although our diversity brings creative potential, it is also accompanied by tension—or at least a difference of opinions.

One way of looking at the progress we have made is to compare the story that opens Chapter 1—the founding of the Institute for Supply Management (ISM) by a savvy salesperson at the *Thomas Register*—to the launch of Procurious in 2013, almost exactly a century later. Procurious is completely online, dedicated to growing procurement's vision, and founded and driven by procurement professionals. E. B. Hendricks founded ISM because he recognized that the purchasing professionals at the time were unable to find a way to network on their own. Tanya Seary founded Procurious because she believes LinkedIn and all of the other social platforms available do not meet our total need. As it says on the Procurious website, "Procurement has a new face. It's smarter, more ambitious, more global and more mobile than ever before. But procurement and supply chain professionals are a widespread and disconnected community—they haven't had anywhere to collaborate online. Until now."[3] While the problem in 2013 was the same as the one in 1913, a fragmented professional community, today's solution is new—as is the source of that solution. Procurement has practically unlimited potential to grow in strength and agility, at least if visionaries like Seary have anything to say about it.

Like any example of evolution, not everything is preserved in the process of natural selection. Some professionals may find themselves out of alignment or out of a job if they are unable to keep up with the changes taking place. In addition to experienced procurement professionals who are under pressure to adapt to a faster, more competitive landscape, associations are challenged to continue providing value through the right channels as expectations and demographics change. The race is on to see who will be around, and who will be dominant, at the end of the next procurement century.

Has Procurement (Finally) Come of Age?

For a long time, procurement professionals have pushed for a seat at the executive table. Today, however, we recognize the fact that just like all of the other structures and frameworks we work inside of, this traditional indication of relative status has changed.

Coming-of-age is a process, not an event, just as success is a journey rather than a destination. We must expect it to take time to understand and internalize all of the changing factors that should be allowed to shape our maturation. The most important thing about this shaping is that we are not truly prepared to act in an appropriate manner until the process is over. While the resulting delay may create a frustrating period for many professionals, each tension we feel has a purpose. It forces us to consider our options and make conscious decisions about which path we will choose. The source of each tension also helps us focus our attention on the areas where we are out of alignment, such as communication, performance, or execution.

What procurement should really pursue on this growth journey is influence. Not only does influence often come with greater opportunity and potential than a title or a seat at a specific table, we don't have to wait for anyone to bestow it upon us. We can strike out on our own and earn it directly. We should also consider the idea that our best bet for success will be through an entirely new organizational path, such as a chief relational officer, or through closer alignment with operations. If change is to be the new normal, we have to position ourselves to see clearly and to work unfettered by legacy notions about the importance of a C-level title.

Is Procurement Strategic?

No. Okay, maybe (at least sometimes). Without realizing it, procurement has sometimes been our own worst enemy. We allow annoyances such as quantitative metrics to have far too much of an impact on who we are and how we interact with others. Since we are not going to be able to move away from them any time soon—if ever—we have to find a way to look beyond them. For guidance, we should look to our colleagues in marketing and sales.

Even the most complex concepts must be clearly delivered. Less is more, because an opportunity to make a pitch to an executive does not come along often and certainly doesn't last long when it does. Believe it or not, reincarnating the *elevator pitch* approach from the days of, well, elevators, may just save procurement from itself when it comes to building internal support and rapport. Any idea that is too abstract to be communicated succinctly will probably be considered suspect—both in terms of its ability to gain traction and its likelihood to generate the promised results.

Although we are sometimes our own worst enemy, we are not our only adversary. Procurement is often goaded into tactical behavior by other functions: finance, operations, and executive management. Even when filling the *bad cop* role offers us the chance to play an important part in some short-term effort, we need to shake this stigma if we are to advance and attain higher-level achievement.

As hard as it may be to swallow, we can also learn a few things from the sales team. First and foremost, no function has more quantitative performance metrics than sales, and yet none is considered as strategic. Part of how they navigate the balance this requires is by doing all kinds of things that do not lead directly to revenue—value creation you might say—and accepting their investment of effort as the cost of doing business. Procurement will need to reconcile similar competing demands for their time at the crossroads of savings and value. Doing so by adopting a business development mind-set may pleasantly surprise our colleagues and demonstrate just how strategic we really are.

Is There Truth behind the Numbers?

Yes. No. Maybe—sometimes? Just like procurement's efforts to demonstrate our strategic value, we are engaged in a constant back-and-forth about needing to provide more numbers while also proving that those numbers are both *real* and representative.

To make things even more complicated, advances in analytical capabilities, the advent of big data, and the Internet of Things give us more numbers to work with and more ways to work with them—all the while still looking to prove that our data does not chain us to the past. Predictive analytics is an area of increasing interest to executives and other decision makers for obvious reasons, so the race to satisfy that need and perfect the associated techniques and skills is on.

Since access to data is no longer the challenge, and the automation required to manage it is improving by leaps and bounds, the crossroads that remains is knowing how to wield that data. The experience required to apply the resulting intelligence in the most effective way may provide procurement with a new opportunity to create value and competitive advantage—but in order to do so, we have to be willing to move beyond known processes and into unstructured and unknown areas. Procurement must translate analytics into basic, attainable strategies that management supports and which serve to build further respect for the value we add.

Are Win-Win Collaborations Really Possible?

If advances in data and analytics are key influencers on the future path that our technology will take, learning to truly collaborate is the key to a successful future with suppliers. Learning to work as equal partners with a select group of strategic suppliers is more than many of us can take. In fact, the alterations in mind-set that are required will make it all but impossible for some of the more traditional thinkers in our field to engage in this way.

In addition to rethinking our supplier interactions, collaboration will require us to alter our approach. The first pin to fall will be the efficiency paradigm that procurement and strategic sourcing were essentially created to execute. You can't collaborate while also looking to leverage economies of scale and consolidate the supply base. It is not a scalable approach. Collaboration requires an artisan skillset, along with mindful attention to detail and a careful pace. Reconciling the differences in approach and capabilities will be a challenge, and may require the involvement of nonprocurement professionals, whose experience qualifies them to be successful under these alternate conditions.

In the case of collaboration, procurement needs to take what seem like opposing forces—scalability and artistry—and help them reach alignment. Although there are many experts and thought leaders who can help companies that aspire to be more collaborative, whether in general or for one project, those companies need to do more than just hire consultants. Being collaborative requires professionals to think collectively and believe in the effort. Otherwise, they will never be able to cross the chasm.

Do We Really Need Another Chapter about Finance?

Hint: the answer to this question is no, although we almost fell into the trap of assuming we needed to dedicate an entire chapter to the procurement finance relationship, just because it is such a frequently addressed topic. Like all other *dinosaur* traps, acting without careful consideration allows us to slip back into an endangered mind-set.

When we look at the interfunctional dynamics of the entire enterprise, it becomes clear that procurement is not the only group undergoing a fundamental change. After many years inside the confining structure of the procurement silo, we are being encouraged to break free and become part of a more fluid corporate structure. But with this increased freedom comes lack of definition—of our role and of our responsibilities.

There are other consequences of this freedom as well—not the least of which is increased cross-functional competition for the same talent pool. If strong general skills are acceptable—even desirable—then any qualified candidate might be equally successful in procurement, finance,

It was clear the world had changed forever when Simon
discovered how to order birdhouses online.

information technology (IT), operations, etc. The challenge becomes finding a way to identify those who really do belong in procurement and winning them over to the idea.

Can Procurement Technology Benefit from the Uber Effect?

As we considered each topic in this book, we repeatedly saw that nothing is quite what it seems. That being said, surely a chapter on technology is about technology—especially for a field like procurement, where we owe so much of our success and identity to the solutions we employ. Well, think again. Even our discussion about technology is really about people: those providing the solutions and those using them.

Thanks in large part to the cloud, small providers have made significant progress in a competitive market. It is no longer considered absolutely wise to select the largest solution any more than it is considered absolutely foolhardy to select the newest or smallest. Procurement needs to use entirely new ways of deciding which solutions to implement, and this requires us to think less about features and functions than agreement with the provider on the stability of their vision, strategy, and finances. The ripple effect of this shift has not worked its way through all of the organizations who cover procurement technology—minimizing the applicability of their evaluations in proportion to the part of our decision that is actually based upon the technology itself.

Procurement is ripe for disruptive innovation—just like Uber founder Travis Kalanick has brought to car and taxi service markets the world over. Procurement cannot play a passive role when it comes to making decisions about technology, especially since we are already practiced in the art of evaluating suppliers on their total profile rather than just comparing pricing, delivery, and specifications.

Are the Differences Between the Public and Private Sectors Real or Perceived?

Thank goodness, finally a topic that we all know will unfold just like we expect. After all, everyone knows that the public sector is bloated, inefficient, and ineffective—constantly being outpaced by their infinitely more capable private sector colleagues.

This near certainty has also been eroded by years of cross sector pollination and collaboration. In many cases, old stereotypes of public sector procurement are propagated by the kinds of stories about them that are most likely to make the news: stories that never see the light of day about the private sector. Well, all of that is about to change. Not only is the public sector starting to achieve better performance through strategic privatization, the private sector is being exposed to more negative press as they increase their spend with suppliers relative to total revenue. Both sides have a lot to learn from each other. And while they should not necessarily expect to become more alike, they may both become better.

The Media and Procurement: Are We Really Covered?

Procurement is fortunate to have a diverse and experienced media sector of our very own. Sure, over time some of the journals and analyst firms have faded into the sunset or been acquired, but there are lots of blogs and analyst firms dedicated to covering the practices and providers in our industry. Besides, the diminishing role of print media in procurement tracks in line with what is being seen across the entire media industry.

Although our industry has been covered by a group of qualified analysts, we have not always gotten the whole story. Unfortunately, the traditional analyst model has gotten in the way of true and reliable journalistic coverage. How can a site honestly cover the same companies that they rely upon for revenue? In some cases this paradox has resulted in what looks like certain stories—especially negative ones relating to established players—being given a good *leaving alone*.

This issue became crystal clear with the example of the Periscope Holdings versus Perfect Commerce NIGP #CodeGate story. While the events that unfolded during *Procurement Insights'* coverage of #CodeGate are important for procurement decision makers to be aware of, they almost didn't come to light. In fact, other than *Procurement Insights*, no blog or news site covered the story at all. This disparity of coverage raises the question about what objectives are setting the priorities of the sources we look to for breaking news in procurement.

AND NOW, FOR A FEW FINAL THOUGHTS

Writing this book has been an intense journey. The sheer amount of thought leadership that we needed to read, think about, and synthesize with our own experiences has been dizzying. Our realizations and conclusions have not always been in line with what we expected, and they have not always been what we wanted to see. You may not agree with us on everything, or anything for that matter. After all, we don't agree on everything and there are only two of us. Our ardent wish is that we have given you enough to consider so that you can make a choice about which direction to pursue at the current crossroads—and the future crossroads to come.

JON'S PERSPECTIVE: *Act Like You Have the Influence and Respect You Deserve*

This is the statement I made to open my second session at the 25th Annual Public Procurement Forum in Virginia: "Procurement professionals are great at delivering value, but terrible at promoting their value to their organization and beyond."

Titled "Strategically Speaking: Procurement, the Organization, and You," I focused on the significant changes that are taking place, not only within our own profession, but within the larger business world as a whole. This included a detailed breakdown on how both finance and IT professionals are also going through major transformations and what it all means in terms of the dissolution of the functional silos that have, for far too long, restricted rather than stimulated enterprise-wide collaboration.

The fact is that procurement's strategic importance is already globally recognized and widely embraced. The lingering problem is what I would refer to as being the Rodney Dangerfield effect, one that continues to cast its pall over the profession. Even though some of you may be unfamiliar with Dangerfield, you are likely aware of his famous tagline, "I get no respect."

This has, to a degree, become the universal and ubiquitous cry of procurement professionals—at least those who belong to the older or former generation. The Generation Next professionals do not suffer from the same lack of self-worth or poor self-image that has been cultivated and nurtured by those who came before them. It is also another example of Handfield's definite and definitive divide between the current and emerging generations.

It is within the observatory wisdom of the Handfield generational chasm that the relevance question is answered as well as the pondering of where we go from here. So what is the answer? We have to start by recognizing that old skill sets will inevitably cede way to new ones.

It also means that we have to understand and accept that technology will, through the advent of wearable devices and 24/7 mobile access, redefine the supply chain as we know it. As a point of reference, the extent of this change was revealed in an article by cloudBuy's Nilesh Gopali, when he talked about a study asserting that the average business person 35 years or younger has never used a desktop or notebook PC. How is that for a major generational wake-up call!

Finally, we have to stop asking for respect and start acting like we already have it, because we do.

In the end, our future in this profession starts and ends with our perception of who we are and the value we bring. When we reach this point of epiphanic awareness, we will also be in a better position to adapt to the broader, external changes in the business world as a whole. Then and only then, will we assume our rightful place in the new hierarchy of organizational influence.

KELLY'S PERSPECTIVE: *Carpe Diem—Today*

Procurement has been incredibly good to me. In just over a decade, I have gone from not knowing what strategic sourcing was, to becoming a practitioner specializing in hired services, to working as the associate director of consulting at a solution provider, to covering the space from a not-too-distant but always fascinating vantage point.

On December 13, 2013, I received an e-mail from Jon which read only the following:

> *Maybe we should co-write a book . . . we can call it Procurement in the Next Decade.*
>
> *Have a Merry Christmas.*
>
> *Jon*

It is amazing that it took us twenty percent of a decade to tell a decade's worth of story. When we started working, I made an initial prediction that the procurement team of the future would be like a SWOT (strengths, weaknesses, opportunities, threats) team, responding with lightning strike accuracy to each need for strategy or spend management. And while it was a cool vision of the future, it was isolationist at its core. At the time, I gave no thought to the relationships, partnerships, and extended opportunities that it would deny us and our organizations—not to mention the fulfillment of our real potential.

If I had to make a prediction about the future of procurement today, it would have far more to do with slowing down, absorbing information, and considering every opportunity to continue learning and creating value—regardless of contribution to our savings metrics. I like how Tim Cummins summed up our current crossroads in a June 2015 *Commitment Matters* post, "Unless procurement also recognizes the importance of shifting away from its focus on control, compliance, categories and process, it will rapidly become irrelevant."[4] Far from being a negative or alarmist viewpoint, he titled the post "Embrace the Future—It Is Here Today." That can-do spirit is what carried procurement from the 19th-century railroad industry to the 21st century. It is the same spirit that will continue to create opportunities for the procurement function in general, and talented procurement professionals in the future—whatever it happens to look like.

Carpe diem. Seize the day—today.

Others' Perspectives: #FutureBuy

In May 2014, we put out an open call to anyone in procurement or otherwise who wanted to make a prediction or wish about the future of procurement. As we wrote at the time: "If we knew what the future held for procurement, we would undoubtedly change some of what we are doing today. Since it is impossible for any of us to be certain about the future, our best option is to form a vision for what we *hope* the future will hold and align our initiatives to that vision."[5]

The responses we received were as diverse and compelling as the individuals and organizations who offered them up. Here are a few of our favorites:

Dr. Thomas DePaoli, Management Program Director at Marian University, supply chain management & purchasing consultant, published author
The future of the supply chain and relationships will radically change. Normally the procurement professional tells or indicates to the suppliers, logistics partners, or links along the supply chain train what is needed. Procurement is usually the engine driving the supply chain train. In the future, with the advent of mega-data analysis, the supply chain will become more self-sustaining. Each link along the chain will become more predictive. They will anticipate demand and just execute. To some this may seem like a scary loss of control, but it depends on suppliers being just as knowledgeable or more knowledgeable than procurement. They can predict changes accurately and just execute. They

will follow the axiom of "It is better to ask forgiveness rather than permission." Multiple shared data warehouses and databases will make this possible. Thus the supply chain train will be driven by every car in the train! It requires a broad and deep understanding by everyone along the supply chain, but access to mega-data will make it possible and the norm.[6]

Patricia Moody, author, publisher, management consultant, driven visionary
The New Monroe Doctrine: The U.S. and Mexico reach a new geopolitical arrangement, beyond NAFTA, beyond immigration, that leverages the resources of Mexico—workforce, manufacturing centers, oil, and in combination with Canada's oil, redefines and strengthens The Americas' global trade powerhouse. Other American countries follow.

Water, even in the U.S., becomes the new oil. When I said this to a BP vice president, we joked about slicing off a piece of Antarctica and floating it up to California. They've got the tools to work it.

The Chinese Box that Morley and I envisioned in *The Technology Machine, How Manufacturing Will Work in the Year 2020*, is just about here in plastics and electronics.

Blinded by the buzz: 3D printing capabilities far exceeded by vision systems impact.

Brick and Mortar: Even the Cloud sits on brick and mortar—it's the moats and bunkers that differentiate. By the time companies figure it all out, they will be too addicted to data to walk it back.

The United States of the Americas: Redrawn geopolitical trade agreements effectively kill the illegal drug and human trafficking trades.[7]

Rolf Zimmer, Founder and Managing Director at riskmethods
Increasing internationalization, global networking, and shifting of value-added processes are a real development. Disruptions in the supply chain—be they of an economic, structural, political, or ecological nature—can have fatal consequences for security of supply in terms of organizations and their corporate success. A research study by PwC (Global Supply Chain and Risk Management Survey, 2013) revealed that more than 60% of respondents saw their performance indicators drop by 3% or more in 2012 as a result of a disruption in their global supply chain. This means that besides suppliers, supply-related risks along all transfer points, interim storage sites, and logistics hubs must be monitored in order to secure supply.

We are convinced that the trend in the future is going to be towards transparency over the entire supplier network, including location and country risks of 1-n tier supply routes. Previous supplier-centric approaches in terms of quality, stability, and price of partners must be supplemented by supply security aspects along all supply routes as well as compliance aspects as regards 1-n tier relationships. Companies in all sectors must continue to focus on their suppliers and supplier relationships—they will, however, have to take this a step further, namely to include the entire supply chain into their management.

So, we are not predicting that supplier management will no longer be relevant—but a holistic 1-n tier supply chain management approach will enter a new era: the conversion of SRM and SCM has started.[8]

Bill Kohnen, Purchasing Leader and Senior Solutions Consultant for Innovative Global Organizations
Purchasing tools and process will be transformed as what is common for consumers with mobile, social, and applications is integrated with Corporate Purchasing Solutions and Process. Some specific broad trends:

Open Requirements—The idea that a product or service can be reduced to only the elements you really need and then you can source those and build as needed. The concept really has seen tremendous results from technical groups at organizations like Facebook which did not accept the need to accept what was offered by the traditional enterprise server and router companies which has resulted in massive purchase and total cost savings.

Everything as a Subscription: Even physical things being acquired as a subscription over the total life cycle and returned at end for disposal.

Thought Leadership: Purchasing and Supply Chain thought leadership and best practice is being equally driven between the U.S. and other parts of the world: India and China in particular.

Logistics: Again consumer-like expectations prevailing with Amazon-like delivery options. Transparency of reporting through supply chain and ultimately 3D printing eliminating the need for shipping of some items altogether.

KPIs: Reflecting more direct contribution of value to the organization as well as getting supply chain risk reduction right.

It is debatable whether the skill set of a Buyer today is correct to meet future requirements which creates a threat that other organizations will take the lead. From an individual point of view, Buyers must try to forget the things they used to do.

Become immersed in your key supply chains. Your contribution and value to your organization will come from your work that takes place with your product development groups, at your key suppliers, optimizing logistics and ensuring end customers needs are met.

For Purchasing Managers and Directors looking for a position: Rebrand yourself as an experienced technical expert in the category you are best at. High-level experts [and] Category Managers' salaries approach and exceed that of Department Managers.[9]

Alun Rafique and Nick Drewe, founders of Market Dojo[10]
As technology develops and the knowledge of eSourcing expands, the number of people using eSourcing will increase. We will hopefully begin to see true commoditization of the process and tools, so it really does just come down to price in the lower end of the spectrum. Eventually, it won't just be large- and medium-sized enterprises utilizing eSourcing, the smaller SMEs will be aware of and embracing it too.

Centralized eSourcing teams move in conjunction with local self-serve teams who even use the tools to get quotes on low value tenders of a few hundred pounds.

REFERENCES

1. John Hagel III, John Seely Brown, and Lang Davison, *The Power of Pull: How Small Moves, Smartly Made, Can Set Big Things in Motion*, (New York: Basic Books, 2012), 13.
2. Eric Hoffer, *Between the Devil and the Dragon: The Best Essays and Aphorisms of Eric Hoffer* (New York: Harper & Row, 1982), 146.
3. "Our Story," *Procurious*, Accessed July 8, 2015, https://www .procurious.com/static/our-story.
4. Tim Cummins, "Embrace the Future—It Is Here Today," *Commitment Matters*, June 19, 2015, http://commitmentmatters.com/2015/ 06/19/embrace-the-future-it-is-here-today/.
5. Kelly Barner, "Open Call for Predictions: What does the Future of Procurement Hold? #FutureBuy," *The Point*, May 1, 2014, http:// buyersmeetingpoint.com/blogs/bmps-qthe-pointq/entry/open-call -for-predictions-what-does-the-future-of-procurement-hold -futurebuy.
6. ———, "Open Call for Predictions: What does the Future of Procurement Hold? #FutureBuy," *The Point*, May 2, 2014, http://buyers meetingpoint.com/blogs/bmps-qthe-pointq/entry/open-call-for -predictions-what-does-the-future-of-procurement-hold-futurebuy.
7. Patricia Moody, "Flash Forward: A #FutureBuy Perspective from The Mill Girl at Blue Heron Journal," *The Point*, June 3, 2014, http://

buyersmeetingpoint.com/blogs/bmps-qthe-pointq/entry/flash
-forward-a-futurebuy-perspective-from-the-mill-girl-at-blue-heron
-journal.

8. Rolf Zimmer, "The Future of Procurement—Take 1," *riskmethods blog*, September 13, 2014, http://www.riskmethods.net/de/blog/the-future-of-procurement---take-1/101.

9. Kelly Barner, "Open Call for Predictions: What does the Future of Procurement Hold? #FutureBuy," *The Point*, May 2, 2014, http://buyersmeetingpoint.com/blogs/bmps-qthe-pointq/entry/open-call-for-predictions-what-does-the-future-of-procurement-hold-futurebuy.

10. Alun Rafique and Nick Drewe, "The eSourcing eVolution Part III - The Future," The Secret Diary of Market Dojo, October 21, 2015, http://blog.marketdojo.com/2015/10/esourcingrevolutionpart3.html.

This book has free material available for download from the
Web Added Value™ resource center at *www.jrosspub.com*

EPILOGUE

What If We Are Wrong about the Future of Procurement?

We have just spent hundreds of pages, not to mention the last two years of our lives, looking into the future of procurement and our options to improve it. We believe our field currently is at a crossroads because there are changes taking place on so many fronts: generational shifts, technology, organizational structure, and skills requirements. As we make the corresponding decisions in rapid succession, we increase the likelihood that our future trajectory will significantly deviate from our past. We prefer to think of this as an evolution rather than a departure, and yet some characteristics and habits will have to be left behind because they conflict with the procurement profile of the future.

On February 16, 2015, we were among 34 procurement experts asked by the Next Level Purchasing Association to make predictions about what 2015 will mean to the future of the profession. We, along with colleagues from a variety of positions, companies, and perspectives, shared unique and optimistic speculations about education, technology, and relationships with external business partners.[1]

Every person—without a single exception—made reasonable suggestions about the positive events likely to take place, or the areas of development or investment that we need to prioritize for investment. No one responded with, "2015 is the year I will get my resume up-to-date, because, let's face it, procurement is a sinking ship. Every man for himself!" Each of us believes in the predictions we made—and why not? We all enjoy working in procurement and want nothing but the best for our profession and all of the individuals building careers in it. Our predictions are also representative of what we aspire to achieve in the coming year and beyond. However, anyone who is focusing on maximizing the potential contribution of procurement to the organization as we are has probably forgotten to consider a very real possibility.

We could all be wrong.

In a February 16, 2015 article in *USA Today*, "Disruption is cheap; cravings are profitable," Michael Wolff discussed the fact that although technology firms seem like the best bet for return on investment today, they are very new players on a stage with a long history. Wolff cited data that suggests it is not the new and disruptive innovations that generate return over the long haul, but the things that consistently tempt us to indulge, things such as alcohol, television, and sports. "The recent study by Credit Suisse that sin businesses, most notably tobacco and alcohol, have, since the beginning of the 20th century, outperformed every other business sector is a bracing reminder of what is constant in this time of radical change."[2] This is true even given amazing recent growth and earnings accomplishments of firms like Apple. They are still isolated (albeit spiked) points on a very long scale.

The constants, according to Wolff, that really make an industry, company, or solution a long-term success, are the habits that support basic human needs and wants. If we can feed into human habits—preferably those that already exist—we have a better chance at traction and long-term impact. "It's not disruption that wins the race, but habituation—serving and understanding basic human impulses and needs. ... This is a teaching moment type of revelation, particularly for the media and tech businesses, where high valuations go to the new and the next instead of to the fixed and proven."[3] Apply this concept to the seeming evolution playing out in procurement, and it becomes clear that there is more than one possibility for what will be evident when we look back at this field and this time one hundred years from now.

One possibility is that the service and supply needs and habits of buyers and other professionals within an organization will be met by a combination of tactical procurement and automation. The disruption that seems to be fueling our evolution could be as fleeting as compact discs ended up being in the music space. Companies may not want a procurement function that is agile and strategic. Since executive teams are already skeptical about the need for real change in the role of procurement, a lack of interest on the part of our stakeholders would seem to be the final nail in the coffin of that idea.

The other possibility is that those of us pulling for a revolution are somehow clinging to a function that we have personally outgrown but are not yet ready to let go of. The fact that our ideas are even being entertained gives some evidence to our promise. That being said, we still need to consider how much executives believe in procurement as a function and how much they believe in the skills and knowledge of the individuals within it. We have to acknowledge the possibility that there is nothing wrong with procurement as it is today, no matter how much we might like for it to transcend its tactical history and rise to a permanent role in the C-suite.

We're not condemning procurement professionals to a dystopian future of transaction processing in bland grey suits and sterile offices. There is unquestionably value to be gained from time spent building analytical skills and understanding the critical role the supply base plays in the long-term success of the enterprise. We do need to consider the possibility, however, that significant change will never come to pass in the majority of procurement organizations. If this happens to be the case, we will all be okay. The cream always rises to the top, as the saying goes, and whether the top happens to be in procurement or not, it is unlikely that any of us will regret for a moment the time we spent in the field. There is a unique business perspective afforded to procurement professionals and those who learn from that experience will have increased their personal intellectual property greatly. That knowledge is highly desirable and valuable in many aspects of modern business outside of procurement.

In *The Procurement Value Proposition*, Gerard Chick and Robert Handfield cited the credo that Peter Thiel, cofounder of PayPal, gave to his venture capital firm, "We wanted flying cars and they gave us 140 characters."[4] Indeed. Clearly, suspicion is merited for any future prediction. Yet, as long as we are paying attention and willing to make the most of the circumstances that arise, there may not be a downside. The world is being changed 140 characters at a time, but who really needs a flying car? The real takeaway is to seize every opportunity that arises and not to think that we know what the *right future* must hold. As long as procurement continues to be tempted by a promising tomorrow, we are simultaneously making the very most of today.

Perhaps the best way to sum it up in terms of how procurement professionals should see the future, can be found in this quote from the recently deceased pastor, motivational speaker, and author Robert H. Schuller, "I'd rather attempt to do something great and fail, than to attempt nothing and succeed."[5]

For us, the time has come to attempt something great!

REFERENCES

1. Greg Uhlren, "34 Procurement Experts Predict 2015 Trends," *Next Level Purchasing Association* blog, February 18, 2015, http://www .nextlevelpurchasing.com/blog/2015/02/34-procurement-experts -predict-2015-trends.html.
2. Michael Wolff, "Disruption is cheap: cravings are profitable," *USA Today*, February 15, 2015, http://www.usatoday.com/story/money/ columnist/wolff/2015/02/15/sin-business-like-alcohol-and -tobacco-top-performers/23353383/.
3. Ibid.
4. George Packer, "No Death, No Taxes," *The New Yorker*, November 28, 2011, http://www.newyorker.com/magazine/2011/11/28/no -death-no-taxes.
5. "55 Motivational Quotes That Can Change Your Life," *Bright Drops*, Accessed July 19, 2015, http://brightdrops.com/best-motivational -quotes.

 Web Added Value™

This book has free material available for download from the
Web Added Value™ resource center at *www.jrosspub.com*

APPENDICES

Interview Transcripts

In the process of reading and researching third-party insights for this book, we consulted articles, blogs, audio, and video. While doing so, we realized how much more difficult it is to cite or reference audio and video content—which means most people probably don't bother. Unless you are working from a transcript, you have to listen to an excerpt multiple times in order to capture the wording accurately as opposed to just retyping or copying and pasting a statement from an article. You also can't scan as easily for a specific statement. So while it is possible to search for a term or phrase within an article, in audio, unless you remember the timing marker of the statement, you are stuck listening in real time until the desired segment is found.

We live in a multimedia age. Audio and video are quickly becoming as popular as blog posts for sharing thought leadership. The comments people make in interviews about subjective topics—such as the ones we cover in this book—are often much more interesting than what is available in the written alternative. The editing and polishing process that any professional feels compelled to conduct on a piece of written opinion might make it *tighter* but it also strips away some of the spirit that made it so compelling in the first place.

There are three interviews we feel are particularly relevant to any consideration about the current and future potential of procurement. They are with Thomas Derry; Kate Vitasek and Phil Coughlin; and Rob Handfield. We selected them based on their content and the profile of the speakers. We have created transcripts of all three and included them as Appendices A, B, and C in this book. Our hope is that by doing so, more people will be exposed to the content and future writers will read and reference their comments. All three interviews and all four speakers are deserving of additional consideration.

We have edited these transcripts for readability only—cleaning up expressions and repeated words so that they flow comfortably in written form. If you are interested in any of the following transcripts—and why wouldn't you be?—we encourage you to listen to the original audio as there is an unquestionable richness added to the content once the inflection and tone of each speaker is added back in. All of the interviews, ranging from 30-40 minutes in length in their audio form, are available on the PI Window on Business Blog Talk Radio channel.

We would like to thank all of these interviewees, not only for agreeing to participate in the interviews in the first place, but also for reviewing and approving the following transcripts for inclusion in our book.

WHY THESE THREE INTERVIEWS?

Many interviews take place every year on the PI Window on Business channel. The participants represent independent thought leaders, writers, executive level practitioners, and pioneers at both startup and established solution providers. These three are relevant to the subject matter of this book and involve well-known and much respected members of our professional community.

Most importantly, however, each contains a bold point of view about how we can bridge from the procurement mind-set of the past to what the future will require of us.

Appendix A: Thomas Derry, CEO of the Institute for Supply Management

Thomas Derry's position as the chief executive officer (CEO) of the Institute for Supply Management (ISM) might have been enough to earn it a spot in our book alone. The thoughts he offered up in the interview, which took place shortly before the ISM annual conference marking their 100th year, would have merited inclusion, regardless of the speaker. In this interview, Derry demonstrated that he has a firm grasp on the changes and challenges facing procurement today. Not only that, he recognizes the specific changes that ISM may have to make in order to continue serving longtime members while meeting the expectations of up-and-coming professionals and enticing them to join.

Derry, who ironically has a background in finance rather than procurement, knows what's at stake for ISM at the current crossroads. This positions him extremely well to lead the organization into their second century. For anyone who might assume he has the *dinosaur* mind-set that we discussed at length in this book, this interview will quickly dispel that as myth.

Appendix B: Kate Vitasek, Author, Educator, and Architect of the Vested Business Model, and Phil Coughlin, President of Global Geographies and Operations for Expeditors International

Kate Vitasek is a well-known expert and author in outsourcing and collaboration. Her Vested series of books has changed the way many professionals and companies look at outsourcing. Since she doesn't identify herself as a procurement professional, she has a somewhat more objective point of view on the development of our field. This allows her to see us as one piece in the complex corporate puzzle. In this interview, she makes her point about needing the procurement *dinosaurs* to, well, go the way of the dinosaurs, before there can be significant change. This statement, one that is brought back up a number of times during the discussion, ended up being central to our philosophy.

Phil Coughlin's point of view is just as valuable as he brings a supplier perspective to the discussion. He has seen the transfer of costs and risks to suppliers; and procurement organizations looking to bring their logistics spend under management under the old efficiency and scalability model. He describes the procurement approach in the logistics industry as *blood-sport* and makes no bones about what will need to change before relationships and value creation become more than a rarity. In a somewhat ironic twist, Coughlin looks at legacy procurement practices from a supply chain provider point of view—demonstrating that while procurement and supply chain are often lumped together, we still do not understand the variables driving their cost model.

Appendix C: Rob Handfield, Author, Bank of America University Distinguished Professor of Supply Chain at North Carolina State University, Executive Director Supply Chain Resource Cooperative

Rob Handfield also played a critical role in the development of the philosophy on which this book is based. Not only was it this interview that led to the *Procurement Unplugged* series of interviews that included the other two transcripts featured in this book, but he also coauthored *The Procurement Value Proposition* with Gerard Chick. Come up with a pressing need or challenge facing procurement today, and their book will have an insightful and considered answer.

As with Vitasek and Coughlin, Handfield's larger supply chain perspective gives him a broader understanding of the changes taking place in procurement. His description of a paradigm shift as well as a definite break between old and new procurement were absolutely part of the inspiration for this book, as was the idea that no approach or initiative launched by procurement can succeed without enterprise-wide support. Handfield manages to balance a clear understanding of the hurdles we face today with an adamantly held belief that we are fortunate to be involved in the most exciting time for procurement to date.

APPENDIX A

Interview with Thomas Derry, CEO of the Institute for Supply Management

This interview originally took place on April 15, 2015, via Blog Talk Radio. Although we have edited it for readability, the content remains the same. The original interview can be heard *on demand* at: http://www.blogtalkradio.com/jon-hansen/2015/04/15/procurement-unplugged-the-three-most-important-questions-for-2015

Jon Hansen: Today is Wednesday, April 15th, 2015, and as always, I'm your host, Jon Hansen. Now, since January we've been airing a series of informal, off-the-cuff interviews with a number of executives and experts, and industry thought leaders from the procurement world. And we've been focusing on what we consider to be the three most important questions in our industry for 2015. I want to preface this by saying these aren't the only questions, but the reason we're asking these is that you, as our readers and listeners, have indicated that these are something that really represent areas of interest for you.

Today we are going to pose these questions to ISM Chief Executive Officer (CEO) Tom Derry, who's joining us from Tempe, Arizona. We're going to develop some of the ideas and concepts in relation to where the industry is heading, what impact it's going to have in terms of these key areas, and what we might expect even beyond 2015. Without further delay, I want to welcome to today's segment, Tom Derry. Tom, how are you?

Tom Derry: I'm well Jon, thank you very much.

JH: We had a chance to speak, ever so briefly, in the virtual green room, but having had three of the Top 30 Under 30 up-and-coming stars on our show the other day, I know ISM and ThomasNet worked hard to bring that about. It's interesting in terms of the fact that the length of time that ThomasNet has been around, and ISM—you're celebrating your 100th anniversary at your conference this year—that the longest-standing professional association jumped onto the fact that we have to start engaging this next upcoming generation, identifying them more effectively. What was the thinking behind ISM's involvement with the program?

TD: Well, it really is responding to a simple demographic fact, which is that within 10 years, three quarters of the workforce in the United States, actually around the globe, will be in the Millennial Generation— those folks born from 1980 onward. And that's just a stunning change to the nature of the workforce as it is currently made up today. So we need to reach out to these young people and introduce them to the fascinating career of procurement and supply management and explain how strategic it is to corporations and the personal benefits of a career in the field. And if we don't do it, we'll be missing out on one of the most significant demographic changes industry has faced in the last 50 years.

JH: Now let me ask you this, because there are two lines of thinking here. Number one is that by reaching out in such a way you're developing a presence for the industry and drawing more of these Millennials, more of the up-and-coming talent, and the best and the brightest to the profession itself. I think of it as almost like developing a farm system, to a certain degree, by recognizing and engaging them in such a fashion. Would that be a fair description?

TD: No question—and we've been doing it for more than 10 years through our Richter Scholar program, which we jointly sponsor with the Richter Foundation. Gene Richter was a preeminent thought leader in our profession, and a top practitioner at companies like Hewlett Packard and IBM, and so, we now recognize more than 60 preeminent young undergraduate scholars entering the field. And the 30 under 30 program, specifically looking at the manufacturing industry in the United States, is the second initiative. We've got our own young professionals initiative within ISM itself, so we've been doing quite a bit to develop this up-and-coming generation. We recognize that they bring an additional set of skills that are absolutely going to be necessary to be maximally effective—optimally effective—in the profession, in the coming decades.

JH: Before we get to the first question, one of the things interesting in terms of this is, considering the long history of ISM, and again of Thom-asNet, how has it been different cultivating or developing this genera-tion from generations past? I mean, let's face it, you have over a century doing what you're doing. Is it intrinsically different from the past in terms of drawing people into the industry? Because I can remember Tom, speaking in front of audiences of all sizes and asking, "How many people chose to be in purchasing or procurement?" And five, ten years ago, if you got one or two hands, that would have been a lot. Is there a difference in terms of how you're engaging the next up-and-coming generation than in the years and decades past? And why is there a dif-ference?

TD: There is no question about it, and like any business, we look at things like the consumption habits of our customers and members—and they're clearly shifting. People are comfortable with the Internet now as a basic media distribution technology, whether that's going to webpages and looking at basically, what would have been printed information 30 years ago, but just not represented on the Internet. But increasingly, like in this case, we're doing this live audio segment via the Internet, and mobile platforms are clearly in the ascendancy. I remember reading a very interesting piece a few years back about eBay, and the new CEO of eBay was confronted with a classic problem that companies who en-joyed success have—which is "All right, we're eBay, we dominate our space on the Internet and the Internet auction area, and we've had this tremendous run of success," and the CEO was absolutely adamant that they had to reinvent themselves as a mobile platform business, not as a desktop platform business, because that was the future. And he faced classic resistance within his own team that said, "Hey, listen, don't mess with the success we've had."

ISM faces a similar kind of strategic imperative, just like any business. We have to become more digital in the distribution of our informa-tion—that's why our online learning courses are so popular and grow-ing. We have to understand how our members and customers want to consume, and need to consume, information confronting the kinds of lives they live today. Let's face it, most households are two income households and if you are raising children, you're certainly working long hours. You're not going to be able to access information during a nine-to-five kind of format the way you might have been able to, say, even 25 years ago. So there's lots of significant underlying changes in consumer behavior and we have to track with those or we just won't be relevant.

JH: This is an interesting point that you just made about being relevant with the current generation. I would imagine that there's still an existing or a previous generation with which you must maintain that same kind of relevancy. I don't know what your demographic mix is between what you would call the established base as well as the up-and-coming base, but how do you do that? Because this leads into our next question, "How do you bridge that generational divide of engagement?"

TD: Well, we think of ISM as a content business, and that's what we do—we provide learning and development opportunities and content to the profession, and on behalf of the profession. And so like any classic media business we're managing a transition from an old print-based dissemination methodology to one that's much more digital. You have to continue to meet the needs of your existing customer base while you layer in on top of that, newer modes of technology that address how your up-and-coming and future members and customers want to consume information. So, as we layer in the more digital applications we'll gradually wind down the more traditional channels of dissemination and, just like any business, manage that transition carefully, so that we don't alienate any one group while we prepare for the future.

JH: So it's like content timing. I read a study somewhere saying that unlike any other time in business, within the same enterprise you could have up to four different generations employed simultaneously. So when you talk about content management, you're not just talking about the type of content, but the way in which it's disseminated. Is it safe to say that ISM is attempting to serve as the bridge between these generations, not from a theoretical standpoint and not just from a technological standpoint, but in a practical standpoint to create a consistent message?

TD: That's absolutely the case, and we do that in any number of ways. We have more than half a dozen apps that we offer at ISM, as a small example. And those are increasingly popular with young people. But as we do our own internal strategic market research, we recognize that we generate something like 4,000 unique web visitors every day on our website. That continues to be the most popular method of interaction with ISM, so that channel has to be well managed by us. And we continue to print 45,000 copies of our award-winning magazine, a traditional print magazine which is also highly valued by people. We have to manage across that whole spectrum.

JH: Now let me ask you this, going into managing that spectrum, being that bridge of connectivity and shared insight and content and knowledge, one of the things, and I refer to Dr. Robert Handfield here, in his book (*The Procurement Value Proposition*) he talked about the definitive or definite break between the older or past generations and new ones. Basically what he said is that unlike previously where one generation had something worthwhile in knowledge to hand off to the next generation, right now in the procurement world this doesn't exist. That the knowledge that went beforehand and the perception of what defined our profession and the job, and objectives, and understanding our role in the world, what was passed on is no longer valid in terms of what's needed going forward. He referred to that as saying that it's almost like the new generation is starting from square one again. What do you think when you hear that?

TD: Well, I mostly agree with that premise. There are a few areas where, say, critical negotiation skills are going to be as fundamental to this job in 50 years as they were 50 years ago. That's just a human dynamic, that doesn't change. But in terms of some of the skills that are being applied, there is no question that we're in a brave new world. Whether that means the advent of the Internet of Things and the information flows we'll be managing in the supply chain in addition to the product and service flows that we've been managing historically. That's a whole new way of looking at managing flows, whether it's embedded information about a product or subassembly or component or financial information about that transaction, or even information about the ultimate end customer of the component. That's a whole new way of understanding the flows across national boundaries that will become fundamental to how we manage supply chains.

Supply chains are so strategic to firms these days that the firms that have the most speed and the most agility in the supply networks are the ones that win. So the ability to analyze massive amounts of data, make intelligent business decisions, and do it quickly is going to be the key critical advantage for the next generation of practitioners in our field.

JH: Okay, now the skills you alluded to, because I remember reading a blog post, I think it was on the Nipendo blog by Eran Livneh, who said, with the Internet of Things, 90% of the functionality that was handled manually or as part of the orientation process or the job requirements of the profession will now move away, freeing up humans to focus on the more strategic elements. And I take it when you talked about the more strategic element, by making reference to negotiation and contract management, is that the biggest difference overall is that traditionally the procurement professional or purchasing professional was more functional in their role in executing those at a day in, day out level, where now they have become more strategic and more capable in areas that maybe they weren't necessarily traditionally?

TD: Yes, there are two key points here, I think, to respond to your question, Jon. The first is that the CPOs that I interact with—and I have the good fortune of interacting with CPOs from around the globe and managing global teams—they're moving the traditional purchase order processing function out of the organization. It's not even seen as part of procurement. It was entirely procurement 30 or 40 years ago, but CPOs today put it in a shared service center and say, "You know, it's not even part of my global supply chain team." So that's one critical change. The other thing is the role of innovation in the global economy today.

I love this example that I stumbled across. Last summer I was reading a transcript of an earnings call and Bob Shanks, CFO for Ford Motor Company, was giving his remarks along with Ford's CEO. Ford is a great example because they're in a classic industry in our profession—automotive—and also one of the companies that's been at the forefront on innovation and development of the profession and spawned some great talent in our field. So, I'm reading the transcript, and one of the investors on the call from Barclays Bank was asking Bob Shanks about the sustainability of the cost reductions that Ford had achieved in some of its key product lines. And he addressed the point by saying "Yes, you know what, we're very good at that, we're very good at engineering cost out of our product, we're very good at our internal processes." He said "You know, I wouldn't focus on that." This is really interesting, and I think it marks a sea change for our profession. He said, "You know, in our industry we've been experiencing absolute declines in consumer prices that are paid for automobiles over the past 10 years. But what we're seeing now is that new innovation in the industry, particularly around navigation systems and entertainment systems—and by the way, we've got cars that are wired to the Internet now—those kinds of features and functions are creating pricing opportunities. Consumers are willing to pay more for a car that contains those features."

That innovation comes from their suppliers—from Ford's suppliers. So having that critical conversation, and automotive is a good example because it's a famous example of the OEMs beating up on their supply network sometimes to drive cost out. You can't maintain that kind of interaction with your supply base if you're going to rely on them for these critical innovations that are ultimately going to increase your bottom line at the OEM level. So for him to point out why supplier innovation is so critical, I think marks a significant mind shift for our profession.

JH: You see, that's an interesting point you just raised because it opens the door to the concept of the relational models advocated by people such as Andy Akrouche, Kate Vitasek, and the like, who have said that what's changing with the past, given the strategic importance of the relationships and the role that suppliers play, that the mind-set has to change from a transactional model where you're negotiating best price and focusing just on cost reduction, to one where you truly become partners. The key, then, is finding the right model by which you manage those relationships. Is that one of the areas where there is a major shift away from what you might call the older generation and how they were taught to do business? I can remember the days of using ThomasNet's industry catalogs, flipping through pages with paper clips trying to find the best price to one where you have to be able to manage relationships, to one when you have to recognize the collaborative necessity to achieve an end result—and that isn't just negotiating the best price. Is that one of the big differences?

TD: Yes, there are a lot of things that drive that difference, Jon, and one of them is very fundamental in terms of how industries and companies organize themselves. It's remarkable that the typical cost structure of an S&P 500 firm, since 1970, has changed in terms of the total cost spent outside of the firm. This has moved from about 60% to more than 80% over that 45-year period. That represents a shift to a bigger supply base, moving more of your cost structure outside of the four walls of your firm. So in an outsourcing world, over the last 25 years, you had incredible opportunities to leverage suppliers against one another, to consolidate spend, and leverage the amount to spend—and that was the natural first phase. So it's not a surprise that over the last 25 years, companies—the buyers—have realized that tremendous power to leverage their position and get costs lower. That makes sense. Well, you know what? The opportunity for expanding the global supply base is rapidly reaching the point of diminishing returns. We've only got so much geography that we can move to.

So, we're shifting, I think inevitably, to this next phase where, cost reduction is important—it'll never go away—but now a different set of skills, understanding how you manage supplier relationships, in a win-win situation, to use that tired old phrase, becomes important. Because today, if we stopped in time today we'd have to recognize that profits tend to pool at the OEM level and get squeezed out of every tier and supply base below them. That model really isn't sustainable in the long run, it has to be changed. And companies are clearly working in this new environment: economists refer to it as factory-less goods production. You used to be a manufacturing firm, or you were a services firm, and there's this new third entity called the factory-less goods producer, where Nike designs products but doesn't actually make them, as a classic example. And that's what's been driving a lot of this change.

JH: There are two streams of thought here. I want to get into the latter in terms of redefinition—like Nike designing, but not manufacturing. But when you were talking about the nonsustainable nature of decreasing costs, I was reminded of a CAPS study, and I think ISM was involved in this study, if I'm not mistaken, back in 2005 when reverse auctions came onto the scene. They wrote in that study that they found that after the initial event, when the market had corrected itself through the efficiency of reverse auctions, that savings dramatically declines. In other words, it wasn't sustainable at the level when it was first launched. That's initially what I thought of when you talked there, so going back to 2005 and what you're talking about now, it would seem that that's the manifestation of that, isn't it?

TD: It absolutely is. There will always be opportunities as we move across categories. One of your previous guests talked about how buyers are leveraging their power to commoditize and effect transportation. And there's a point of view about whether or not that should be commoditized, but the reality is that companies recognize they've got that buying power, and it's not surprising that they're going to try to exercise it. In certain industries that are not as far advanced in adopting our discipline—the health care industry is a great example that's really lagging; industries like automotive, pharmaceuticals, and others in terms of embracing what can be delivered—we're going to be going through what we've already experienced over the past 20 years, in health care, in the next 10 years. In fact the learning curve will be shortened, but we'll be going through the same cycles in that industry that we've already gone through in other industries. But overall, the big picture is quite clear.

JH: All right, so here's the other side of that question. I read an article recently indicating that there should be a whole new role set up called chief relationship officer, or CRO, but I remember reading about a survey with CIO Magazine saying chief information officers and IT are saying, "We have to redefine ourselves now." Finance, in terms of still being the focal point or the heartbeat of the enterprise, they themselves are going through shifts and changes. And of course, so are CPOs and procurement. Is a CRO, a chief relationship officer, something that we're likely to see emerge as what you call an amalgam of all those other disciplines of areas of practice?

TD: I think it's going to be critical. Just think about the world of technology for a moment. You really have got four basic ecosystems in the consumer technology world: you've got a Microsoft ecosystem, you've got a Google ecosystem, you've got an Amazon ecosystem, and, well, you could argue whether there's a fourth. You have to understand how you're going to play, and you have to choose which ecosystem you're going to operate in, or maybe ecosystems, but increasingly companies are going to try to own their entire space and you may be shut out. If you're at a Google shop, maybe you're not in a Microsoft shop, going forward. Apple is the other famous ecosystem. So you have to understand this: there's a shifting landscape. It doesn't mean that we own technologies exclusively, but it does mean that we're operating in a sphere where we have to interact with partner firms, and companies have to understand what the strategic landscape looks like. Which companies are going to be critical to providing the capability they need to be successful and make sure that they've got good relationships?

JH: Thus the relationship element becomes critical—I'll jump ahead to the third question. When we're talking in the context of what we've just spoken about, is there a difference between the public and private sector and what is it, in terms of this evolution?

TD: Well, I think that's a great question. It's really interesting to me, Jon. I think in many ways, what distinguished the public and private sector in the past is now converging. Specifically, the public sectors classically had to layer into its purchasing role some societal goals that were imposed by government. Well, these kinds of societal goals are being imposed on the private sector in a way that they never had been before. The famous example, obviously, is the conflict minerals provision out of the Dodd Frank law. But that's only one example. Remember back in October of 2012, the House Intelligence Committee released a report saying that Huawei and BT posed a national security risk to U.S. firms because of concerns about the technology that might have been embedded in their routers and switches.

They didn't go so far as to legislate, but they certainly put a big flag in the ground saying, "Hey, listen, be careful about who you're doing business with." Back in 2010, the Rain Forest Action Network showed up at General Mills with a protest and said, "Listen, we think you're contributing to deforestation of rain forests around the world because of your use of palm oil." And four years later General Mills published a policy that formally addressed their sustainable sourcing of palm oil around the world. It wasn't imposed by a legislator, it was imposed by activists and consumers. So we increasingly have to factor in these kinds of pressures, and companies that *get it* will do this proactively. Otherwise they'll be blindsided by a social media post that goes viral and will realize that their business is being very much impacted.

JH: It's interesting because when you talk about public sector procurement, it's often seen as a vehicle for driving innovation. You look at industrial regionalized benefits in terms of strategic procurement that help build up a particular region's economic strength and all these other factors, and what you're saying is, in the private sector there also has to be an increasing social awareness of the impact of what they're doing. They're not operating in a vacuum. So that's where the similarities exist between both public and private sector procurement professionals. Am I getting that right?

TD: Yes, absolutely. So you look at local contact requirements for an oil or gas firm that's setting up an exploration project in a different part of the world. We had to deal with local contact requirements for a long time. But the way that companies engage there is entirely different. They look at the entire economic ecosystem in that area. They sometimes have to build up capability that doesn't exist in that country. I'm aware of an example of an oil and gas firm that built a bakery near its production facility, because culturally it was important for their local workers to be able to have access to that daily source of bread and they had to travel 60 miles to get it otherwise.

So they created a local business, they built up a local economy, and they provided a valuable service for their employees because it was good business. So it was doing good, to do good business, and the private sector companies recognize that and are doing it more and more.

JH: Now, are there any industries within the private sector that are getting that message sooner than other sectors? Who's leading the charge on this increased social sensibility on the private side?

TD: Well, if you are a classic B2C business, you have to be absolutely aware of it. I really admire what's happening, for instance, at Patagonia, which makes clothing for outdoor adventure and camping and all of that. One recent example that impressed me was how they've reinvented the wet suit. A lot of their customers use the wet suit. The wet suit is not biodegradable and so you might wear it for 10 years, but when it has to be replaced it ends up in a landfill. Well they figured out a way to create a cotton wet suit that is biodegradable, that has all the performance characteristics of the classic rubber wet suit. So, in keeping with their own values and in keeping with the values of their customers, they've created a product that performs just as well without the harmful side effects environmentally.

Companies who are engaged with consumers are really at the forefront of having to understand what the new expectations are.

JH: Obviously, that's an impact of the public sensibility into the private sector. What from the private sector is migrating or moving over to the public sector in terms of impacting the procurement professionals in that area?

TD: Well, certain best practices are clearly more adopted, and you mentioned e-auctions earlier. Increasingly government entities are able to utilize those kinds of best practices to improve the velocity with which they can source, and the efficiency and effectiveness of their sourcing process. So that would be a good example there.

JH: Okay, and again we're familiar with the new public management mind-set that seemed to permeate the public sector in the late '90s, which suggested that the private sector had figured it all out and that their model was the one to emulate. I think you're talking about a little bit more than that, aren't you? I mean, there are best practices and things along that particular line, but in terms of the private sector influencing the public sector, I mean, it stems beyond that though, doesn't it?

TD: Well, I think it does. We're able to access leading-edge technology, unless you're in a classic defense-related field, where the leading edge technology and thinking is happening in a way that's typically funded through the public sector. But in all other areas the best thinking typically is emerging from private sector innovation. And so that makes its way into commerce generally, and then it's eventually introduced into the public sector via the private sector.

JH: So within the private sector you have much broader freedom to innovate and be creative and prove the ideas or the new emerging technologies than you would within the public sector, and that is where the greatest gain is.

TD: Yeah, it's like Joseph Stumpeter's creative destruction, aimed at capitalism and that power. So we see that all the time. A well-known example is Eastman Kodak, who was well ahead of the curve in inventing digital technology for photographs. They made the wrong strategic decision to remain a film company and not a photography company. They actually owned a lot of the patents around digital photography and just didn't see the promise. So Eastman Kodak is barely in existence and digital firms have replaced them. That happens all the time and it's not that companies don't see the wave of the future, many companies do see what's coming but sometimes they don't have the ability to react as quickly as they need to, or they miss the key insight and the result is they get overtaken by events.

JH: You know, what's kind of funny, I'm smiling when you say that. This will be a topic for discussion for another day but I remember actually working very closely with Eastman Kodak out of Rochester when they first were converting their continuous tone printers and trying to find a more commercial use for them because they explained it to me; their printers at that point had been used extensively in the military during operation Desert Storm. And again a continuous tone is obviously far more vivid resolution than the dot matrix that the corporate world was used to. And I remember the enthusiasm they had in developing the Kodak engine to convert regular cameras into digital cameras, and all of that. And then it just stopped, and I think that goes into what you were saying, they realized the future, but it's sometimes comfortable to keep your foot on first—but it makes stealing second base that much more difficult.

TD: Yeah absolutely. That adds a lot of depth to my example, and that's the challenge for any of us who are leaders in business, to not get comfortable with the success that we're enjoying at the moment, because that's a recipe for being out of business very quickly.

APPENDIX B

Interview with Kate Vitasek, Author, Educator, and Architect of the Vested Business Model, and Phil Coughlin, President of Global Geographies and Operations for Expeditors International

This interview originally took place on January 28, 2015, via Blog Talk Radio. Although we have edited it for readability, the content remains the same. The original interview can be heard *on demand* at: http://www.blogtalkradio.com/jon-hansen/2015/01/28/procurement-unplugged-the-three-most-important-questions-for-2015

Jon Hansen: Today is Wednesday, January the 28th, 2015. I'm doing a series of what you could call informal, off-the-cuff interviews with a number of executives and experts from various areas of the procurement world. And, I'm focusing on what I consider to be the three most important questions for our industry in 2015. I didn't come up with these questions in a vacuum, but over the past year, looking at some of the interviews I've done, some of the discussions and the feedback and the response from you, the listeners and readers, to the *Procurement Insights* blog.

These three questions are centered around themes or topics that appear to be the most important to you. What matters the most to you. And so, by bringing in these experts and these industry thought leaders, the hope is to shed some light on the different variables out there that we're dealing with within the context of these three important or specific areas. And joining me today to carry on the discussion is Kate Vitasek who is one of our industry's top experts, an author of five books including *Vested* and *Getting to We*; and Phil Coughlin, who's the president of global geographies and operations for Expeditors International.

Without further delay, I'd like to welcome to the show, both Kate Vitasek and Phil Coughlin. Welcome. How are you today?

Phil Coughlin: Great, Jon. Thank you for having me.

Kate Vitasek: Good, glad to be on again. It's always nice to be on your show.

JH: One of the things that I liked about our discussion in the virtual green room is the fact that we can really get into it in this sort of informal setting. And one of the three questions we're going to focus on, starting with Robert Handfield and Gerard Chick's assessment in their recent book, *The Procurement of Value Proposition*, is that there is a definitive and definite gap between the old purchasing or buying professional and the new procurement professional. And I use those two words, purchasing and procurement, with deliberate intent, but more so in the content of what we're talking about.

One of the issues that you raised in terms of the T and Cs, or the approach to supplier relationships that is derailing a lot of the initiatives, and the outcomes that people are hoping to achieve. And so maybe just to pick up on that conversation, Phil, when you talk about T and Cs, and having a negative impact on suppliers and vendors, can you elaborate a little bit more? I know you mentioned Apple and such in terms of lopsided deals, but why is this important in terms of an issue we have to address? And, in terms of the generational divide that Handfield referred to; is change on the horizon?

PC: Yeah, Jon. I guess to briefly touch on this, what's transpired over the last several years in the logistics space is that the terms and conditions have become more and more aggressive. We've moved away from industry standard and liability regimes around the world like Warsaw Convention and Montreal Protocol. We've gone to each customer or shipper or consignee crafting their own terms and conditions. And those terms and conditions have extended payment terms out to a significant amount of time. They've shifted the risk that's inherent with the shipper or consignee over to the carrier or the service provider. And they've just gradually expanded the amount of exposure, liability, and risk while simultaneously, through the procurement organization, driving pricing down to somewhat of a commodity type process.

So what that has really done is, it's begun to push away the more strategic thought leaders and to become much more of a transactional "How do I manage this and avoid the risk?" type relationship, rather than this collaborative, strategic partnership. It's become much more of a commodity shifting-of-risk-type relationship, which is not really helpful, considering some of the supply chain challenges and things that most shippers want to take on.

JH: I have to interrupt you, Phil, because Kate, when we talked in November about the Minnesota Bridge rebuilding project, you had mentioned that the risk element to which Phil has just referred was dealt with on an equitable basis—or maybe I should use the word a *conciliatory* basis that took into consideration all stakeholders. That project was successful. Why is that not the same approach across the board?

KV: Well, I think you have to look at the fact that buyers inherently have power, right? And so rewind to 1983, with Peter Kraljic, and at the time pioneering the two-by-two Kraljic model that said, "We're going to classify and segment our spend." So if I look at the category such as what Phil says, with freight and expediting worldwide supply chains, a lot of times people take those categories and then go, "Oh, that's just a shipment. That's just Point *A* to Point *B*," or, "That's just facilities in real estate. No big deal, just cleaning." And we tend to put those in noncritical buckets, or a bucket called *leverage*.

So even though we may have these strategic suppliers, I think what we try to do is to, as Phil said, we over-commoditize, because buyers naturally have power. You've heard the golden rule: those who have the golden rule and Peter Kraljic taught us to leverage. Michael Porter taught us, "If you don't have power, do what you can to shift the power to what you're doing." So instead of having a deal around how to reduce your overall supply chain management cost, it's, "How do you change the price from Point *A* to Point *B* freight?" And I'm going to drive that down to something that's very standard. I'm going to pit the suppliers against each other so I can get the best price. And by the way, the lawyers are really smart. If the suppliers come back and fight back about price, we can hit a lower price by shifting Ts and Cs in our favor.

JH: Okay, you know what, and I've got to say this, though, and remember in the context of the Handfield divide, isn't this a characteristic of the old buyer mentality that you're referring to? I will go back to Phil and then come back to you, Kate, after I hear from Phil on this. But is this something, Phil, that will jump that chasm that Handfield talks about this new generation of procurement professionals, who have chosen to be in the profession, who are part of this strategic renaissance? You could call it strategic renaissance, where we recognize now that it isn't just getting the best price. There's strategic elements to it. And I'll talk about an automotive industry study shortly, but is this where it ends or is this going to jump the chasm and, even with the insights and the perspective of the next generation, we're going to fall in the same traps?

PC: Yeah, Jon, I would say that there are some exceptions out there, but they are few and far between. And if there is a strategic renaissance going on in my world, it's at the very beginning stages. There's clearly a well-entrenched philosophical approach to procurement in my industry, which is more tilted towards negotiations being a competitive, almost blood-sport if you will, where the buyer has such a disproportional amount of power, and there are so many competitors out there that they wind up using a very powerful grip to squeeze what they need to squeeze. So there are exceptions to be sure, but they are few and far between.

I think it's going to take more time and more realizations that, as they continue to attract service providers that are willing to agree to these types of terms and conditions, they're going to continue to get mediocre results. And I think when they begin to value supply chain services and logistics services as something more strategic than a commodity, I think perhaps then, maybe we'll begin to deal with some of the more advanced and sophisticated procurement folks. But right now, we deal almost exclusively with folks that are more interested in extracting value from the relationship than creating value in the relationship.

JH: Okay, I have to turn to you next, Kate, because of a couple of things. First of all, let's talk about the lopsided deals with Apple, etc., but also that automotive industry study that I alluded to, where they're talking about the fact that a product that is ultimately produced by the auto manufacturers is directly now linked to the satisfaction that the vendors have in terms of the relationship with the buyer or with the manufacturer themselves. In essence, and we see in the SupplierPay initiative signed by the Obama administration, the recognition that we have to compress the payment times as opposed to throw someone in his industry, where you're looking at extending and transferring the risk.

There seems to be all these building blocks in place to driving a more strategic or relational approach. Yet, as Phil indicated, we're still at the very early stages. Is the writing not clearly on the wall to people? The bridge example, the SupplierPay example, the industry study showing that the ultimate product that is delivered to the end consumer by the buying company, whether it be the auto manufacturer or otherwise, is tied to the satisfaction that vendors have with the relationship. Do we have to get hit in the face with a two-by-four?

KV: Well, I do think we have to get hit in the face with a two-by-four because sometimes that's what it takes to change. Look at when we have a bad habit. How hard is it to try to stop smoking or if you're addicted to drugs, right? So I think buyers are addicted to being able to get the short-term win by bringing out the hammer, and so they don't have the impact until later. Look at Apple/GT Advanced, right? It was touted as a strategic deal. And Apple is probably rolling over in their grave, because the judge ordered that a lot of the details of that contract come out. GT Advanced didn't have all the information. You could say that it was a bad deal and that shame on them, and they should have never signed the deal in the first place. But they got in and they said, "Hey, I'm under water." You know what? Apple said, "Sorry, you're not allowed to change the price." And every day they were losing cash, which eventually led to them going out of business.

So I think that if I use the analogy of a river, we're to the point where the water in the river is down and we're exposing the rocks. So, as you say, getting smacked in the face—GT Advanced going bankrupt smacked Apple in the face. They're a big, powerful company with lots of cash, and they could probably go to another supplier in the short-term, but if that happens over, and over, and over again, you have companies like Expeditors saying, "You know what? Take your business. I can't do business with you." We need to have suppliers who are willing, like Phil, to be more transparent with their customers and say, "You've pushed too far. This doesn't make sense."

JH: Right. Let me ask you this: that ability to stand up and say, "You've pushed too far," from where does that originate? Again, I will go to this new generation of procurement professionals coming into the picture, they know what's wrong. They know what doesn't work, so there'll obviously be some push back potentially from the rank and file. But within your organization, does that have to achieve higher up? It seems like for any meaningful traction or scalability to be gained, you have to have leadership who is informed and understands the consequences of their actions rather than merely adhering to a contract if the best interests of the vendors or other stakeholders be damned. Where does that originate, Phil?

PC: Yeah, Jon, I think what I'd like to describe to your audience is that . . . I would say the vast majority of the time, the contracts that I'm dealing with and I'm positive my competitors are dealing with, they're not tailor-made or custom-made for the business at hand or the industry. In many cases, they're sort of generalized contracts that may deal loosely with transportation or logistics or warehouse and distribution. And then being a template, they continue to get additional provisions and sections added to them by the, let's say, general council or financial officer, until you have this quilt of a contract, bits and pieces sewn together around a centralized service, right?

So what can happen is, in the transportation space you can wind up with a contract that might have a commercial value of let's say $5 million, but the liability exposure and the liability expectation because of the general terms that have come in could be $50 million or $100 million. They're so disproportionate between the commercial benefit versus the risk imposed, and it becomes this debate where perhaps the procurement person doesn't really understand logistics, or in the opposite, the logistics person negotiating doesn't understand the terms of indemnification and liability regimes. So you get stuck in this world where they are like, "Just sign it. Everybody else has."

It's a difficult discussion to have, because it's the commercial value vs. not even a proportional risk. It's something that's quite out of whack. The problem is that we have people signing them. So you're stuck in this . . . "I'm going to win on principle, but I'm going to lose on profit" kind of a thing. It's quite frustrating at times, but we just need to get another dialogue going out there, another discussion that these contracts come with some significant teeth and we need to make sure that there's proportionality. That's really the crux of the matter.

JH: When you talk about proportionality, is the problem originating with the buyer? Is the problem originating with upper management or corporate direction rewarding the wrong motivators? I remember, Kate, you talked about your years at Microsoft and the rewards for saving money. In other words, you were rewarded and acknowledged for getting the better of the vendor rather than for collaborating with the vendor to everyone's mutual benefit. So is it the buyers, let's say the older generation of buyers, who looked at this and said, "Well, that's just the way it is, and I'm going to do it. I'm not going to lose my job." And the newer generation is going to come along and say, "Wait, this doesn't work," and you've got to pay attention. Now is the time because we're having these kinds of conversations, which five years ago probably weren't possible—at least to the same degree they are now. Where does the origin of this problem come from? Is it from buyer acquiescence of just accepting that's the way it is, and management is rewarding the wrong things? Where does it start changing?

KV: Well, I think that things can start changing in a couple of ways. Sometimes, as you said, people have to be smacked in the face. But other times, people are in alignment. So we are seeing people come and be highly interested in our work at the University of Tennessee about the Vested sourcing business model—which is a value-based partnership. We are definitely starting to see procurement and supply chain professionals say, "You know what? We are not just buying a shipment from Point *A* to Point *B*. That's not a commodity. What we need to buy is supply chain and distribution as a strategic weapon." What we are seeing is a slow shift with companies moving to a mind-set to create value instead of extracting value.

You're going to start to see two paths. One is the enlightened people, and one is those who have been smacked in the face because they have an Apple-GT kind of a deal that went south, and they've been burned and they are now scratching their heads saying, "Wow, I need to change." In addition, you've got the new people coming in, the younger generation that has a totally different mind-set. Yes—it's going to take time because like it or not, the old generation are the ones that have the power in the companies today. But there is a shift happening, and it will continue to happen. Think of it as if you have a world full of dinosaurs. It takes time to let the dinosaurs die.

PC: I couldn't agree more.

JH: Using your example, Kate, isn't that going to deter more people? Are they going to hit a point of frustration?

KV: I think that they're just going to go to the companies who have different types of values. You'll see them want to go and work at the Zappos' of the world, who have a value-creation mentality. So you're not just seeing this in the procurement space. You're seeing this mind-set shift across businesses, and the most talented people will shift to the businesses with a pie expansion mentality instead of a dog-eat-dog mentality, because that's a better environment for the new folks. You know what, if you're a supplier, Jon, you're going to take your best people and go to your best accounts. Why would an *A team* person want to get stuck on a C *team*, working with a client who doesn't value them?

JH: All right. So here's an interesting thing; this is like a *Good to Great* example from Collins' book. Ultimately, Phil, corporations who do adopt what you're championing and what Kate is championing, which we all know to be the right direction, they are ultimately going to attract the newest, most innovative talent. And that is going to give them a competitive advantage in the marketplace, especially if we are to believe the surveys from the automotive industry saying a supply base that is liquid, well-paid, or fairly paid, and happy with their buyer-supplier relationships because they're part of the process, is ultimately going to enable the company to deliver the highest quality of products and services. That, in and of itself, is really going to be the key point. That's going to be the competitive advantage, or the tipping point. Is that a fair assessment?

PC: Yes, Jon. I think the best way for me to describe what you just mentioned is if you think about it, I'm also a buyer. Expeditors is probably one of the largest purchasers of transportation in the world, bigger than most of my customers. I'm buying directly from the airlines and directly from the steamship lines. We treat our relationships with those asset-based carriers entirely different than how we're treated by our customers. We treat our service providers, the airlines, and the steamship lines, very strategically. Our relationships with them are very open and transparent, and win-win. Because, frankly, we need them, and without them we'll be stuck buying planes and boats, and we don't know how to do that.

So we practice that on our side, and we see the benefits of it. We think it actually gives us a strategic advantage in the field, in the competitive arena, because we have very strong carrier partnerships with the guys who put the cargo on planes and boats. That hasn't made it over to me as a seller, or to my customers, because they still treat it as, "How much value can I extract from the relationship by way of longer payment terms, shifting more inherent risk, greater user exposure, while purchasing at a commodity base?"

So there are elements of that in the industry where it's more strategic, but it hasn't drifted over into the traditional buyer-seller relationship in the logistics world. And that's not going to happen until more and more companies realize that when they buy that way, they're going to get a certain amount of resources. And those customers that buy more strategically in a more collaborative environment will get the cream of the crop resources. I see that every day, both in my own situation as well as in pursuing business. You can always tell when you're pursuing a potential customer, what type of resources they're getting access to with their current provider. So eventually that will begin to take shape, but we've got a lot to do in that area.

JH: This is interesting, because I want to move on to the next topic, which is the emergence of eCommerce and technology obviously having an impact. And whether or not the power of technology, wearable technology, buyers wanting the same experience at work that they do at home and buying on the Internet, whether or not that actually hurts or helps the cause that we're talking about.

But at the end of the day, is it still safe to say that the success with the Minnesota Bridge rebuilding, which you're talking about, Phil, is grounded in terms of how you are able to practice what you preach? Ultimately, is the driver for the overall scalability and massive change that needs to take place based in the next generation coming up? Is that the competitive advantage once it really manifests itself? When a company is seen as having clear profitability, gaining market share, gaining strength, offering better products at lower prices or whatever it may be because of the strength of their relationships. Is that the overall shift that we're ultimately going to see? Is that the Atlas Shrugged kind of moment?

KV: Yes, I think so, and that's one of the reasons why we're really big on case studies. People come and learn about the Vested methodology and they implement it. We really encourage them to submit their case studies and to make those public. Case studies allow more people to realize that win-win isn't just a nice thing to say—it's real. Every day we get more and more people who have gone through our classes, and they come back and say, "Wow, I changed the way I worked with that supplier, and it made all the difference in the world. I was fair, I was candid, I was transparent, I allocated risk instead of shifting risk, and it makes a big difference."

So the more we get those case studies, the more the movement will grow. It's just like a virus that spreads. You've read, I'm sure, Malcolm Gladwell's *The Tipping Point*, right? So we're in the early stages of getting an idea to spread, and the more that people try it, the more they say, "Wow, this is great." The more that folks like Phil come out and say, "You know what, I'm a buyer and a supplier, and this is how I do work. And this is why we have a competitive advantage in the industry because I'm a buyer, and I believe in this. And this is how we gain our competitive advantage."

I think you'll see it, it's just going to take time because, as you mentioned, and as Handfield has mentioned, there's the old school mentality and the new school mentality, and like it or not, the old school mentality has the power jobs in the companies today. And so maybe the dinosaurs have to die, or maybe we need to educate them.

JH: We're hearing that the line between B2C, B2B is really disappearing. The buyers are saying, "Why can't I have the same experience at work that I have at home in terms of ease of use?" We see all these platforms, cloud-based solutions. What used to take years, and millions upon millions of dollars to implement, we now have applications and solutions that can be implemented within a matter of weeks, if not days, and produce results. Do these things help to facilitate a relationship-based approach to procurement, or does technology undermine it?

PC: Well, technology is a huge game changer for this industry. I would say, when people talk about the same experience they have in their personal life as they do in their professional life, and again, referring to my industry, it's because when I shop for Christmas or I shop for the holidays, I can quickly find out, "Where is my stuff and when will it be delivered to me?" Those are two simple questions, two very important things I want to know.

But when you're in the business world, and you have all the complexities of volumes, and units, and colors, sizes, governments, airlines, and ocean freight—and you try to answer those two questions in the same manner... they are very simple questions that are incredibly complex to answer. But technology is beginning to provide visibility to the answer to those questions, but it's still a long way off because of the disparate nature of the supply chain. There really is no single window into, "Where is my stuff and when will it be here?" There are bits and pieces that technology can bolt together, but it's still not there.

Now there're some great platforms out there, and they're having a dramatic effect. I'm sure we're going to get there, given the pace of technology and the change that comes with that.

But I think what's really going to wind up happening with technology and the move towards the single platform of visibility, what comes with that is also a single source of data, and that data will be one version of the truth. And from that, procurement groups will have better information regarding volumes of commodities, types of volumes, trends and patterns in those volumes and spend. And so when they begin to go out to bid, and when they begin to put things out for review, they will have much more reliable information regarding services, volumes, and spend.

Right now it's more art than science when bids go out. I think technology will have a dramatic impact, but again, the gap between the simplicity of me buying something online and having it delivered to my home, versus managing a complex, disparate, global supply chain is a quantum leap.

KV: I think technology is going to do some great things as well as, potentially, some not so great things. Let me explain. So, I do think it will help compare apples to apples. It's going to streamline how we work. Reaching one version of the truth is absolutely critical. We have to remember that we need to use data in a positive way and not to use it to make our case, but not be transparent with the supplier. So the more we can use that as one version of the truth, as Phil said, is great.

But I fear—here's my negative thought about technology—I fear that just because we have technology and we can use it, it will further over-commoditize. So instead of buying freight optimization, or supply chain optimization, we buy *Point A* to *Point B*. So we optimize the commodity and we leave money on the table, because we haven't solved the bigger picture. And so the more technology enables us to have to have auctions or reverse auctions—that's actually bad if you have a strategic category.

I'll point to McDonalds: is beef a commodity, or is it a strategic weapon? It's a strategic weapon. So if we start to see freight and logistics and warehousing as a commodity, I think we'll lose the ability to create value from that category. So just because we have technology, we need to use it in the right way, versus use it as a way to further commoditize.

PC: Technology is a double-edged sword.

JH: So it is a two-edged sword. It can be good or bad depending on how it's wielded. Let me ask you about the public sector versus the private sector. There's always been this traditional view that one is different than the other. One would think that in the public sector, which has to focus more on other factors like industrial, regionalized benefits, or economic benefits, or social responsibility, that it would be more conducive to the kind of relationship that you and Phil are talking about, because there's more opportunity for that. Is that true or is that a fallacy?

KV: I would actually say there is more opportunity in the public sector because traditionally, it is not as efficient. However, it is a bigger mind-set change than in the commercial sector. So when your procurement or contracting officer can get sued for using best value, it's probably not going to be a driver of change. They don't want to try best value techniques because it's risky. In the commercial sector, it's not as risky. In the commercial sector, we have an enemy called *bonuses* or just *price variances*. So until management says, "It's stupid to have a buyer being rewarded on price reduction," you're probably not going to see change.

JH: One of the things about the public sector that I discovered in Virginia was the fact that they do have a clause that gives the buyer power to be able to make best value decisions without consequences. I'm not saying that's present in every state to the same degree. I guess what I'm looking at here is the fact that people don't want to take the risk to step outside of the box to look at that kind of legislation, and so they just accept it as, this is the way it is.

Just like on the other side, Phil, with the private sector industry, or the commercial industry, as Kate calls it, these incentives are created by people within the organization, so they can be changed by people within the organization. Granted, it is a lot easier than widespread legislative change, but nonetheless, both originate with people's views of protecting themselves. In the public sector, everybody has the right to do business, which I don't always think should be the case. But these are all, for lack of a better term, *people-made* issues, aren't they?

KV: Yes. You nailed it. That's one of the things I teach in my classes: we always end with the *barriers discussion*. What are the barriers that prevent you from doing the things that Handfield says? We find that almost all barriers are perceived to be bigger than they really are. Yes, there may be a *policy* that prevents you from doing something. But you know what? Those policies are made by people. So I don't see any real obstacles. I see a mind-set obstacle, and this is where I go back to the idea that, maybe dinosaurs just need to die.

Handfield's spot on. There is a divide, and the cool thing is, years ago, you weren't seeing this. Today, it is coming to the forefront, because you're seeing these tensions in buyer-supplier relationships: the lawsuit between Apple and GT Advanced around their bankruptcy. In Europe, you've got all kinds of companies that are really being exposed if they've had bad procurement practices, muscular practices that have really harmed the supply base. Obama's payment initiative: when the government has to step in and say, "Hey, let's maybe think about being a little fair how we pay our suppliers." That's probably a sign that we've gone a little too far.

JH: Phil, would you concur with that? Are these the factors that are going to change? Gartner coined the term the *Postmodern ERP era*, referring to the fact that the old ERP platforms never really delivered on their promise, and now we're in a new era. So of course, cloud-based solution's all this. Are we going to have a similar postmodern contract, or T&C era here? Is that something that's going to happen?

PC: I think the two things that I find interesting and concerning about the underlying trend going on is as the public sector of the government begins to source more and more privately, what they've done is, if you are a direct contractor with the government, they've taken the governmental policies, social engineering policies, other types of governmental policies, and you accept them as-is. Not only that but, within those contracts, they have pass-through rules that trickle down right to all their suppliers. So the number of people doing business with the government is growing at a rapid pace, and through sort of osmosis, public terms are now becoming integral parts of commercial private contracts. And so if I'm a second- or third-tier provider, I'm still getting exposed to governmental procurement terms, which is getting tricky.

KV: People have to start thinking about the total cost of what they're doing, and looking at value and how they're going to create value, versus simply exchanging or extracting value from their partners. Are you extracting value, exchanging value, or creating value? Maybe it's time to think about your supply base, and ask, "Which suppliers need to fall in which one of those categories?"

APPENDIX C

Interview with Rob Handfield, Author, Bank of America University Distinguished Professor of Supply Chain at North Carolina State University, Executive Director Supply Chain Resource Cooperative

This interview originally took place on October 30, 2014, via Blog Talk Radio. Although we have edited it for readability, the content remains the same. The original interview can be heard *on demand* at: http://www .blogtalkradio.com/jon-hansen/2014/10/30/the-procurement-value -proposition-a-discussion-with-robert-handfield-phd

Jon Hansen: Welcome to another segment of PI Window on the World. As always, I'm your host, Jon Hansen. When Robert Handfield reached out to me regarding his new book, *The Procurement Value Proposition*, I was obviously interested, for a number of reasons. Handfield is considered to be a thought leader in the field of supply chain management, and he is also an industry expert in the fields of strategic sourcing, supply market intelligence, and supplier development. So suffice to say the gentleman knows about which he speaks. However, it is the focus of his latest book on procurement's changing value proposition in the context of a more global viewpoint—and not just from a geographical standpoint but from a practical standpoint—that really interested me and we are going to focus on that today. Now without further delay, let's welcome to the talk show, Dr. Robert Handfield. Robert, how are you today?

Robert Handfield: I am great, Jon. Thank you for hosting me on your show. I am a big fan of you and your blog, and your show, so it is really an honor to be here today.

JH: Well the honor is mutual because when you look at the length of time, and the insights and the perspectives that you have garnered over the years, this next book, what you'd call a critical transition point, a paradigm shift, in what the industry was and what it is going to be—that is really what your purpose is with this, isn't it?

RH: That's right. I think I've been footing around the procurement world for close to 25 years now, which is incredible when I think about it. But I think we're going to be talking about what's in the book, and what we tried to do is say, "Hey, look, there is something going on here that is really exciting for people that are in the procurement field, and we want to talk about it." And really the intent is to get the dialogue going because we think everybody should be included in this dialogue, not just people in procurement.

JH: Now, when you talk about 25 years, maybe you could give our listeners a little bit more of a background in terms of where you are today and what those 25 years encompassed.

RH: Sure, well I started out as a traditional academic, studying organizations and operations and early on, I became really interested in what was happening in the world of procurement—and this was probably in the early '90s—1990 or 1992 timeframe. And I started working with a group of folks, I took a job at Michigan State University, and during that period Bob Monczka and a group of people were doing some really interesting work looking at best practices through something called the Global Procurement Benchmarking Initiative.

And as part of that, we were talking to people in organizations all over the world. I got to travel to Japan and talked to people at Honda. I went to Europe and talked to people at BMW. So there are some really exciting things that were going on all over the world and as a part of that I really started to learn more about emerging best practices in procurement.

I left Michigan State in 1999 and came to North Carolina State and at that time we had an idea that in the procurement world there was a talent shortfall—that we really needed people who had skill sets in this area. One of my favorite authors wrote that business school should follow more like the medical school model, where you have a patient and the physician and the student all in it together, and the student is actually working on the patient. And if you can't bring the patient to the classroom then you bring the classroom to the patient. So that's what I started to do there to create something called the Supply Chain Resource Cooperative.

I basically sold the idea to, at the time, Dave Nelson who was at John Deere—and he loved it. I sold it to him on the way to the airport. He got to the airport, he said, "This is great." He picked up a phone and handed over some funds and said, "Let's get this going because this is the best way to develop talent in procurement." And the rest is history, really. We have taken off and we have some 25 odd companies, and every single day we're working on different problems with procurement—and every problem is new, and every problem is different, and very often it is the same approach and the same methodologies that are consistently applied. So that's what I do, I love working with students and I love working with companies—and I am doing a lot of that these days.

JH: So what you have really garnered your expertise on, or gained your knowledge on, was the practical elements: not just theory, not just the functional requirements of a position, but you are actually looking at creating real experiences from which you can learn, from which you can provide insight and/or direction and that's what was unique about what you've been doing all these years, isn't it?

RH: It is. And I think that was really fundamental to this: you can't just take people and put them through a procurement class with Power-Points and case studies. You really have to throw people into an experiential process that says you have got a problem here, you've got multiple stakeholders, price and cost is only one parameter. There's risk, there's stakeholder requirements, there's quality, there's delivery, there's service, and you have this entire internal world of stakeholders you have to deal with and this entire external world of suppliers and external third-parties. Procurement is in the crosshairs of that upstream and downstream world. It is really an exciting place to be because no other business function, except maybe for sales, has that same leverage point, and it is really an opportunity. It's one that I think we have to step up to. There's no better way to do that than to have the learning experience of getting into a problem and working it.

JH: Now, you mention in the book that these ideas and concepts have been kicking around for a long time. Why this book, and why now?

RH: Well there's a story behind it, as always. In this case I happened to be in London with my family, and I e-mailed Gerard Chick. Gerard is a brilliant guy; he is one of these people who is constantly spouting off new ideas and concepts. I said, "Gerard, let's go for a coffee." So we went down to Brampton Road in London and we had coffee together and we were there for probably about two hours. Gerard at the time was leaving CIPS, Chartered Institute for Purchasing & Supply. He was frustrated a little bit by what he had been seeing and his experience with CIPS. So we sort of had a group therapy session, if you will, and I was also seeing the same challenges. I was doing the future procurement study with KPMG and I was hearing the same stories from executives. People were saying, we're not getting the right traction, and we're not getting enough recognition, we're not getting a seat at the table, you know, a lot of sort of whining and complaining. I said, "Look, there is an opportunity here, but somehow people aren't expressing that opportunity very well to others. They're not taking advantage of it, they are not fully exploiting it, and they're not communicating it effectively to drive change."

Gerard picked right up on that and he said, "Absolutely, I see the same thing here in the UK. We're not maximizing the potential of what procurement is. We are challenged to communicate the potential of what it can achieve—especially in this rapidly changing world." At that point we left; I had to leave, and I said, "Right, we're going to write a book." And that was it. And so we both got started over the next couple years sort of writing it in bits and pieces and exchanging ideas via e-mail and Skype; and it just came together really, that is sort of how it occurred.

JH: I have to ask you this because the timing has to be right for the message. It's a matter of the market's receptiveness to what you are talking about. Going back to your work with John Deere, they were the right organization with which to do that with because obviously, with some other organizations, perhaps the majority of them back at that time, your idea wouldn't have taken off or have been as well received. Looking at where we are today and the general evolution of the procurement world, we have long-time buyers and then there's the next generation, let's call them procurement professionals. I am wondering who this book is directed towards? Who is going to *get it?*

You have talked about the fact that there is a new reality evolving, which you refer to as being the social and economic challenges taking place outside of the organization. With traditional buyers their mandate and focus was quite narrow. Now you've got the emerging professionals and their awareness and a more holistic view of the enterprise, even beyond the enterprise, certainly seems to be something that they are gaining insight into. Who is this book going to resonate with the most?

RH: That is a great question. Let me go back a little bit. As I said, if I think back 25 years ago I was going to meetings of the National Association of Purchasing Managers, or NAPM. At the time, the people going to those meetings were buyers. They were people who sort of had the eye shades or a stack of purchase orders and they would show up at a conference—and they would basically go to these meetings where they would get badges and pins and there was a lot of heavy drinking involved. It is not what I would call a professional networking atmosphere. It was an excuse to go out and have some fun and drink.

Over the years I think we started to see the change. I think the first change was the strategic sourcing era where it basically came down to *let's bundle up our demand and let's stack them higher and buy them cheaper.* And there was this whole era of the group purchasing organization that is still around in healthcare and other areas that embody that philosophy. And then, of course, there was the Freemarkets era. Freemarkets was a brilliant idea where people would say, "Let's take advantage of the excess capacity or requirements of the supply market." But unfortunately, that approach has been misused and in some cases abused, if you look at, for instance, some of the government procurements that is going on.

Then you have this whole era of the beginning to understand that procurement, there is something else here. There is more than just price, there is more than just bundling, there's something about really getting to a deeper understanding of the business and starting to understand not just price, but the underlying cost drivers. And as you get into that you start to get into more analytical approaches towards understanding costs and cost drivers. Some of the early work that Jimmy Anklesaria at the Anklesaria Group did around cost management was really brilliant. As that evolved, the sort of the red-meat-eating buyer that was out there to destroy suppliers and drive down price, that position went away and that person really isn't relevant anymore. What you're looking at is a professional now who, I would say, is almost a consultant—someone who is solving people's problems and contributing to the top line growth.

The people who get that are the CEOs, the CFOs, the CIOs; they understand the contribution and service that procurement delivers to the organization. And they are looking for people who have that same mind-set.

JH: In your book and the insights you're delivering through it, let's say for that *red-meat-eating buyer* or whatever term you used, the point is for them to really understand the book and then apply it. It would seem, then, based on what you said, they would have to go through an *unlearning process.*

Let's face it—10, 15 years ago I can remember speaking to an audience, regardless of whether it was 20 or 400, and asking how many chose to be in the profession. If you got one or two hands you were lucky. Most fell into it; where today, people are choosing to be in it. Do they now have to unlearn everything? Is it possible for the long-established buyers to unlearn something, or is there going to be an evolutionary divide where the knowledge and experience they have has a shelf life that ends and there's not really any transferring of the torch. And then, what you're talking about can start to resonate and be more readily adapted by newer procurement professionals. Is this the divide between the generations?

RH: The short answer is yes. I think this is definitely a major divide between the people who get it and the people who don't. And I think there's another piece to this, which is that it takes two to tango. I think sales people also have to unlearn behaviors that have been useful to them in the past and have worked in the past, but which are no longer working. Let me give you a great example of that. I was at a meeting one time of IACCM, which is the International Association for Contracts and Commercial Management, and there was a presentation by a sales organization and by a procurement organization. They were all talking about sort of holding hands and singing Kumbaya and working together and collaborating, and I stood up and I said, "Look—if I look at your professional sales organization, you have a webinar there that talks about how to get around procurement; and procurement, you have a webinar that says how to beat up your suppliers on price."

These are behaviors. People are saying one thing but not really getting it. I think there's a major shift in the cultures and the behaviors of individuals who are going to drive this procurement value proposition. I think that begins with the understanding that price is only one of the components of value and that there are many different sources of value. Essentially, the internet has changed that. Price is visible now. Benchmarking is visible, but what is becoming more important is the underlying cost drivers; being able to understand the contribution to fixed capital and to working capital, the total cost of ownership, the level of risk that an organization is willing to pay for and withstand and stomach.

Most important is the value of the brand. People are seeing that procurement can impact the brand, and as corporations expand globally into new regions of the world, you have to find ways to develop local suppliers to start to identify sources of supply that can meet local requirements and local demand: a diverse supply base, one that is representative of your customers and addresses the area of intelligence, building a repository of intelligence and knowledge. Procurement isn't just the guy who goes and gets you a good deal. He's the guy who can tell you everything you need to know about that market—what is happening, the trends, the issues, new technology—and can advise you on how to make a better sourcing decision if you're in a business. That is a different type of person than a so-called *red-meat-eating buyer* who is going to hammer suppliers and drive down their prices.

JH: You raise an interesting point here, because part of the adoption standpoint is that these concepts and ideas that you've talked about have yet to materialize in more than a handful of organizations. Let's say associations, and I don't want us to go too far off the path, but if associations have a membership composition that has 60% of the old time buyers, the *red-meat-eaters*, and the younger generations are just starting to join in, how do they introduce these ideas without potentially alienating traditional buyers? That's got to be a challenge, isn't it? Even within an organization, how do you, if you have a large base or a substantial percentage of these traditional buyers who have to unlearn—and may be unwilling to unlearn—and may not be able to unlearn—does that create a barrier to entry that slows it down but also makes it even more of a risk?

RH: It's a huge risk and it is a huge problem. The other problem is that you have these old time buyers, the ones who have been there for 20, 30, or 40 years, and you can't just discard those people. They have a wealth of information and knowledge in their heads about the organization, and about the supply base, and about the market—and I think you have to find a way to integrate these people. So you say, "Look, we're going to make this a fact-based decision, and we're going to use data to make the best decision not just gut feeling, going into negotiation with a gut feeling that we're going to win." That doesn't work anymore. As you start to build cross-functional sourcing teams that are composed of stakeholders who have an equal voice in decisions, that is when you start to get people around the table expressing their opinions and having a debate and a dialogue, and procurement becomes a facilitator of that information. You are going out there and you're collecting the market data, or the market intelligence, and you're presenting the data and having a discussion or debate, as opposed to a single individual who's just going out there for blood.

A perfect example of this is in the healthcare environment. I have been working with some hospitals that have actually said, "We can't make decisions if we don't have physicians and nurses on board." So they have developed a physician-executive team that are leading their category teams and these physicians go out and essentially sell the idea to other physicians in the network. It's a data driven approach, so they collect the data on cost of these devices, the cost for operations, the cost for physicians, and they're using the data to the benchmarking and to say, "If you look at all of our operations and you group them by physician, certain physicians have a lower cost than others; and why is that? Well the device that they're using and the supplier they're using, there is different pricing, there are different costs."

All of the sudden the debate becomes, "Why are we paying more for certain physicians to do the same operations in the same parts of the hospital?" That's a very different discussion point that generates the right to switch, or leads to the right decision over time and becomes a group position as opposed to a single individual who is making that decision.

JH: You talk about the integration of procurement across the business not being the responsibility of a few, but rather a challenge that must be embraced company wide. One of the things that I thought of in terms of this is with the changes that are happening in purchasing and procurement. The same changes are happening within the field of operations with chief financial officers and chief information officers. In fact, I remember a CIO survey from a couple of years ago where they said they're even contemplating changing the designation of chief information officer to reflect a shifting focus to a broader understanding.

When you look at the changes within the framework of procurement, but also the changes that are happening simultaneously within these other areas of practice within an enterprise, how do you align all three to coordinate the collaboration that is necessary? It's no longer hard-divided as functional silos is it? You have to look at it from the procurement side, but also how those organizations and those departments within the enterprise have also expanded their view. Is that a major challenge to coordinate all of these shifting realities?

RH: It absolutely is. So what that entails, as you have just pointed out, is being able to truly embed yourself into a business function and to be able to understand their world. If you have a procurement person with a business degree, they don't understand anything about technology. They may understand very little about medical devices or stents. They may understand very little about financial instruments or outsourcing of labor or temporary labor, or may know less about travel for instance, and different travel benefits.

So what organizations are doing is they're realizing that they have to create procurement people that have functional specialties. We need someone to work on a category for information technology who feels, looks, and maybe is recruited out of that technology organization. And one of the thoughts that we're promoting here is we really need people who have that same vernacular, who have the same language, who can talk the talk and walk the walk with the people in that area, because that is the only way they're going to get the respect and the engagement and the level of understanding that will help integrate those decisions into sourcing decisions. Countless organizations that I am talking to are saying we need to find people that can lead a category team, that have specialized in electronics in IT, or in healthcare, or in financial risk, that have specific skills that can contribute to the category but can also work and lead and develop a category team and lead a procurement organization and help write an RFP.

That is the skill set we're seeing: a specialized set of people that could sit in on staff meetings, even though 90% of what is said in the staff meeting isn't relevant to procurement, but 10% that is said you've got to be there for and understand it to be part of the discussion.

JH: One of the questions that comes to mind here is, whether associations and traditional institutions are keeping pace in terms of providing this education? Where can a procurement professional go to get the kinds of insight you are talking about? Because based upon what you just said, category management takes on a whole new dimension of importance, doesn't it?

RH: It absolutely does. I think that is where a lot of organizations are moving to right now. Everybody I've talked to is talking about category management. I think there are certain industries that have been at it longer and are further along. If you go into a lot of industrial manufacturing organizations, especially at the moment, they have people that own and manage categories and that is all they do. They know everything there is to know about that particular category down to the level of resins or to the plastic injection molding cards. These are very specific category levels that they acknowledge and may become experts in.

The people who really started this, years ago, were Honda and Toyota. Organizationally what they did was to put procurement people next to engineering people. So the engineer owns the specification and the technology and procurement owns the commercial piece and they have 50% decision rights on that. They are physically colocated, so they have to work with one another on that sourcing decision on that new product life cycle.

You can't do that in every industry because (a) you may not have enough people to spread across these industries and (b) you may just not want them there to begin with. There's cultural change when you start thinking about how you get this going. I'll probably get myself in trouble here, but I don't think there are many professional organizations that are doing this at all. I think the majority of them are giving you the standard run of the mill PowerPoint deck and there is not a lot of training on how to engage and how to influence, how to get people on board, how to present facts and data, how to do research that brings the data forward. That is what I see lacking in a lot of the professional procurement organizations today.

I think to develop that level of engagement requires that people be thrown off the deep end and it requires that they do workshops, as I call them. I've done a lot of these where you organize people into category teams and you say, "Okay, let's do a marketing assessment, let's do a stakeholder map, let's do a value stream map—let's understand what is happening." As the team works through their specific categories there are moments of insight—I call them the Ah-ha moments—when everybody sees, "Oh, that is what is going on." Suddenly the strategy unfolds in front of them and it becomes clear. This is what we need to do to drive value that is going to meet all of our requirements. It is that process of engagement that has to happen; no one is teaching that right now.

JH: So what you're really talking about are relational elements, as much as anything else. The fact remains that there are obstacles and road-blocks. Progress has not been made to the degree that it should have been made, but ultimately, *is the determining factor that the market has changed?* We are seeing realities changing. There is interest in the fact that paying suppliers on a timely basis has a positive impact on the whole value proposition. They did an automotive industry survey and discovered that the suppliers that were most satisfied with dealing with the buying organization offered far better products. The fact is that the timing is right for this now because the market is starting to dictate so—even if there is resistance, even if there are obstacles, change is inevitable and it is better to embark on it now than wait and do it later.

RH: Absolutely. I think it is something that organizations are throwing themselves into because they are seeing there isn't time to wait. We can't let this progression take two, three, five years to complete. We have to accelerate this because, quite frankly, we need to generate results quickly. Getting back to the beginning: yes, these ideas have been around for 20 or 25 years, but they are coming to the forefront now because we live in a risky world. We have global events and tsunamis. The global supply chains that we have created are very fragile and they have shocks to them that ripple globally throughout the world. All of a sudden people are recognizing, "Holy smokes—we've outsourced everything; we are buying it from all over the world; and we've just increased our risk and our potential for disruption that much more.'

You can see this happening everywhere. The number one issue— when I talk to people in Brazil, in Europe, in China, in Russia, and in India—they all say the same thing; you have to get the right people into supply chain. Supply chain is about people: it's about the soft skills, it's about analytical skills, it's about people who are good listeners, who are humble, who are smart, and who can influence. The organizations that get that and are bringing those people on board—those are the ones who are going to succeed in this complex, challenging, difficult world.

Index